He Mele Aloha
A HAWAIIAN SONGBOOK

He Mele Aloha
A HAWAIIAN SONGBOOK

Compiled by Carol Wilcox

Musical Notation
Vicky Hollinger and Kimo Hussey

Orthography and Translation
Puakea Nogelmeier

'Oli'Oli Productions, L.L.C.

Copyright © 2003
by 'Oli'Oli Productions, L.L.C.
P.O. Box 10558
Honolulu, Hawai'i 96816

Softbound Edition Printed 2008, 2009, 2011

All rights reserved. No part of this publication
may be copied or reproduced without written
permission from the publisher.

ISBN 978-0-9742564-2-9

Printed in China

Distributed by The Islander Group
www.booklineshawaii.com

Book design by Carol Wilcox and Cindy Turner
Photography by Hugo de Vries

Profits from the sale of this book
go to Lunalilo Home
www.LunaliloHome.org

Table of Contents

Hoʻolauna iv

He Mele

ʻĀ ʻOia! 1
Adiós Ke Aloha .2
Ahe Lau Makani 3
Ahi Wela 4
ʻAhulili 5
Aia Hiki Mai 6
ʻĀina ʻO Molokaʻi 7
ʻĀinahau 8
ʻAkahi Hoʻi 9
ʻAkaka Falls 10
ʻAlekoki 12
ʻĀlika 14
Aloha Ka Manini 15
Aloha Kauaʻi .16
Aloha Kuʻu Home Kāneʻohe 17
Aloha Nō Wau I Ko Maka 18
Aloha ʻOe 19
Aloha Week Hula 20
Alu Like 21
ʻAnapau 22
Beautiful Kahana 23
Beautiful Kauaʻi 24
Blue Lei 25
Cockeyed Mayor of Kaunakakai 26
E Hīhīwai 27
E Hoʻi I Ka Pili 28
E Kuʻu Tūtū 29
E Maliu Mai 30
E Naughty Naughty Mai Nei 31
ʻEkolu Mea Nui 32
ʻEleu Mikimiki 33
Farewell for Just Awhile 34
Fiftieth State Hula (Aloha Week Hula) . . .20

For You a Lei .35
Green Rose Hula 36
Haleʻiwa 37
Haleʻiwa Pāka 38
Hāliʻilua 39
Hanalei Moon 40
Hanohano Hanalei 41
Hanohano Ka Lei Pīkake 42
Hanohano Olinda 43
Hanohano Wailea 43
Haole Hula 44
Hawaiʻi Aloha 45
Hawaiʻi Calls .46
Hawaiʻi Ponoʻī 47
Hawaiian Cowboy 48
Hawaiian Wedding Song (Ke Kali...) . . .122
He Aloha Kuʻu Ipo 52
He Aloha Nō ʻO Honolulu 50
He Hawaiʻi Au 53
He Inoa No Kaʻiulani 54
He ʻOno 55
He Punahele Nō ʻOe 56
He Uʻi 57
Heha Waipiʻo .58
Henehene Kou ʻAka 60
Hiʻilawe 62
Hilo Ē 64
Hilo Hanakahi 65
Hilo Hula 66
Hilo One 67
Hole Waimea .68
Holoholo Kaʻa 69
Honolulu City Lights 70

Honolulu I'm Coming Back Again 71	Kāne'ohe 110
Honomuni 72	Kāua I Ka Huahua'i 111
Ho'okena 73	Kaua'i Beauty. .112
Ho'okipa Pāka 74	Kauanoeanuhea 113
Ho'onani I Ka Makua Mau 75	Kaula 'Ili. 114
Hu'i Ē. 76	Kaulana Nā Pua 115
Hukilau Song. .77	Kaulana 'O Waimānalo 116
Hula Breeze 78	Kawaihau Medley 117
Hula O Makee .79	Kawaipunahele. 118
I Ali'i Nō 'Oe 80	Kawohikūkapulani 119
I Kona. 81	Ke 'Ala O Ka Rose. 120
I Mua Kamehameha. 82	Ke Aloha 121
I Will Remember You 83	Ke Aloha O Ka Haku *(Queen's Prayer)* 239
Iā 'Oe E Ka Lā E 'Alohi Nei 84	Ke Kali Nei Au 122
I'll Weave a Lei of Stars for You. 85	Ke Ka'upu 123
'Imi Au Iā 'Oe. .86	Keaukaha 124
'Iniki Mālie. 87	Keawaiki 125
Island Medley. .88	Kilakila 'O Haleakalā. 126
Ka 'Ano'i 89	Kimo Hula 127
Ka Beauty A'o Mānoa 90	King's Serenade *('Imi Au Iā 'Oe)*. 86
Ka Lehua I Milia 91	Kinuē 128
Ka Makani Kā'ili Aloha. 92	Kipikoa *(Stevedore Hula)* 247
Ka Mana'o Nō Ia *(Me Moloka'i)* 170	Kīpū Kai. 129
Ka Na'i Aupuni 93	Kōke'e 130
Ka Ua Loku 94	Kona Kai 'Ōpua 131
Ka Wai Māpuna. 95	Koni Au I Ka Wai 132
Ka Wai O Nāmolokama. 96	Kō'ula. 133
Ka Wailele 'O 'Akaka *('Akaka Falls)*. . . .10	Kūhiō Bay 134
Ka Wiliwiliwai. 97	Kupa Landing. .135
Ka'ahumanu 98	Ku'u Hoa 136
Ka'ahupāhau *(Pūpū O 'Ewa)* 235	Ku'u Home *(Old Plantation)* 206
Kaimana Hila. .99	Ku'u Home O Nā Pali Hāuliuli *(Aloha*
Kaimukī Hula. 100	*Ku'u Home Kāne'ohe)* 17
Kalama'ula. 101	Ku'u 'I'ini 137
Kaleleonālani .102	Ku'u Ipo I Ka He'e Pu'e One 138
Kalena Kai 103	Ku'u Ipo Pua Rose 139
Kaleponi. 104	Ku'u Lei Aloha. 140
Kalua 105	Ku'u Lei 'Awapuhi. 141
Kamehameha Waltz. 106	Ku'u Lei Mokihana *(Maika'i Kaua'i)*. . .160
Kanaka Waiwai 108	Ku'u Lei Poina 'Ole 142
Kananaka 107	Ku'u Pua I Paoakalani 143

Laimana 144	My Little Grass Shack in Kealakekua, Hawai'i 182
Lanakila Kawaihau 145	My Sweet Gardenia Lei 183
Latitū 146	My Sweet Sweeting 184
Laupāhoehoe Hula 147	My Yellow Ginger Lei 185
Lē'ahi 148	Nā Ali'i 186
Lei Aloha, Lei Makamae 149	Nā Hala O Naue 188
Lei Hali'a 150	Nā Hoa He'e Nalu 189
Lei 'Ilima 151	Nā Kuahiwi 'Elima 190
Lei Nani 151	Nā Lei O Hawai'i 191
Lei No Ka'iulani 152	Nā Makani 'Ehā 192
Lei 'Ohu 153	Nā Moku 'Ehā 194
Lei Pīkake 154	Nā Pua Lei 'Ilima 195
Lovely Hula Hands 155	Nāmolokama Lā 196
Mahina 'O Hoku 156	Nani Haili Pō I Ka Lehua 197
Mai Poina 'Oe Ia'u 157	Nani Hanalei 198
Maika'i Ka Makani O Kohala 158	Nani Kaua'i 199
Maika'i Kaua'i 160	Nani Nu'uanu 200
Maile Lauli'i 161	Nani Wale Līhu'e 201
Maile Lei 162	Niu Haohao 202
Maile Swing 163	No Ka Pueo 203
Makalapua 164	Noho Paipai 204
Makee 'Ailana 165	Now Is the Hour 205
Malihini Mele 166	Old Plantation 206
Manu 'Ō'ō 167	On the Beach at Waikīkī 207
Maui Girl 168	'Ōpae Ē 208
Maunaloa 169	Pa'ahana 210
May Day is Lei Day in Hawai'i 170	Pā'au'au Waltz 212
Me Moloka'i 170	Pālolo 213
Mele O Lāna'i 171	Pane Mai 214
Meleana Ē 172	Pāpālina Lahilahi 215
Mī Nei 173	Pauoa Liko Ka Lehua 216
Miloli'i 174	Pidgin English Hula 217
Moanalua 175	Pō La'ila'i 218
Moanike'ala 176	Pōhai Ke Aloha 219
Moku O Keawe 177	Pretty Red Hibiscus 220
Moloka'i *(Honomuni)* 72	Pua 'Āhihi 221
Moloka'i Nui A Hina 178	Pua Carnation 222
Moloka'i Waltz 179	Pua Hone 223
Manowaiopuna *(Kō'ula)* 133	Pua 'Iliahi 224
Muliwai 180	Pua Līlia 225
My Hawaiian Souvenirs 181	

Pua Līlīlehua 226	To You Sweetheart, Aloha. 256
Pua Mae ʻOle 227	Toad Song 254
Pua O Ka Mākāhala. 228	Tūtū 257
Pua ʻŌlena 229	Ua Like Nō A Like 258
Pua Tuberose 230	Ua Mau. 260
Puamana. 231	Ua Noho Au A Kupa 259
Pulupē Nei ʻIli I Ke Anu 232	ʻUheʻuhene 262
Punaluʻu 233	ʻŪlili Ē 263
Pūpū Hinuhinu 234	Uluhua Wale Au 264
Pūpū Aʻo ʻEwa 235	ʻUlupalakua 265
Puʻuohulu 236	Uluwehi ʻO Kaʻala 266
Puʻuwaʻawaʻa .237	Uluwehi O Ke Kai 267
Queen's Jubilee 238	Wahīikaʻahuʻula 268
Queen's Prayer. 239	Wahine ʻIlikea .269
Radio Hula. 240	Wai O Ke Aniani 270
Roselani Blossom 241	Waiʻalae 272
Royal Hawaiian Hotel 242	Waikā 273
Sanoe 243	Waikaloa 274
Sassy 244	Waikīkī. 275
Song of Old Hawaiʻi. 246	Wailua Alo Lahilahi *(Nani Wale*
Song of the Islands *(Nā Lei O Hawaiʻi)*. 191	*Līhuʻe)*. 201
Stevedore Hula. 247	Waimea Corral. 278
Sweet Lei Mamo 248	Waiomina. 276
Sweet Lei Mokihana 249	Waipiʻo. 279
Sweet Leilani 250	Waltz Medley. .280
Sweet Someone 251	White Ginger Blossoms 282
Tewetewe. 252	White Sandy Beach 283
That's the Hawaiian in Me. 253	Yellow Ginger Lei *(My Yellow...)* 185

ʻUkulele Chords. 284
Chord Transpositions. 285
Mahalo. 286
Bibliography 287
Index of Composers. 289

Baritone ʻukulele on the back and inside covers courtesy of Kahauanu Lake

Hoʻolauna

The word *kanikapila*, literally "play music," has come to mean gathering together informally to sing and play. It was not so long ago that *kanikapila* was part of our daily lives in Hawaiʻi. Somehow over the last generation music has moved from the garage party to the concert stage. It has become something to listen to rather than participate in. There is a sense today that singing is reserved for those who are really good at it. Still, many people yearn to *kanikapila*.

He Mele Aloha: A Hawaiian Songbook is intended to encourage the tradition of kanikapila. The lyrics are large for easy reading. Chording is designed for the beginning and intermediate ʻukulele player. The emphasis is on accurate Hawaiian lyrics and translation.

Melody and phrasing is not provided—you must know the song to sing it. Most of these songs have been recorded, and one purpose of this book is to encourage support of Hawaiʻi's composers and entertainers.

Chording

Simple chording is shown for each song. If you are uncomfortable singing in the key provided, there is a guide to transposing to a different key in the front of this book, along with a chord chart.

Songs and Translations

He Mele Aloha is a collection of over 260 songs, listed alphabetically, about 40 of which are hapa haole songs.

Translations in this book favor a less than literal approach, as the translator tried to capture not only the specifics of the language but the essence of the song. Many of these songs have hidden meaning concealed in metaphor and analogy, known in Hawaiian as *kaona*. Kaona is an integral component of Hawaiian chants and *mele* and an essential reason why it is considered lyrical poetry. While the English translations may offer some insight into the veiled Hawaiian meanings, much of the multi-layered, sophisticated word play that constitutes Hawaiian poetry defies easy translation.

Existing translations were edited in order to provide a level of consistency, and were sometimes adjusted to reflect more recent understandings of the poetry. When translations were not available, they have been written anew. In cases where translations by others are used intact, those sources are acknowledged. Queen Liliʻuokalani, Mary Kawena Pukui and Mahiʻai Beamer provided models of clarity and poetic expressions.

Hawaiian spelling, markings and word separations have been standardized to help with clarity and provide a common base. Hawaiian diacritical marks, the ʻokina and the *kahakō*, are added throughout the text. Contractions, although often sung, are not usually shown. Again, it helps to know the song, and to sing it with friends.

Certain conventions have been adopted. Song titles are in italics. Hawaiian words that are part of everyday conversation in Hawaiʻi are generally not italicized. If part of a place name alone doesn't identify the location it is shown as a single word, for instance, "Maunaloa" rather than "Mauna Loa." When two or more people have collaborated on a song, the lyricist was listed first if that is known. The *hui*, or chorus, is indicated by ☞ and indentation. An effort has been made to format one song per page, and so, as a general rule, repeated lines are not included. Two-page songs are on facing pages, which sometimes required a slight shift in alphabetical listing.

Sources

There is relevent material in the copyright office and music divisions of the Library of Congress, the Bishop Museum Archives, the State of Hawaiʻi Library System, the University of Hawaiʻi Hamilton Library's Pacific Collection, and various neighbor island collections. As a general practice, lyrics were selected from the earliest available published sources, which can be loosely grouped into five categories.

Song and lyric books: Much of the early Hawaiian music that survives has done so because it first appeared in published compilations. Most of these were songbooks, with lyrics and scoring for the piano. Others were simply books of lyrics, possibly reflecting the understood reliance in Hawaiʻi on kanikapila to perpetuate melodies. At least 22 such song books have been published, 12 of these before 1930. The earliest of these was in 1888, a book of lyrics by Keakaokalani and J.M. Bright called *Ka Buke o na Leo Mele Hawaii*. The most comprehensive of these publications were those by Edward Holstein, Charles E. King, Johnny Noble and Johnny Almeida. King, Almeida and Noble were composers and published their own work along with that of others. Other songbooks have been published since 1950 but they tend to be reproductions of earlier works.

Scholarly texts: In more recent times, two sources of a more comprehensive nature stand out: *Nā Mele o Hawaiʻi Nei*, by Samuel H. Elbert and Noelani Mahoe, which includes lyrics, translations and notations, and *Hawaiian Music and Musicians* by George Kanahele, an extensive and interpretive history. In addition, there are several publications that deal with individual composers, such as *Songs of Helen Desha Beamer* and *The Queen's Songbook*, or subjects, such as *Nā Mele Paniolo*.

Sheet music: Sheet music refers to songs published individually, usually with a decorative cover, and is generally considered an excellent source of primary information.

Sheet music is relatively rare for the Hawaiian songs in this collection, or at least was not in the archival sources mentioned above. And sometimes even this good source can be misleading. An exception to the former and a good example of the latter is *Aloha 'Oe*, written by Queen Lili'uokalani. There are 27 distinct pieces of sheet music for this song at the Library of Congress, some of them with basic inaccuracies such as being variously credited to "Lihuokalani," and "Lvokalan" and claiming publication dates right up to 1934. While some are clearly derivative works, others do not appear the least altered from the original 1884 music. One can only wonder at the dependability of any source.

Covers: Record, tape and CD covers and liners, along with programs for various events such as song contests, annual meetings and award events contain a wealth of information provided by those many, mostly unnamed, writers, scholars and students, family members, and other usually knowledgeable people.

Internet: Moving into the 21st century, the World Wide Web provides the lyrics to many songs. The most useful site was *Huapala.org*, managed by Kaiulani Kanoa Martin.

Notes

The notes that accompany each song provide attributions, dates and information about the song. These are intended to add a little dimension, but are by no means definitive. Much more detailed information about the songs, their history and composers is available in the works referred to above and other primary sources not referenced in this work.

Identifying composers of any folk music is often difficult. In Hawai'i, musical composition was a rich, progressive, creative process, built on the work of the past, added to, and passed to the future through kanikapila. Hawaiian composers often turned to ancestral chants for words, form and imagery. They coupled this with Western musical tradition introduced primarily through hymnal singing. While there were many original compositions, it was also common practice to augment or revise earlier music.

In addition, collaboration was common. A frequent collaboration was between the poet and the melody maker. Another was between the composer not fluent in Hawaiian and a native speaker, essential to ensure that the Hawaiian poetry was authentic. Because of these collaborative, layered and oral traditions, identifying composers was often difficult, resulting in the enigmatic "traditional" attribution. Furthermore, the distinction between the composer and the person who arranged and published a song was often vague at best.

It was tempting to keep out of this thicket and not try to identify any but the most easily acknowledged attributions. The more difficult and thorny route was taken in the notes, which attempt to acknowledge all composers associated with each song.

Dating these songs also was difficult, for all the reasons stated above. Some songs are based on earlier chants, which themselves are not dated in this work. In many cases the earliest reference is in compiled songbooks, so that a date is used for songs that were written in some unspecified earlier time. If you weren't forewarned, you might think there were incredible bursts of musical creativity in 1888, and again in 1897 and 1916. To help place the song into some historical context, the earliest date is provided in the notes, whether it was first written, referred to, published, copyrighted, sung or performed.

Hawaiian Music

Hawaiian music is one of the largest and most diverse bodies of folk music on earth. It enjoys world-wide recognition and appeal. From the time the missionaries introduced the concept of melody after their arrival in the 1820s, Hawai'i's *ali'i* quickly became sophisticated and prolific song writers. They ensured the perpetuation of Hawaiian *mele* by conducting public contests and publishing their work. With the introduction of the 'ukulele and guitar in 1879, tools for composition became more accessible to the general population. This launched a period of unsurpassed creativity among all the people of Hawai'i.

Of the 267 songs in this book, over half were composed before 1930. About 100 were published between then and 1970, including almost all of the hapa-haole songs. About 30 are by contemporary artists. There are 190 composers represented in this collection, a testament to the importance of music in everyday life in Hawai'i. This body of music, taken in its entirety, offers a unique, intuitive history of Hawaiian culture written by the people themselves, one that is also accessible through the English translations.

The quintessential Hawaiian act is a gift of song, often bestowed as a present from the composer — a name song for a child, a song of love for one's sweetheart or homeland, a thanks for gracious hospitality, a tribute to a hero. This collection is a gift of love created over time by the people of Hawai'i.

Let's kanikapila.

xiii
He Mele
Aloha

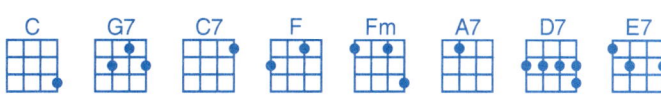

'Ā 'Oia!

'Ā [C] 'oia! A e lilo ana [G7] 'oe ia'u, aha[C]hana
Onaona ko maka i [G7] 'ane'i e ka ipo, [C] wahine u['C7]'i
He u'i [F] 'i'o nō ka wahine [Fm] leo hone
He manu [C] leo le'a ia o ke [A7] kuahiwi
Na'u [D7] 'oe, na'u nō e lei ha[G7]'aheo
Li'a [C] wale aku nō ka mana[G7]'o lā i laila, ho[C]'ohi[C7]hi
Ua noa [F] ko nui kino na'u ho'okahi [E7] wale nō
Me [A7] 'oe au, pumehana kāua
Me a'u [D7] 'oe, 'olu nei pu'uwai
Aia [C] lā! Lilo ana, [G7] lilo 'oe ia['C]'u

    That's it! I am going to win you — Oh! oh!
    Your pretty eyes are attracted hither, oh lovely dear
    You are pretty indeed and your voice is so sweet
    Like a sweet-voiced bird of the mountain
    You are mine, mine to cherish with pride
    For my thoughts are drawn there to you my fancy taken
    You are all mine and mine alone
    With you, I find the warmth of love
    Having you with me soothes my heart
    There now! You are won, won by me

This lively song of the 1940s is by John Kameaaloha Almeida, who was a gifted composer and a collector of traditional and contemporary Hawaiian songs. Over the years from the 1880s until the 1940s, about a dozen people collected and, more importantly, published Hawaiian songs, preserving them for the future.

This translation is by Mary Kawena Pukui, the acknowledged, and sometimes unacknowledged, source of translation for hundreds of songs and chants, both published and in archival collections.

Much of the music that survives does so because of Edward Holstein, Charles King, Johnny Noble, Johnny Almeida, Mary Kawena Pukui, Vivienne Mader, Helen Desha Beamer, George Kanahele, Samuel Elbert, Noelani Mahoe and all those others who have worked to preserve things Hawaiian and make them accessible to those who follow.

Adiós Ke Aloha

      F   Bb   G7
E kuʻu belle o ka pō laʻilaʻi
   C7   F
Ka lalawe mālie a ka mahina
             Bb   G7
Kōaniani mai nei e ke ahe
 C7   F
Āhea ʻoe e hoʻolono mai?

My sweetheart of the still night
As the moon moves gracefully along
Being carried aloft by a breeze
When will you listen to me?

🎸 *hui*

    F   Bb
Āhea ʻoe, āhea ʻoe
    F
ʻOe e hoʻolono mai?
   D7   G7
I nei leo nahenahe
   C7   F
Adiós, adiós ke aloha

chorus:
When, when will you
You notice and pay heed?
To this gentle voice
Adiós, adiós my love

   F   Bb   G7
E ka hauʻoli ʻiniki puʻuwai
  C7   F
E ke aloha e maliu mai ʻoe
            Bb   G7
Ke hoʻolale mai nei e ke Kiu
  C7   F
Ua anu ka wao i ka ua

Oh happiness that tingles in my heart
My love do consider my feelings
Being urged on by the Kiu wind
The upland becomes cold in the rain

  F   Bb   G7
Hoʻokahi kiss dew drops he maʻū ia
   C7   F
E ka belle o ka noe līhau
     Bb   G7
Eia au lā e ke aloha
  C7   F
Ke huli hoʻi nei me ka neo

One kiss, refreshing as dew drops
Oh belle of the cool mist
Here I am, oh my love
Returning empty handed

*In the 1830s, Spanish-Indian vaqueros were brought from Mexico to Waimea, Hawaiʻi, to share their cowboy skills with the Hawaiians, who called them paniolo. Leleiōhoku wrote this moody and romantic song, reminiscent of the Mexican corridas, sometime in the 1870s, evoking the image of the Hawaiian cowboy. This song was played often by the Royal Hawaiian Band, usually together with **Hole Waimea**. It was the style of the period, a mark of sophistication, to use a foreign word or phrase in the poetry.*

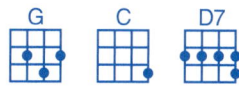

Ahe Lau Makani

G	C	D7	G

He 'ala nei e māpu mai nei
Na ka makani lau aheahe
I lawe mai a ku'u nui kino
Ho'opumehana i ko aloha

There is a breath so gently breathing
So soft so sweet by sighing breezes
That as it touches my whole being
It brings a warmth unto my soul

🎸 hui

E ke hoa o ke ahe lau makani
Halihali 'ala o ku'u 'āina

chorus:
We, fair one, together shall enjoy such moments
While murmuring wind sweeps over my fatherland

He 'ala nei e moani mai nei
Na ka ua noe Līlīlehua
I lawe mai a ku'u poli
Ho'opumehana i ku'u poli

There is a breath so soft and balmy
Brought by sweet zephyrs Līlīlehua
And while wafted to my bosom
It brings a yearning for one I love

He 'ala nei e puīa mai nei
Na ka makani anu kolonahe
I lawe mai nō a pili
Ho'opumehana i ka mana'o

There is a fragrance that saturates
A cool, soft breeze
Brought it to cling to me
Warming me with feelings

He 'ala nei e aheahe mai nei
Na ka leo hone a nā manu
I lawe mai a loa'a au
Ho'opumehana i ko leo

There is a fragrance wafted here
The sweet calls of birds
Brought it to find me
Being warmed by your voice

Also entitled He 'Ala Nei E Māpu Mai Nei, Lili'uokalani attributes this 1868 composition to the "three graces of Hamohamo," possibly referring to herself, her sister Miriam Likelike, and Kapoli; Hamohamo being the Queen's home in Waikīkī. Līlīlehua is a wind and a rain well known in Pālolo, also on Waiehu, Maui. Translation of first two verses and hui by Lili'uokalani, second two verses by Hui Hānai. (Hui 31)

He Mele Aloha

Ahi Wela

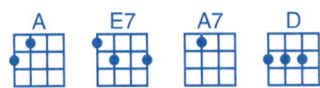

   A   E7
'Elua nō māua
  A
I 'ike ia hana
        E7
La'i wale ke kaunu
         A A7
Ho'onipo i ka poli

Only the two of us
Know of this carrying on
How delightful it was to make love
Romancing the heart

hui

 D   A
Ahi wela mai nei loko
 E7   A A7
I ka hana a ke aloha
 D   A
E lalawe nei ku'u kino
       E7   A
Konikoni lua i ka pu'uwai

chorus:
There is a burning fire within
Due to the workings of love
That envelops all of me
Wildly throbbing here in my heart

 A   E7
'Auhea wale ana 'oe
        A
Ku'u pua i kui a lei
   E7
I lei ho'ohiehie
       A A7
No ke ano ahiahi

I beckon to you
My blossom that I have strung into a lei
An elegant lei of adornment
For the peaceful eventide

The lovemaking theme, usually buried in the kaona, is more readily accessible in this "Fire of Love." This 1891 version of Ahi Wela *is by Lizzie Doiron, a well known singer with the Royal Hawaiian Band, and Mary Beckley, a lady-in-waiting to Queen Lili'uokalani.*

Opposite: Scott Ha'i, a cowboy from Kaupō Ranch, asks "How come you go to that mountain and not to mine?" Word play, a favorite device in Hawaiian song, occurs here with "lili," which means jealous, and "'Ahulili," heaped up jealousy, a prominent peak in Kaupō, Maui, depicted as jealous because it is seldom covered by the light mist that typically settles on mountain peaks. There are numerous versions of this traditional song about a jealous woman. A slightly different, older version has these additional lines: "E ō 'ia e ka lei, Ke 'ala kūpaoa, Ka puana ho'i a ka moe, Ka beauty o Mauna Hape." Respond, oh garland, the powerful perfume, my dream it is, the beauty of Mount Happy.

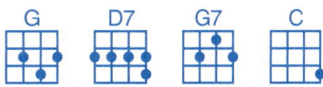

'Ahulili

G
He aloha nō 'o 'Ahulili
D7   G G7
A he lili paha ko iala
C   G
I ke kau mau 'ole 'ia
D7   G
E ka 'ohu kau kuahiwi

G
Eia iho nō e ka 'olu
D7   G G7
Ke 'ala kūpaoa
C   G
Lawa pono kou makemake
D7   G
E manene ai kou kino

G
'Ako aku au i ka pua
D7   G G7
Kui nō wau a lei
C   G
A i lei poina 'ole
D7   G
No nā kau a kau

G
Pa'a 'ia iho a pa'a
D7   G G7
Ka 'i'ini me ka 'ano'i
C   G
He 'ano'i nō ka 'ōpua
D7   G
Ka beauty o Mauna Hape

G
Ha'ina mai ka puana
D7   G G7
He aloha nō 'Ahulili
C   G
He lili paha ko iala
D7   G
I ke kau mau 'ole 'ia

Beloved indeed is 'Ahulili
And perhaps somewhat jealous
At never being settled upon
By the mountain-cloaking mist

Here indeed is relief
A powerful fragrance
Your desire will be sufficient
To make your whole body tingle

I pluck the blossom
I string it into a lei
An unforgettable garland
For ever and ever

Bound and held fast
Is the desire and longing
The horizon cloud is yearning
For the beauty of Mount Happy

Tell then the refrain
Beloved is 'Ahulili
And perhaps somewhat jealous
At never being settled upon

He Mele Aloha

Aia Hiki Mai

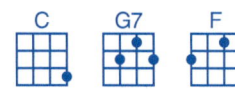

C Ma'ema'e ē Līhau, pō i ka lehua **G7**
Kupu kelakela i ke alo o Malama **C**
Me he lama lā ko aloha e ka ipo **F**
G7 Ke hiki mai, hiki mai **C**

Līhau is perfection, abundant with lehua
Rising so lofty in the presence of Malama
Your love, sweetheart, is like a lighted torch
When it comes, when it comes

hui

C Aia hiki mai ka hali'a io'u nei **G7**
Me he uila lā i ka maka o ka 'ōpua **C**
Ua puīa e ka liko pua o ka hīnano **F**
G7 Ke hiki mai, hiki mai **C**

chorus:
When fond recollections come upon me
It's like lightning in the face of the clouds
Perfumed by the enfolding hīnano blossoms
When it comes, when it comes

C Hiki mai ana kama hele 'alo anu **G7**
I lawea mai e ke 'ala laua'e **C**
Ua hele a puīa i ke onaona **F**
G7 I ka noua e ke kēhau **C**

The traveller who faces the cold arrived
Brought here by the fragrance of laua'e fern
Imbued with the sweet perfume
Pressed onward by the settling dew

C Hia'ai hewa ana au iā iala **G7**
La'ahia nei kino i ko leo **C**
I lei, i home no'u ko aloha **F**
G7 Kuleana ai kāua **C**

I was wrongly drawn to that one
This body is reserved by your voice
Your love is my adornment, a home for me
You and I belong to each other

This Maui song was attributed in 1897 to Emma Kapena, then later to Likelike. This is a good illustration of the difficulty we face today in making definitive attributions, especially when considering the collaborative and evolving nature of Hawaiian music. In the hui, the hīnano referred to is the male hala blossom, its pollen some say is an aphrodisiac.

He Mele Aloha

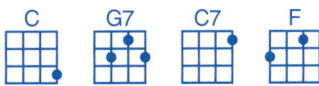

'Āina 'O Moloka'i

[C] He aloha au iā 'oe [G7]
['Āina a'o Moloka'i [C] [C7]
[F] Ho'okipa po'e malihini [C]
[G7] Me ka pu'uwai hāmama [C]

I have a deep love for you
Land of Moloka'i
So welcoming to the visitors
With an open loving heart

[C] He aloha a'o Wailau [G7]
He wahi mehameha nō ia [C] [C7]
[F] He nani nō ke 'ike aku [C]
[G7] E uhi ana i ka ua noe [C]

Beloved indeed is Wailau
Such a very lonely place
But beautiful to witness
Veiled in the misty rain

[C] Hanohano a'o Haka'ano [G7]
Ke kani o ka 'ili kai [C] [C7]
[F] He pu'e one 'ole ia [C]
[G7] Me nā pali ki'eki'e loa [C]

Haka'ano is reknowned
The crashing sound of the sea
With no sandy shore
And backed by towering cliffs

[C] Ha'ina ke aloha pau 'ole [G7]
A'o Kainalu [C] [C7]
[F] Ke 'ala o ka līpoa [C]
[G7] E moani nei [C]

Never ending love is expressed
For Kainalu
The fragrance of the līpoa seaweed
Drifts in on the breeze

[C] Ha'ina mai ka puana [G7]
Nani a'o Kalaupapa [C] [C7]
[F] Ho'okipa po'e malihini [C]
[G7] Me ka pu'uwai hāmama [C]

The refrain is told
Beautiful is Kalaupapa
So welcoming to guests
With an open loving heart

This song by Kai Davis travels in verse from one Moloka'i place to the next, a favorite format in Hawaiian poetry. The song traverses the steep cliffs and deep valleys of the north coast of the island. Translation by Carol Silva.

'Āinahau

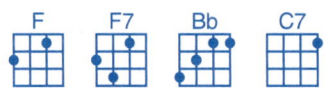

Na ka wai lūkini, wai anuhea o ka rose
E hoʻopē nei i ka liko o nā pua
Na ka manu pīkake, manu hulu melemele
Nā kāhiko ia o kuʻu home

hui

Nani wale kuʻu home ʻo ʻĀinahau i ka ʻiu
I ka holu nape a ka lau o ka niu
I ka uluwehiwehi i ke ʻala o nā pua
Kuʻu home, kuʻu home i ka ʻiuʻiu

Na ka makani aheahe i pā mai ma kai
I lawe mai i ke onaona līpoa
E hoʻoipo hoʻonipo me ke ʻala kuʻu home
Kuʻu home, kuʻu home i ka ʻiuʻiu

It is perfume, the cool essence of the rose
That is drenching the buds of the flowers
The peacocks, those golden feathered birds
Are the adornments that grace my home

chorus:
So beautiful is my home, elegant ʻĀinahau
ʻMidst the swaying of coconut fronds
The lush greenery and the fragrance
    of the flowers
My home, my home of majestic bearing

The ever gentle wind that blows in
    from the sea
Brings the wonderful scent of the līpoa
The fragrance of my home
    stirs love and longing
My home, my home of majestic bearing

Composer Likelike was the sister of Hawaiʻi regents Kalākaua and Liliʻuokalani. Her daughter Kaʻiulani was beautiful, urbane, and heir apparent. Ruth Keʻelikōlani gave ʻĀinahau (literally, land of the hau tree) to Kaʻiulani at her baptism in 1875. ʻĀinahau was located where the Princess Kaʻiulani Hotel now stands. Upon Kaʻiulani's death in 1899, at the age of 24, the estate passed on to her father, Archibald Cleghorn. When he died in 1910 he left it to the Territory of Hawaiʻi as a park, but the legislature did not accept the gift.

'Akahi Ho'i

    F   Bb
Aloha wale
C7   F
Pua hinahina
         Bb
I lei hoʻohie
C7   F
No kuʻu kino

     The heart always yearns
     For the hinahina flower
     As an elegant wreath
     To adorn my person

hui

    F   Bb
'Akahi hoʻi
  C7   F
Ka hikina mai
       Bb
Ka haliʻa ʻana
 C7   F
Hone i ka lipo

Chorus:
Only now
Comes the arrival
Loving remembrance
Teasing my soul

 F   Bb
'O loko hana
C7   F
Nui ka ʻanoʻi
       Bb
Ka haliʻa ʻana
C7   F
Me ke aloha

My heart is stirred
Tremendous is the desire
Loving remembrances
Are filled with affection

The Hawaiian March *was composed and played by Henry Berger at his first appearance as conductor of His Majesty's Band in 1872. Kalākaua later took one of the two melodies in* The Hawaiian March, *put words to it, slowed down its tempo, and called it* 'Akahi Hoʻi, "Tis for Thee Alone." *It was published under Kalākaua's pen name* "Figgs."

He Mele Aloha

'Akaka Falls

C　　G7　　　　　C
Malihini ku'u 'ike 'ana
　　G7　　　　C　　C7
Kahi wailele 'o 'Akaka
F　　　　　C　A7
Wai kau maila i luna
　　　G7　　　　　　　　C
Lele hunehune maila i nā pali

I saw for the first time
The waterfall of 'Akaka
Waters placed there on high
Cascading in misty streams down the cliffs

C　　G7　　　　　　C
Kau nui aku kahi mana'o
　　G7　　　　　　C　C7
E 'ike lihi aku i ka nani
F　　　　C　A7
Ia uka i puīa
　　　G7　　　　　　C
I ke 'ala me ke onaona

The thoughts are drawn there
To catch a glimpse of the beauty
That high land, so redolent
With fragrance and sweet scent

C　　G7　　　　　C
Onaona wale ho'i ia uka
　　G7　　　　　　C　C7
I ka pa'a mau 'ia e ka noe
F　　　　　C　A7
Ia uka kūpaoa
　　　G7　　　　　　C
E moani nei i ku'u poli

Those heights are always sweet
Enclosed within the mists
That perfumed high land
Exudes its scent in my heart

C　　G7　　　　C
I ne'e aku au e 'ako
　　G7　　　　　C　C7
I ka pua o ka 'awapuhi
F　　　　　C　A7
I lei no ka malihini
　　　G7　　　　　　C
Na'u ia a e honihoni

I move to pluck
The blossom of ginger
As a lei for the newcomer
It is I who shall enjoy it

He Mele Aloha

```
    C         G7        C
Na ke Akua mana loa
        G7      C   C7
E kia'i maluhia mai
  F         C   A7
I kēia mau pua
        G7    C
O ku'u 'āina aloha
```
May Almighty God
Guard over in peace
These fair blossoms
Of my beloved land

```
    C     G7             C
Ha'ina 'ia mai ka puana
         G7        C   C7
I kahi wailele 'o 'Akaka
  F           C  A7
Kau maila i luna
           G7              C
Lele hunehune maila i nā pali
```
Tell the story in the refrain
Of a waterfall, 'Akaka
Placid there on high
Cascading in misty streams down the cliffs

Also known as Ka Wailele 'O 'Akaka, this mele credited to Helen Lindsey Parker lauds the beauty of the 442-foot waterfall named after 'Akaka, who is said to have leapt from its heights. His two lovers, Lehua and Maile, disguised as two smaller falls in a nearby ravine, cannot stop their crying.

'Alekoki

    C   C7
'A'ole i piliwi 'ia
 F   C
Kahi wai a'o 'Alekoki
                  D7
Ua ho'okohu ka ua i uka
 G7   C
Noho maila i Nu'uanu

Just unbelievable
Are the waters of 'Alekoki
The rain adorns the highlands
Settling upon Nu'uanu

  C   C7
Anuanu makehewa au
 F   C
Ke kali 'ana i laila
              D7
Kainō paha ua pa'a
 G7   C
Kou mana'o i 'ane'i

I'm overcome with cold
Waiting there
I had mistakingly assumed
Your thoughts dwell on me

  C   C7
I 'ō i 'ane'i au
 F   C
Ka pi'ina a'o Ma'ema'e
            D7
He 'ala onaona kou
 G7   C
Kai hiki mai i 'ane'i

I've been all about
On the climb to Ma'ema'e
You have a sweet perfume
That has come to me here

  C   C7
Ua malu nēia kino
 F   C
Mamuli o ko leo
              D7
Kau nui aku ka mana'o
 G7   C
Kahi wai a'o Kapena

This body is reserved
By your word
Thoughts are drawn to
The waters of Kapena

  C   C7
Pani a pa'a 'ia mai
 F   C
Nā mana wai a'o uka
            D7
Ma luna a'e nō au
 G7   C
Ma nā lumi li'ili'i

Closed off and dammed up
Are the streams of the heights
I am there above
In the little niches

[C]Ma waho a'o Mā[C7]mala
[F]Hao mai nei e[C]huehu
Pulu au i ka hu[D7]na kai
[G7]Kai he'ehe'e i ka [C]'ili

[C]Ho'okahi nō koa [C7]nui
[F]Nāna e 'alo ia [C]'ino
'Ino'ino mai nei [D7]luna
[G7]I ka hao a ka ma[C]kani

[C]E kilohi au i ka [C7]nani
[F]Nā pua o Mauna[C]'ala
Ha'ina mai ka pu[D7]ana
[G7]Kahi wai a'o 'Ale[C]koki

Ma waho a'o Māmala	Outside of Māmala Harbor
Hao mai nei ehuehu	The seaspray is pelting me
Pulu au i ka huna kai	I'm soaked with salty spray
Kai he'ehe'e i ka 'ili	Streaking my skin
Ho'okahi nō koa nui	There's only one great warrior
Nāna e 'alo ia 'ino	Who shall brave that storm
'Ino'ino mai nei luna	It's all blustery above
I ka hao a ka makani	Where the wind is gusting
E kilohi au i ka nani	I gaze upon the beauty
Nā pua o Mauna'ala	The blossoms of Mauna'ala
Ha'ina mai ka puana	The tale is told in the refrain
Kahi wai a'o 'Alekoki	Of the waters of 'Alekoki

'Alekoki is a story-telling song from the 1850s, based on a chant that tells about a rendezvous with a beautiful girl at the 'Alekoki Pool in Nu'uanu Stream. The words were pronounced clearly and carefully listened to, the more stanzas the better. There are several versions. This one comes from Charles E. King, who credits it to Kalākaua and the melody to Lizzie 'Alohikea. The chant is also credited to Lunalilo. It is said he wrote it for Kamāmalu, whom he was forbidden to marry because of "selfish and political" reasons. (Kanahele 3) The lingering rain evokes brooding affection, the storms and wind suggest political uproar and flying gossip.

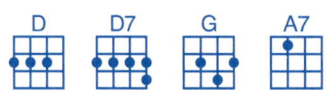

'Ālika

	D	A7 D	D7	G
Aia i 'Ālika ka ihu o ka moku
A7		D
Ua hao a pa'ihi nā pe'a i ka makani

There at 'Ālika is the prow of the ship
The sails are well set in the wind

D　　　A7 D　　D7　　G
Ke liolio nei ke kaula likini
A7　　　　　　　　　D
'Alu'alu 'ole iho nā pe'a i ka makani

Taut are the rigging lines
The sails do not slacken in the wind

D　　　A7 D　　　D7　　G
'A'ole i kau pono ka newa i ko piko
A7　　　　　　　　D
Ka'a 'ē ka huila e niniu i ka makani

The needle is not fixed in the north
The wheel turns, spinning in the wind

D　　　A7 D　　　D7　　G
Ke kau a'e nei ka ihu 'o Macao
A7　　　　　D
Ke iho a'e nei e komo 'Asia

The prow is set, there's Macao
Descending to go to Asia

D　　　A7 D　　　D7　　G
Me ke Kai Melemele, ke kōā o Pelina
A7　　　　　　　D
Nani wale ka 'ikena, nā pua i Sarona

The Yellow Sea, Bering Straits
A lovely view, the flowers of Sharon

D　　　A7 D　　　D7　　G
I noho ka ihu i ka piko i Hīmela
A7　　　　　　　D
Ka hale lau pāma ho'omaha i ke kula

The prow presses towards the Himalayan summit
A palm-leafed house for rest on the plains

D　　　A7 D D7　　　G
Ha'ina 'ia mai ana ka puana
A7　　　　　　D
Aia i 'Ālika ka ihu o ka moku

Tell the refrain
There at 'Ālika is the prow of the ship

There are multiple versions of this song, one of the earliest is credited to Charles Ka'apa. Although Hawaiian historian Samuel M. Kamakau referred to a ship named 'Ālika as having visited Hawai'i before 1792, the 'Ālika in this song refers to a port in South Kona that was overrun by lava in 1926. The prow of the ship entering all these ports might suggest a sailor's life.

He Mele Aloha

Aloha Ka Manini

F   F7   Bb   F
Aloha ka manini me ka pōpolo
G7   C7   F
He iʻa noho ia i ka laupapa

Beloved is the manini and pōpolo fish
Fish that live in the reef shallows

F   F7   Bb   F
Kala, ka nenue, ʻo ka nahawele
G7   C7   F
Moani ke ʻala ke honi aku

Kala, nenue and nahawele
The fragrance is gently carried in, to be inhaled

F   F7   Bb   F
Āhole iʻa piko lihaliha
G7   C7   F
Poi ʻuala kāohi puʻu

The āhole fish with rich, oily belly
Sweet potato poi, sliding down the throat

F   F7   Bb   F
Haʻina ʻia mai ana ka puana
G7   C7   F
Aloha ka manini me ka pōpolo

The refrain is told
Beloved is the manini and the pōpolo fish

Within the context, it seems clear that composer Lot Kauwē refers in the first verse to the pōpolo fish, maiko, a surgeonfish, rather than pōpolo, a well known plant, noted for its small, black, edible berries and medicinal uses. In any event, fish probably have little to do with this song anyway.

Aloha Kauaʻi

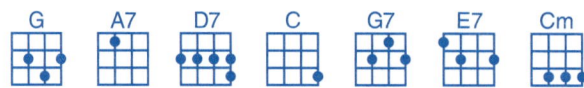

    G   A7   D7   G
Aloha mokihana, pua o Kauaʻi
  A7   D7   G
Wili ʻia me ka maile lau liʻiliʻi
C   D7
Maile liʻiliʻi
   G   A7   D7   G
He uʻi, onaona, he aloha wau iā ʻoe
  A7   D7   G   G7
Me aʻu, me ʻoe i ka puʻuwai

Beloved is the mokihana, flower of Kauaʻi
Entwined with the dainty-leafed maile
Maile so dainty
A fragrant loveliness, I love you
Be close to my heart

  C   Cm   G   E7
Aloha nō ʻo Kauaʻi
  A7   D7
Luana, hoʻokipa malihini
  G   A7   D7   G
Puana, kaulana ka inoa o Kauaʻi
  A7   D7   G   E7
Haʻaheo he nani hiwahiwa
  A7   D7   G
Kauaʻi he nani nō ʻoe

Beloved indeed is Kauaʻi
And the home, Luana, so welcoming to visitors
The story is told of the fame of the name Kauaʻi
Proud, a cherished beauty
Kauaʻi you are beautiful indeed

Maʻiki Aiu wrote this for the Malina family and their home, Luana, with the help of Lei de Fries, Claude and Kia Malina. The mokihana berry and maile lau liʻi are twined together to make a fragrant lei symbolic of Kauaʻi. 1950s.

He Mele Aloha

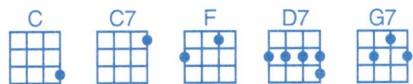

Aloha Kuʻu Home Kāneʻohe

   C   C7   F D7
Aloha kuʻu home a i Kāneʻohe
      G7   C
A me nā pali hāuliuli o nā Koʻolau

Beloved is my home in Kāneʻohe
And the green cliffs of the Koʻolau mountains

   C   C7   F D7
Noho aku i ka laʻi o kuʻu home
      G7   C
ʻUpu aʻe ka manaʻo no nā hoaloha

Staying in the peacefulness of my home
Brings up thoughts of dear friends

   C   C7   F D7
I laila mākou i hiʻolani ai
      G7   C
A me ka wai noenoe e pipiʻi ana

It is there that we found such pleasure
With the misty waters bubbling up

   C   C7   F D7
Hoʻokahi ka manaʻo i kualono
      G7   C
A me ka leo aloha e hoʻokipa mai

One thought of those lofty mountains
And the voice of hospitality beckons

   C   C7   F D7
Haʻina ʻia mai ana kuʻu home
      G7   C
A me nā pali hāuliuli o nā Koʻolau

Tell the refrain of my home
And the green cliffs of the Koʻolau range

Also known as Kuʻu Home O Nā Pali Hāuliuli, *Louisa Hopkins composed this tribute to her home, Halekou, in 1939. The phrase "a i Kāneʻohe" is short for "aia i Kāneʻohe," a form often seen in songs.*

Aloha Nō Wau I Ko Maka

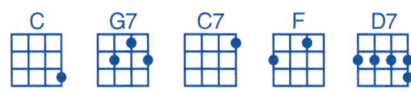

    [C]'O 'oe nō ka'u aloha[G7]
Ku'u ipo noho i ka 'iu[C]
E noho [C7]'oe a mana'o mai[F] [D7]
A he [G7]kuleana kou i 'ane'i[C]

🎸 *hui*

    [C]Aloha nō wau i ko [G7]maka
    Kou ihu waliwali ka'u i [C]honi
    Koe a[C7]ku kou piko wai'[F]olu [D7]
    Ua [G7]kapu na ka mea wai[C]wai

[C]Ua like nō 'oe a [G7]like
Me ke onaona Ia[C]pana
Ka [C7]hoene i ka poli[F] [D7]
Koni[G7]koni i ku'u pu'u[C]wai

[C]Someone is tall and [G7]handsome
Someone is fair to [C]see
[C7]Someone is kissing some[F]body [D7]
[G7]Under the light of the [C]moon

[C]I wish I had someone to [G7]love me
Someone to call my [C]own
[C7]Someone to sleep with me [F]nightly [D7]
Cause I'm [G7]tired of sleeping a[C]lone

You are my beloved
My sweetheart of lofty position
Do dwell and consider me
For you have privileges here

chorus:
I do adore your face
Your smooth nose I have kissed
Reserving your gentle piko
Sacred to one of importance

You are so very like
A sweet Japanese perfume
The way it murmurs in the bosom
Throbbing here in my heart

It's not known who added the English verses to this song from the 1890s by Leleiōhoku.

Aloha ʻOe

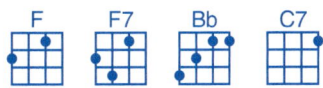

[F] [F7] [Bb] [F]
Haʻaheo ka ua i nā pali
[C7]
Ke nihi aʻela i ka nahele
[F] [F7] [Bb] [F]
E hahai ana paha i ka liko
[Bb] [C7] [F] [F7]
Pua ʻāhihi lehua o uka

Proudly swept the rain by the cliffs
As on it glided through the trees
Still following ever the liko
The ʻāhihi lehua of the vale

🎸 *hui*

[Bb] [F]
Aloha ʻoe, aloha ʻoe
[C7] [F] [F7]
E ke onaona noho i ka lipo
[Bb] [F]
A fond embrace a hoʻi aʻe au
[C7] [F]
Until we meet again

chorus:
Farewell to thee, farewell to thee
Thou charming one who dwells in shaded bowers
A fond embrace ʼere I depart
Until we meet again

[F] [F7] [Bb] [F]
ʻO ka haliʻa aloha i hiki mai
[C7]
Ke hone aʻe nei i kuʻu manawa
[F] [F7] [Bb] [F]
ʻO ʻoe nō kaʻu ipo aloha
[Bb] [C7] [F]
A loko e hana nei

Thus sweet memories come back to me
Bringing fresh remembrance of the past
Dearest one, yes, thou are mine own
From thee, true love shall neʼer depart

[F] [F7] [Bb] [F]
Maopopo kuʻu ʻike i ka nani
[C7]
Nā pua rose o Maunawili
[F] [F7] [Bb] [F]
I laila hiaʻai nā manu
[Bb] [C7] [F]
Mikiʻala i ka nani o ka liko

I have seen and watched thy loveliness
Thou sweet rose of Maunawili
And ʼtis there the birds oft love to dwell
And sip the honey from thy lips

Although Liliʻuokalani intended this as a love song, it was immediately embraced as a song of farewell. Aloha ʻOe was internationally popular from its first publication in 1884, and was sung at the closing ceremony of the 1932 Olympic Games in Los Angeles. Translation by Liliʻuokalani.

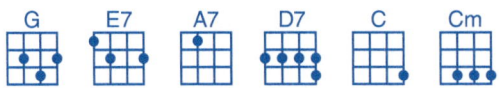

Aloha Week Hula

G   E7
Little hula flirts in hula skirts
A7
Winking at the boys in aloha shirts
          D7
That's the way they do
                   G
The Aloha Week hula

G   E7
Around the isle, mile by mile
A7
Take a detour in Hawaiian style
          D7
That's the way they do
                   G   G7
The Aloha Week hula

🎸 *hui*

          C   Cm
For a brand new step you can try and match
G   E7
Tūtū walking in the taro patch
A7
Clap your hands, the music is grand
                        D7
Do an 'ami'ami for the boys in the band...hey!

G   E7
Beat that drum, dum-dee-dum
A7
Wiggle in the middle, it's a lot of fun
          D7
That's the way they do
                   G
The Aloha Week hula

This song, also known as the 50th State Hula, was written by Jack Pitman when Hawai'i became a state in 1959. Aloha Week, a cultural celebration of Hawai'i's music, dance and history, was started in 1946 by the Jaycees Old-timers of Hawai'i. Once a week-long celebration, it has grown to span two months and all the islands.

He Mele Aloha

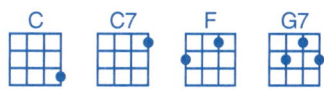

Alu Like

hui

    C   C7
E alu like mai kākou
  F
E nā 'ōiwi o Hawai'i
     G7   C
Nā pua mae 'ole
  C   G7
Nā pua nani ē

  F
E hana me ka 'oia'i'o
        C
E hana me ka ha'aha'a
  G7   C
E 'ōlelo pono kākou

     F
E nānā aku i ke kumu
    C
E ho'olohe mai
   G7
E pa'a ka waha
           C
E hana me ka lima

chorus:
Let us work together
Natives of Hawai'i
The descendants (flowers) that never fade
The beautiful, handsome descendants
The beautiful, handsome descendants

Let us work with sincerity
Let us work with humility
Let us speak with righteousness

Let us look to the source (of our strength)
Let us listen (to that source)
Let us work not so much with the mouth
Let us work more with the hands

This song by Haunani Apoliona incorporates 'ōlelo no'eau, statements of traditional wisdom and guidance. 1979.

'Anapau

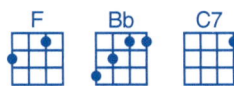

F / Bb / F
He aha e ka hana 'Anapau lā
C7 / F
Holo lio e ka hana, 'Anapau lā

tag
C7 / F / C7 / F
'Ea'eā, 'ea'eā

F / Bb / F
He aha e ka hana 'Anapau lā
C7 / F
Ho'olewa e ka hana, 'Anapau lā

F / Bb / F
I luna a'e 'oe, 'Anapau lā
C7 / F
I luna loa a'e, 'Anapau lā

F / Bb / F
I lalo iho 'oe, 'Anapau lā
C7 / F
I lalo loa iho, 'Anapau lā

F / Bb / F
He aha e ka lole, 'Anapau lā
C7 / F
He silika e ka lole, 'Anapau lā

F / Bb / F
Ha'ina ko hana, 'Anapau lā
C7 / F
'Anapau i ka lewa, 'Anapau lā

What does Frisky do?
Frisky goes horseback riding

What does Frisky do?
Frisky swings her hips

Reach up high, O Frisky!
Away up high, O Frisky

Reach down low, O Frisky!
Way down low, O Frisky

What does Frisky wear?
Frisky wears silks

Tell now of your deeds, Frisky
Frisky, you do it so well, O Frisky

"Perpetuation of life and of people was a sacred endeavor in old Hawai'i, especially where the ali'i were concerned, so the life-creating organs were named and honored with chants and hula. 'Anapau' (Frisky) was the name given to Lili'uokalani's ma'i, and this song, usually subtitled 'He Mele Ma'i No Lili'uokalani,' was originally a hula chant, with the hula danced entirely in the 'ai 'ami style. That type of hula involves little foot movement, but the dancers' hips revolve continuously throughout the dance." (Hui 280). 1880s.

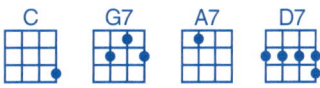

Beautiful Kahana

    C   G7
Mau loa nō koʻu mahalo nui
                   C
I ka nani pūnono o Kahana
        A7   D7
Ka moani ʻaʻala anuhea
  G7   D7   G7 C
O nā pali aʻo Koʻolauloa

My great admiration is eternal
For the beauty of Kahana is unsurpassed
The fresh and sweet fragrance is wafted
From the cliffs of Koʻolauloa

hui

   C   G7
ʻO ka home ia o ka wahine
                C
Puʻuwai aloha a ʻĪnia
          A7   D7
He pua ua miliani ʻia
  G7   D7 G7 C
E ka Mālualuakiʻiwai

chorus:
That is the home of that noble woman
Who is beloved of India's hosts
A flower held precious and dear
Caressed by the Mālualuakiʻiwai breeze

C   G7
ʻO Kalāhikiola nō ka ʻoi
               C
He puʻulena ia na ka maka
         A7   D7
Kohu kīhene pua ka uʻi
  G7   D7 G7   C
I luluhe i ka ʻae o ke kai

Kalāhikiola is unsurpassed
A vision for the eye to behold
With charm like a floral bouquet
Cascading to the edge of the sea

This is one of many beautiful songs written in appreciation of special homes, places and welcoming hosts. In this mele, Mary J. Montano honors Mary E. Foster, her country home in Kahana, Oahu, and her hospitality to those who brought the Baha'i faith to Hawai'i from India. 1915.

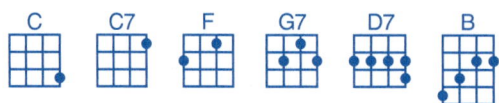

Beautiful Kaua'i

C   C7 F   C
There is an island across the sea
      G7   C
Beautiful Kaua'i, beautiful Kaua'i
                    F   C
And it's calling, yes calling to me
      D7   G7   C   C7
Beautiful Kaua'i, beautiful Kaua'i

        F
In the midst of Fern Grotto
          C   B   C
Mother nature made her home
      D7
And the falls of Wailua
     G7
Where lovers often roam

      C   C7   F   C
So I'll return to my island across the sea
      G7   C
Beautiful Kaua'i, beautiful Kaua'i

Rudolph (Randy) Haleakalā Farden, Jr. wrote this while at the Coco Palms Hotel on Kaua'i. A hotel where, at dusk, a lucky visitor could witness the famous and fabulous torchlighting ceremony created by hotel manager Grace Buscher Guslander. Under her management from 1953 to 1985 the hotel was noted for its joyful celebration of Hawaiian song, dance and spirit.

The composer's family sung the line "In the midst of Fern Grotto." Don Ho recorded the same line as "In the mist of Fern Grotto." This is credible, as there is indeed a hanging mist in the air of Fern Grotto. Since we don't have a written record by the composer himself, we cannot be certain of his original intent. This is a good example of how easy it is for variations to develop in an oral tradition, and why there often is no "right" answer. 1967.

He Mele Aloha

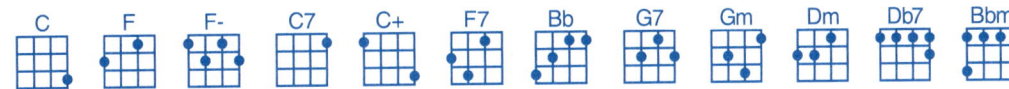

Blue Lei

C   F
You were wearing a blue lei
          F-   C7
The day that I first met you
And we wandered on the sand
          C+   F
By the blue, blue sea

           F7
With not a cloud in the sky
     Bb
To distress us
     G7
Not a care had you or I
     C7
To suppress us

     C+   F
I shall always remember
              C7
The moment when I kissed you
       Gm
For the smile upon your lips
         Dm
So heavenly sweet

F7   Bb   Db7
When your blue eyes looked into mine
     F- F
It was then the sun began to shine
    Gm   C7
That day in May
     Bbm   C7   F
You wore a blue, blue lei

R. Alex Anderson composed his first hit song, Haole Hula, in 1927, and continued composing hapa haole music for the next fifty years. He wrote this with Milton Beamer in 1940.

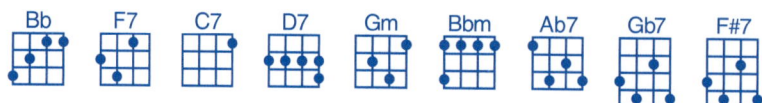

Cockeyed Mayor of Kaunakakai

    Bb   F7   Bb   F7
He wore a malo and a coconut hat
Bb   C7   F7   Bb
One was for this and the other for that
                          F7 Bb
All the people shouted as he went by
F7   Bb   C7   F7   Bb
He was the cockeyed mayor of Kaunakakai

    Bb   F7   Bb
He wore a lei and he wore a smile
F7   Bb   C7 F7   Bb
He drank a gallon of 'oke to make life worthwhile
                    F7 Bb
He made them laugh 'til he made them cry
F7   Bb   C7   F7 Bb
He was the cockeyed mayor of Kaunakakai

      D7
The horse he rode was skinny
                   Gm
A broken down old female
     C7
He placed a green pānini
                F7
Right under that horse's tail

    Bbm   Ab7   Gb7   F7
He made her buck and he made her fly
   Bbm   Ab7   F#7 F7
All over the island of Moloka'i
       C7   Bbm   C7
You could hear the kānes and wahines cheer
                    F7
As they gave him a lei of kīkānia

F7   Bb
Now you've heard my story
    F7   Bb
About the mayor of Kaunakakai
G7   C7
All his fame and glory
                 F7
On the island of Moloka'i — auē

This R. Alex Anderson song provides an early example of political correctness when, in 1936, "CBS, NBC and ABC radio stations all refused to play it. They claimed that the song made fun of mayors and ridiculed people who had such a deformity as being cockeyed." The stations got over it once comic dancer Hilo Hattie made it famous. (Stone 92)

He Mele Aloha

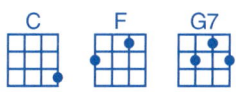

E Hīhīwai

[C] Aia i ka nani
[F] O Moloka'i [C] lā
I nā pali weliweli o ke Ko'o[G7]lau [F] [C]

Hea mai ka leo hone
[F] I ke ahiahi [C] lā
I ka makani 'Ekepue o ke a[G7]wāwa [C]

hui

[C] E hīhīwai lā lae lae
[F] E ho'i mai kāua [C] lā
I ka 'āina uluwehi o [G7] Wailau [F] [C]

Hanahano wale nō
[F] Ka wailele Kahiwa [C] lā
A me ke kuahiwi [G7] 'o Oloku'i [C]

[C] Mele kākou nei a pau
[F] I ka mele 'āina [C] lā
O ka nani mae 'ole o ke [G7] ola mau [F] [C]

'O ka makani ku'u leo
[F] 'O ke kai ku'u [C] pu'uwai
'O ka 'āina uluwehi [G7] ku'u nui kino [C]

There in the beauty of Moloka'i
Amid the awesome cliffs of the windward side
The sweet voice beckons
In the evening hours
On the cold 'Ekepue wind of the valley

chorus:
O hīhīwai lā lae lae
Let us two return
To the lush beautiful land of Wailau
Simply glorious
Is the waterfall Kahiwa
And the mountain peak of Oloku'i

Let us all sing together
The song of the land
Of the never fading beauty of life eternal
The wind is my voice
The sea is my heart
The lush and beautiful land is my whole being

Dennis Kamakahi extolls the beauty of the remote valley of Wailau, on Moloka'i. 1978.

He Mele Aloha

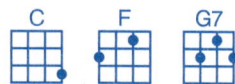

E Hoʻi I Ka Pili

C
E hoʻi i ka pili
F   **C**
E kuʻu ipo
G7
E neneʻe mai, e nanea mai
F   **C**
E ke aloha
G7   **C**
E hoʻonipo kāua

Come back to me
My darling love
Cuddle close and relax
Oh my beloved
And let us make love

C
He lei wehi ʻoe
F   **C**
No kuʻu nui kino
G7
Lei ʻala hoʻōnaona lua i ka poli
F   **C**
E ke aloha
G7   **C**
E hanu lipo kāua

You are like a lei
For my whole being
Incomparably fragrant in the heart
Oh my dearest
Let us deeply kiss

C
Ka nehe a ke kai
F   **C**
O Kahakuloa
G7
Kai koʻo hākuʻi, piʻi i ka pali
F   **C**
E ke aloha
G7   **C**
Pulupē iho kāua

The murmuring of the sea
At Kahakuloa
Rumbling on the rocks, splashing
    upon the cliffs
Oh, my love
We are drenched

C
Puana ʻia mai
F   **C**
E kuʻu ipo
G7
E neneʻe mai, e nanea mai
F   **C**
E ke aloha
G7   **C**
E hoʻonipo kāua

Let it be told
My love, my darling
Come cuddle close, and relax
Oh my beloved
And let us make love

This song by Kealiʻi Reichel beckons the loved one to return and enjoy the delights and passions of the relationship. 1990s.

He Mele Aloha

E Kuʻu Tūtū

G
Aloha au i kuʻu tūtū lā
D7   **G G7**
I ka nui lokomaikaʻi
C   **G**   **A7**
E lohe mau ʻia ana lā
D7   **G**
Kona leo heahea

I love my grandmother
For her good and kindly nature
Always heard will be
Her welcoming voice

G
ʻO ka holokū kalakoa lā
D7   **G G7**
Ka muʻumuʻu lima nui
C   **G**   **A7**
Ka hainakā lei kilika lā
D7   **G**
ʻO kona wehi mau ia

The calico holokū
The puffy-sleeved muʻumuʻu
The silk handkerchief worn about as a lei
Those are always her adornments

G
ʻO ka humu kapa pohopoho lā
D7   **G G7**
Ka ulana i ka pāpale
C   **G**   **A7**
ʻO ke kui lei pua ʻala lā
D7   **G**
A ʻo ia kona makemake

Stitching quilted blankets
Plaiting woven hats
Stringing leis of sweet flowers
Those are her favorite things

G
Aia ma kona lumi lā
D7   **G G7**
He noho paipai nui
C   **G**   **A7**
He mea hoʻoluliluli lā
D7   **G**
I kāna lei moʻopuna

There in her room
Is a large rocking chair
Used for gently rocking
Her precious grandchildren

G
Haʻina mai ka puana lā
D7   **G G7**
No kuʻu tūtū aloha
C   **G**   **A7**
E lohe mau ʻia ana lā
D7   **G**
Kona leo heahea

The story, then, is told
About my beloved grandmother
Always heard will be
Her welcoming voice

Mary Kawena Pukui and Maddy Lam collaborated on many songs, including this one in 1955. It includes an often used poetic reference to children, especially one's own children or moʻopuna, as lei. He lei poina ʻole ke keiki, an unforgettable lei is the child.

E Maliu Mai

   G
E maliu mai   Please heed my voice
  G7   C
E ku'u ipo   Oh my beloved
        D7   G   D7
Me ke aloha pumehana   With all your warm affection

hui
     D7   G
E maliu mai   *chorus:*
  G7   C   Come close to me
E ku'u ipo   My beloved
        D7   G
Me ke aloha lei makamae   With your love, like a precious lei

G   G7
Ko'u 'i'ini   My desire
    C   Is that you be mine
Na'u 'oe   With your soft, gentle voice
    A7   D7
Me kou leo nahenahe

Irmgard Aluli wrote this for her husband, and as a song to be played at weddings. 1950.

He Mele Aloha

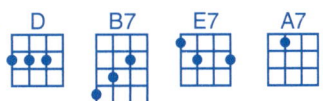

E Naughty Naughty Mai Nei

D   B7   E7   A7   D
When you make with the hula, you are so happy and gay
         B7   E7   A7
You do a slow 'ami'ami

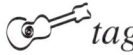 *tag*

                                D   A7   D
   E naughty naughty mai nei, 'eā 'eā, e naughty naughty mai nei

D   B7   E7   A7   D
Your smile is so full of mischief, why do you tease me this way?
               B7   E7   A7
You're driving my poor heart crazy

D   B7   E7   A7   D
When you move so enticing, your lovely eyes seem to say
        B7   E7   A7
Aloha dear how's about it?

D   B7   E7   A7   D
Your hair is long and it ripples, like the moon on the bay
            B7   E7   A7
With every 'ami you beckon

D   B7   E7   A7   D
You don't kiss 'cause you love me, nor when you give me your lei
          B7   E7   A7
You're up to something, I think so

D   B7   E7   A7   D
Ha'ina should be the ending, of every song that they play
         B7   E7   A7
But with you it's beginning

Entertainer and composer Mel Peterson, like many island musicians, spent much of his professional career on the mainland, an indication of the popularity of Hawaiian music throughout the United States and indeed the world. 1940s.

'Ekolu Mea Nui

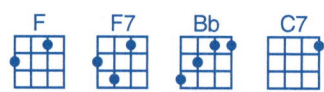

'Ekolu mea nui ma ka honua
'O ka mana'o'i'o, ka mana'olana
A me ke aloha, ke aloha ka i 'oi a'e
Pōmaika'i nā mea a pau

E nā mākua, nā keiki
Nā mamo a Iuda me 'Epelaima
E pa'a ka mana'o i ka pono i 'oi a'e
Pōmaika'i nā mea a pau

Three important things in the world
Faith, hope, and love
Of these love is foremost
Everyone, then, is blessed

Oh parents, children
Descendants of Judah and Ephraim
Think always of the foremost virtue
Everyone, then, is blessed

Robert K. Nāwāhine composed this song for a Congregational church song contest in 1925, basing it on a passage from Corinthians, "And now abideth faith, hope, love, these three; but the greatest of these is love."

'Eleu Mikimiki

    F   G7   C7
Kāu hana mau nō ia, 'o ka milimili 'apa

                F   C7
Hala 'ē ka wā kūpono, 'o ka milimili 'apa

                F
Hala 'ē ka wā kūpono

hui

    C#   F   D7
E kala nō 'oe a i a'o mua 'ia ai

  G7   C7   F
Na ka 'eleu mikimiki, nāna ē ka lawe lilo

F   G7
'A'ole nō a he lua

C7   F
A e like ai me 'oe ma ka ho'ohemahema

F   G7   C7
Kapae ka hilahila, e wake up mai ho'i 'oe

                                   F
A laila, 'aka 'oe, no ka mea, 'o 'oe ka best

F   G7
Ua 'ike maka nō 'oe

C7   F
I ka nani lua 'ole o ka lei hulu mamo

F   G7
'O ka puana kāu e ho'olohe mai

C7   F
Na ka 'eleu mikimiki nāna ē ka lawe lilo

That's usual with you
To linger and be so slow
Till the right time passes by
To linger and be so slow
Till the right time passes by

chorus:
You have long ago been warned
That the alert and quick one is the one
    that will win all

There is none other
That could compare with you in being
    so careless

Put aside your bashfulness, you must
    wake up
Then you will laugh because you are
    the best

Surely you have seen
The unsurpassed beauty of the mamo
    feather lei

The refrain, which you should heed
The alert and quick one is the one who
    will win all

Charles E. King cautions "step lively, lazy-bones, the one who pays attention will win all" in this 1930s song.

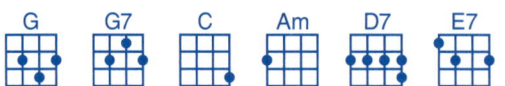

Farewell for Just Awhile

G   G7   C   Am
Farewell for just awhile
D7   G
We're parting with a smile
G7   C   Am
Dreams will keep me near you
D7   G
Farewell for just awhile

G
It's time for us to say farewell for just awhile,
     Am
   for just a little while
D7   G
So let's be thankful that we're parting with a smile,
   it's easy when you smile
G7   C   Am
I'll miss you so but dreams will keep me near you,
  E7   Am
   I know
D7   G
We'll meet again farewell for just awhile,
   D7   G
   for just a little while

Jack Brooks put these English lyrics to a traditional Tahitian farewell song. The second verse can be sung in obligato with the first. 1950.

He Mele Aloha

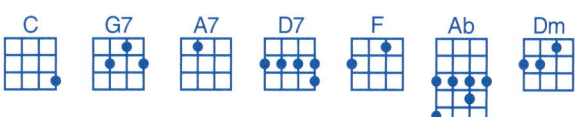

For You a Lei

  C   G7   C   Ab
It is time to say goodbye, dear
G7   C
Dry your tears and don't you cry
A7   Dm
Just one more embrace and a fond adieu
     D7   G7
And here's a lei I brought for you

C   G7   C
For you a lei of flowers rare
         G7   C
For you a lei to hold and wear
        A7   D7
For you a lei to caress while you are away
                               F   G7
Throw your troubles away make you happy and gay

                     C
A lei of love I give to you
        C7   F
To think of me when you are blue
                  Ab   C   A7
Where ever you may be, over land or on the sea
    D7   G7   C
For you a lei to remember me

Composer Johnny Noble was also a collector of traditional and contemporary Hawaiian songs, which he published along with his own songs in several books of collected work, ensuring that these songs were passed on to us. 1929.

He Mele Aloha

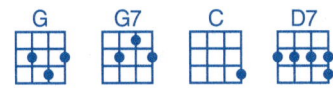

Green Rose Hula

| G | G7 | C | G |
No ka pua lokelau ke aloha
| C | G | D7 | G |
No ka uʻi kau i ka wēkiu

My love goes to the green rose
The blossom I esteem the highest

| G | G7 | C | G |
Ko ʻala onaona i ʻaneʻi
| C | G | D7 | G |
Hoʻolale mai ana e walea

Your fragrance reaches me here
Inviting my thoughts to be carefree

| G | G7 | C | G |
E walea pū aku me ʻoe
| C | G | D7 | G |
I ka hana noʻeau hoʻoipo

O to while the time pleasantly with you
In the delightful pastime of wooing

| G | G7 | C | G |
A he ipo ʻoe naʻu i aloha
| C | G | D7 | G |
Ka ʻanoʻi a kuʻu puʻuwai

You are the sweetheart I love
The darling of my heart

| G | G7 | C | G |
Ka hāʻupu, ka haliʻa, ka ʻiʻini
| C | G | D7 | G |
Me ʻoe mau aku nō ia

May recollection, remembrance and desire
Always be with you

| G | G7 | C | G |
Hoʻi mai kāua lā e pili
| C | G | D7 | G |
ʻOiai ka manawa kūpono

Now, now is the time
For us to be together

| G | G7 | C | G |
Haʻina ʻia mai ana ka puana
| C | G | D7 | G |
Nou nō green rose ke aloha

This is the end of my song
For you, beloved green rose

John Kameaaloha Almeida is said to have composed songs as gifts for the women he loved. The green rose, with its somewhat plain features and its spicy, peppery scent may indicate something about the woman who inspired this poetry, and one wonders at how his blindness might have worked to strengthen his imagery. 1935. Translation by Mary Kawena Pukui.

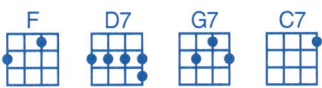

Hale'iwa

F   D7   G7
Hanohano nō Hale'iwa
   C7   F
Ku'u home aloha

Hale'iwa is magnificent
My beloved home

F   D7   G7
U'i nō 'o Pua'ena
      C7   F
Ka 'ehu kai hāwanawana

So beautiful is Pua'ena
With the spray of the whispering sea

F   D7   G7
Kilakila 'o Hale'iwa
      C7   F
Ka hale kipa o ka malihini

Majestic is Hale'iwa (Hotel)
A welcoming place for visitors

F   D7   G7
Ha'ina 'ia mai ka puana
      C7   F
Hanohano Hale'iwa

Tell the story
Hale'iwa is magnificent

Pua'ena Point, referred to in this song by Jennie Nāpua Hānaiali'i Woodd, is an ancient surfing area at the northern end of Waialua Bay, O'ahu, 1934.

Hale'iwa Pāka

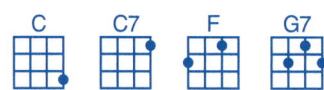

    C   C7 F   C
Hanohano wale 'oe e Hale'iwa Pāka   You are truly glorious, Hale'iwa Park
   G7   C
'Ohu'ohu i ka popohe a ka pua hau   Adorned with the full bloom of hau blossoms

  C   C7 F   C
'O ka luli mālie a ka lau o ka niu   The gentle swaying of the coconut leaves
    G7   C
I ke aheahe 'olu a ka makani kolonahe   In the comforting touch of the gentle breeze

 C   C7 F   C
Laukanaka mau 'oe i ka lehulehu   You are always filled with people
 G7   C
E kipa mau ana e 'ike i kou nani   Who come often to see your beauty

 C   C7 F   C
Ka 'oē a ke kai i ka 'ae kai   The murmur of the ocean at the shoreline
  G7   C
E kono mai ana e luana iki kāua   Invites you and I to relax awhile

 C   C7 F   C
Ua ana ka 'ikena i kou nani   The sight of your beauty is fulfilling
  G7   C
Hanohano mau 'oe e Hale'iwa Pāka   You, Hale'iwa Park, are ever glorious

All the senses are engaged in this lyrical description of Hale'iwa Park by Alice K. Nāmakelua.

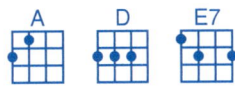

Hāli'ilua

A	D	A
Aloha kahi wai a'o Hāli'ilua lā, lana mālie
	E7	A
'O ke one kaulana o Keōua lā, 'o ka 'ihi kapu

Beloved are the fresh waters at Hāli'ilua, placid and calm
The famous sands of Keōua, of sacred kapu

| A | D | A |
Kapukapu nā maka a'o ka 'ōpua lā, ke 'ike aku
| | E7 | A |
Ka 'anapa i ka luna o Ka'awaloa lā, maoli pua

Faces of the cloud banks are regal to see
Gleaming there above Ka'awaloa, amazing offspring of the land

| A | D | A |
He pua nani 'oe a he mea laha 'ole lā, na ka makua
| | E7 | A |
A he lei 'ā'ī na ke kupuna lā, he mea milimili

You are a beautiful blossom and a rare thing for the parents
A neck lei for the elders and a thing to be cherished

| A | D | A |
Ki'ina ko lei lehua i 'Ōla'a lā, lei 'ia mai
| | E7 | A |
I 'ohu no ka wahine e walea ai lā, me 'ano'i pua

Fetch your lehua lei at 'Ōla'a, and be draped
As an adornment for the woman to enjoy, like a sweetheart

| A | D | A |
Mahalo aku wau lā i ka nani lā, mau mea ho'ohihi
| | E7 | A |
Ka 'ōnohi o ka lā, mālamalama lā, kau kehakeha

I admire the beauty, things that delight
The orb of the sun, shining brightly, set on high

| A | D | A |
'O ke kō a ka hau anu o Ma'ihi lā, 'au i ke kai
| | E7 | A |
Kaomi i ka 'ili o ke kama hele lā, me ka 'eha koni

The surge of cold of Ma'ihi moves along over the sea
Pressing against the skin of the traveler, with a cold throbbing

| A | D | A |
Ha'ina ko lei lehua i 'Ōla'a lā, lei 'ia mai
| | E7 | A |
Ka 'ōnohi o ka lā, mālamalama lā, kau kehakeha

The refrain is told of your lehua lei at 'Ōla'a
The orb of the sun, shining brightly, set proudly on high

This traditional song, noting places on Hawai'i, was taught to Vicky 'Ī'ī by her grandmother, who said it was not meant for children to sing.

Hanalei Moon

    F   G7
When you see Hanalei by moonlight
      C7   F   C7
You will be in heaven by the sea
     F   G7
Every breeze, every wave, will whisper
     C7   F
You are mine, don't ever go away

 F   D7   G7
Hanalei, Hanalei moon
  C7   Bb F
Is lighting beloved Kaua'i
     D7   G7
Hanalei, Hanalei moon
 C7   F
Aloha nō wau iā 'oe

This simple song by Bob Nelson strikes a note of truth and recognition in those who have visited Hanalei by moonlight. The last line, "Aloha nō wau iā 'oe," — I love you — could be directed at someone special or to the place itself.

He Mele Aloha

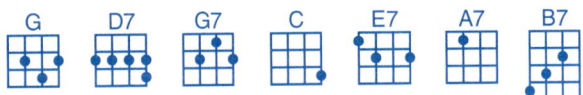

Hanohano Hanalei

G   D7   G
Hanohano Hanalei i ka ua nui
         D7   G G7
I pakika kahi limu o Manuʻakepa
C   G   E7
I laila hoʻi au i ʻike iho ai
   A7   D7
I ka hana huʻi konikoni i ka ʻili
G   D7   G   G7
Aloha kahi one o Puarose
  C   B7
I ka hoʻopē ʻia e ka huna kai
   E7   A7
ʻAkahi hoʻi au a ʻike i ka nani
G   D7   G
Hanohano Hanalei i ka ua nui

G   D7   G
Kilakila kahi wai Nāmolokama
         D7   G G7
I ke kau ʻia mai hoʻi e ka ʻohu
C   G   E7
He ʻohu hoʻi ʻoe no ka ʻāina
   A7   D7
A Hanalei aʻe haʻaheo nei
G   D7   G   G7
Kilohi i ka nani Māmalahoa
  C   B7
I ka hoʻopē ʻia e ke kēhau
   E7   A7
ʻElua wale iho nō māua
       G   D7   G
ʻEkolu i ka hone a ka ʻehu kai

Grand is Hanalei in the pouring rain
Making the moss of Manuʻakepa slick
It is there that I saw
Things that made me tingle
Beloved the sands of Puarose
Wetted by the spray of the sea
Finally I've witnessed the beauty
Grand is Hanalei in the pouring rain

Majestic are the waters of Nāmolokama
Overlaid by the sweeping mists
You are an adornment for the land
That makes Hanalei proud
Gaze at the beauty of Māmalahoa
Moistened by the dew
There was just the two of us
Three with the murmur of sea spray

Although not a direct translation, this accompanying verse by composer Alfred ʻAlohikea expresses as eloquently in English as in Hawaiian the pilina paʻa, solid connection, between the people of Hawaiʻi and the land. 1920s.

> *For beauty Hanalei is unexcelled*
> *Her mountains so majestic are ever verdant*
> *The waterfalls and the beautiful shore*
> *Her charms are rare and ever for her my praises shall ring*
> *The spray from the waves that are always splashing*
> *On the moss covered rocks that cling to cliffs*
> *No land that I know allures and enchants*
> *Hanalei! Home of beauty I ever adore*

Hanohano Ka Lei Pīkake

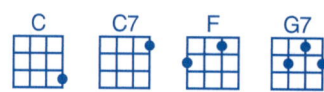

C		C7

Hanohano ka lei pīkake
Ke hoʻolale mai nei
He ʻiʻini nui koʻu

Nāu e hoʻokō mai
I laila koʻu manaʻo
E pili aku me ʻoe
I ka poli pumehana

Glorious garland of pīkake
Strongly stirring
A deep urge within
That only you can satisfy
My desire is to be
Adorned by you
In your loving embrace

Moani mai kou ʻala
A puīa ʻo loko
ʻUpu aʻe kuʻu liʻa

E honi mau aku
I ka hanu anuhea
Pōniu au i ke onaona
I hoʻohihi ai ka manaʻo

Your fragrance is borne here
Infusing my very being
Welling up my desire
To forever take in
Your soft, cool
And heady aroma
That I so desire

Puana mai kuʻu liʻa
Ka ʻiʻini o loko
He ʻiʻini nui koʻu

Nāu e hoʻokō mai
I laila koʻu manaʻo
E pili aku me ʻoe
I ka poli pumehana

Let my desire be known
This yearning in me
A deep urge within
That only you can satisfy
My desire is to be
Adorned by you
In your loving embrace

This composition by Puakea Nogelmeier, set to a melody by Paleka Mattos, describes how certain people, like fragrant pīkake, can entrance the mind. 1989.

He Mele Aloha

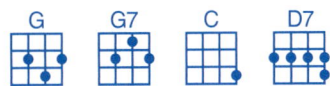

Hanohano Olinda

G **G7** **C** **G**
Hanohano Olinda kuʻu home kuahiwi
D7 **G**
E hoʻopumehana i ke ahi kapuahi

Majestic is Olinda, my mountain home
Get warmed by the blaze of the hearth

G **G7** **C** **G**
ʻO ka neʻe paʻa mai a ka ua Nāulu
D7 **G**
Kohu maka kui kele ʻīnikiniki i ka ʻili

The steady approach of the sudden Nāulu rains
Is like needle points nipping the skin

G **G7** **C** **G**
Haʻina ʻia mai ana ka puana
D7 **G**
Kēhau kakahiaka ʻīnikiniki pāpālina

Tell the story in the refrain
Morning frost that tingles the cheeks

Composed by Alice Johnson for Olinda Vista, home of Maui sugar plantation manager Frank Hutchinson, after which the surrounding area was eventually named.

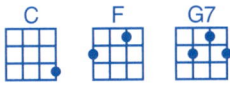

Hanohano Wailea

C **F** **C**
Hanohano Wailea i kaʻu ʻike
G7 **C**
Ka wahine kiaʻi ʻau i ke kai

Honored is Wailea in my thoughts
The guardian-woman who reaches into the sea

C **F** **C**
Pūnāwai ʻiliʻili nehe i ke kai
G7 **C**
ʻAuana ka wai ʻolu i ka ulu hala

Pūnāwai's pebbles clatter in the tide
Cool water winding through the hala grove

C **F** **C**
Halakau ʻo Kaʻiwa i luna lilo
G7 **C**
Neʻe mai ʻo Ahiki i ke kualono

Kaʻiwa rests high above
And Ahiki shifts this way, along the ridge

C **F** **C**
Hoʻolono Kaʻōhao i kēia mele
G7 **C**
O kuʻu ʻāina nani e waiho nei

Kaʻōhao pays attention to this song
Of my beautiful home spread out below

Composed by Kīhei de Silva and Moe Keale. 1984.

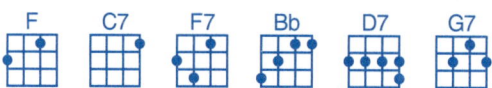

Haole Hula

F   C7   F
Oh, when I hear the strains of that sweet "'Alekoki"
         C7   F   F7
And stealing from a far-off guitar "Penei nō"
    Bb   D7   G7
When "Lili'u ē" makes you sway in the moonlight
           C7   F
I know the reason why fair Hawai'i haunts you so

F   C7   F
The lovely blue of sky and the sapphire of ocean
                              C7   F   F7
The flashing white of clouds and of waves' foaming crest
      Bb   D7   G7
The many shades of green from the plains to the mountains
              C7   F
With all the brightest hues of the rainbow we're blessed

F   C7   F
I hear the swish of rain as it sweeps down the valley
                    C7   F   F7
I hear the song of wind as it sighs through the trees
         Bb   D7   G7
I hear the crash of waves on the rocks and the beaches
              C7   F
I hear the hissing surf and boom of the sea

F   C7   F
I love to dance and sing of the charms of Hawai'i
                  C7   F   F7
And from a joyful heart sing aloha to you
        Bb   D7   G7
In every note I'll tell of the spell of my islands
              C7   F
For then I know that you'll be in love with them too

R. Alex Anderson composed Haole Hula *for Don Blanding's Hula Moon show, performed at the old Princess Theater in Honolulu in 1927. Although written in English, Anderson's songs are thematically Hawaiian, such as this one in which he shares with you the beauty of the islands through sight, sound and motion.* 'Alekoki, Penei nō *and* Lili'u ē *are titles of popular songs, the strains of which would haunt anyone who loved the islands.*

Hawai'i Aloha

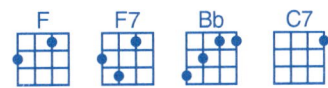

F / F7 Bb / F
E Hawai'i, e ku'u one hānau ē
　　　　C7　　　　　F
Ku'u home kulāiwi nei
　　　　F7　　Bb　　F
'Oli nō au i nā pono lani ou
　　C7　　　　F
E Hawai'i aloha ē

O Hawai'i, o sands of my birth
My native home
I rejoice in the heavenly blessings of you
O beloved Hawai'i

🎸 *hui*

　　F　　Bb　　　　　　　　　F
E hau'oli e nā 'ōpio o Hawai'i nei
　　　　C7
'Oli ē! 'Oli ē!
　　　　F　　　　F7　Bb　　F
Mai nā aheahe makani e pā mai nei
　　C7　　　　　F
Mau ke aloha no Hawai'i

chorus:
Be joyous o youth of Hawai'i
Rejoice! Rejoice!
May the gentle breezes blow
Love for Hawai'i is eternal

F　　　　　　　　　F7　Bb　F
E ha'i mai kou mau kini lani ou
　　　C7　　　　　　　F
Kou mau kupa aloha, e Hawai'i
　　　　　　　　F7　Bb　　F
Nā mea 'ōlino kamaha'o no luna mai
　　C7　　　　F
E Hawai'i aloha ē

May your divine throngs speak
Your loving people, o Hawai'i
The holy light from above
O beloved Hawai'i

F　　　　　　　　F7　Bb　　F
Na ke Akua e mālama mai iā 'oe
　　　C7　　　　　　F
Kou mau kualono aloha nei
　　　　　　　　　F7　Bb　　F
Kou mau kahawai 'ōlinolino mau
　　C7　　　　　F
Kou mau māla pua nani ē

May God protect you
Your beloved mountain ridges
Your ever glistening streams
Your beautiful gardens of flowers

Lorenzo Lyons, better known as Makua Laiana, arrived in Hawai'i in 1832 and remained until his death in 1886. Fluent in Hawaiian, he was a critical force in encouraging Hawaiian as a written language, and in translating hymns into Hawaiian. He wrote these words originally as a poem around 1860, they were later set to the music of I Left It All With Jesus. *This is often the last song at Hawaiian gatherings sung before dispersing. A closing tag of "E Hawai'i aloha ē" — Oh beloved Hawai'i — is often sung as a parting line.*

46
He Mele Aloha

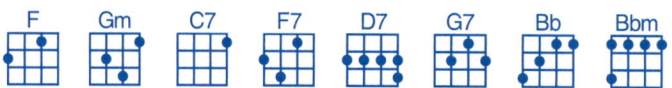

Hawaiʻi Calls

     F   Gm C7
Hawaiʻi calls
                F
With a melody of love dear
     Gm C7
Across the sea
     F   F7
As evening falls

  Bb   C7   F
The surf is booming on the sand at Waikīkī tonight
       G7
Oh how I wish that you were strolling hand in hand
  C7
With me tonight

 F   Gm C7
Hawaiʻi calls
             F
With a message of aloha
      Gm C7
To you sweetheart
       F F7
Where e'er you are

 Bb   Bbm
Reminding you to dream a while
 F   D7
Of happy days we knew
    Gm
Hawaiʻi calls
 C7   F
And my heart's calling you

Harry Owens has captured a truth. Hawaiʻi indeed calls, as almost no place else on Earth, to those for whom it is home and those who have but visited briefly, even to those who may have just read about it or seen a glimpse in a movie or magazine.

He Mele Aloha

Hawai'i Pono'ī

    F   C7
Hawai'i pono'ī
           F
Nānā i kou mō'ī
G7   C
Ka lani ali'i
  G7   C7
Ke ali'i

     hui

      C7
Makua lani ē
           F
Kamehameha ē
      F7   Bb
Na kaua e pale
C7   F
Me ka ihe

  F   C7
Hawai'i pono'ī
         F
Nānā i nā ali'i
  G7   C
Nā pua muli kou
  G7   C7
Nā pōki'i

  F   C7
Hawai'i pono'ī
        F
E ka lāhui ē
    G7   C
'O kāu hana nui
  G7 C7
E ui ē

Hawai'i's own
Be loyal to your chief
Your country's liege and lord
The ali'i

chorus:
Father above us all
Kamehameha
Who guarded in war
With his spear

Hawai'i's own
Look to your lineal chiefs
These chiefs of latter birth
Younger siblings

Hawai'i's own
People of loyal hearts
Thy only duty lies
Listen and abide

For the last two decades of the Hawaiian kingdom this was the national anthem. It continues to be sung today, together with the Star Spangled Banner, at most public events in Hawai'i. Its history is unusually well documented. Henry Berger, conductor of His Majesty's Band, composed Hymn of Kamehameha *for his inaugural concert in 1872. King Kalākaua put these words to that music, and it was first sung in Kawaiaha'o church in 1874. In the original musical score, "Nanai na 'li'i" used five syllables, as it was intended to be sung. When standardized spelling is applied, 'nānā i nā ali'i' appears to have seven syllables, although those familiar with the conventions of spoken Hawaiian will know that the glides that smoothly join vowels allow it to fit the same meter.*

Hawaiian Cowboy

A
He wahi lio Lehua kou inoa lā
D
Kilakila wale 'oe o Hawai'i lā
E7
E like kou holo 'ana me ka 'ō'io lā
A
Ke kolo, ke kuli, ke ku'i kolo iho 'oe

'Auhea wale 'oe te wahine holo lio
D   E7   A
Pua nani a'o Hawai'i lā aloha i ka Hawaiian cowboy

You are a fine steed, Lehua is your name
Majestic one of Hawai'i
Your ride is smooth like the 'ō'io fish
You crouch, work the knees, and you post
Where are you oh horsewoman
Beautiful blossom of Hawai'i who loves the Hawaiian cowboy

A   E7
Ku'u lei, 'o lei lehua, lei lehua, 'o lei lehua
A   D   A   E7 A
Lei lehua, 'o lei lehua, 'o nā lei, lei u'i ē

My garland, lei of lehua, garland of lehua, lei of lehua
Garland of lehua, lei of lehua, the garlands, beautiful leis

A
He wahi lio Roselani kou inoa lā
D
Kilakila wale 'oe o Maui lā
E7
E like kou holo 'ana me ka 'ō'io lā
A
Ke kolo, ke kuli, ke ku'i kolo iho 'oe

'Auhea wale 'oe te wahine holo lio
D   E7   A
Pua nani a'o Hawai'i lā aloha i ka Hawaiian cowboy

You are a fine steed, Roselani is your name
Majestic one of Maui
Your ride is smooth like the 'ō'io fish
You crouch, work the knees, and you post
Where are you oh horsewoman
Beautiful blossom of Hawai'i who loves the Hawaiian cowboy

A   E
Ku'u lei, 'o Roselani, Roselani, 'o Roselani
A   D   A   E7 A
Roselani, 'o Roselani, 'o nā lei, lei u'i ē

My garland, lei of Roselani, garland of Roselani, lei of Roselani
Roselani, oh Roselani, Roselani, oh Roselani, the garlands, beautiful leis

Solomon (Kolomone) Kamaluhia Kekipi Kealiikaapunikukealaokamahanahana Bright was on tour in San Francisco in 1933, playing to a packed house at the Tahitian Hut. When, during intermission a woman was enticing the guitar player to yodel with twenty-dollar bills. Bright composed this song on the spot.

He Mele Aloha

A
Ha'alele mai au i Honolulu lā
D
Ho'i mai au i ka 'āina malihini
E7
Ke kau 'ana aku i ka lio Kaleponi
A
Ua fāfā mai lā 'o Lehua
A
He wahi lio kalakoa ko ka 'āina malihini lā
D
I San Francisco by the Golden Gate
E7   **A**
Aloha i ka Hawaiian cowboy

I depart from Honolulu
Coming back to foreign lands
Mounting a California steed
Lehua said don't do that
The foreign land has a horse of many colors
In San Francisco by the Golden Gate Bridge
  who loves the Hawaiian cowboy

A   **E7**
Ku'u lei, 'o lei 'ilima, lei 'ilima, 'o lei 'ilima
       A   **D**   **A**   **E7**   **A**
Lei 'ilima, 'o lei 'ilima, 'o nā lei, lei u'i ē

My garland, lei of 'ilima, garland of 'ilima, lei of 'ilima
Garland of 'ilima, lei of 'ilima, the garlands, beautiful leis

A
I'm heading for the last roundup
D
'Auhea wale 'oe te wahine holo lio
E7
E like kou holo 'ana me ka 'ō'io lā
A
Ke kolo, ke kuli, ke ku'i kolo iho 'oe
A
'Auhea wale 'oe te wahine holo lio
D   **E7**   **A**
Pua nani 'oe o Hawai'i lā aloha i ka Hawaiian cowboy

I'm heading for the last roundup
Where are you my horse riding woman
Your ride is smooth like the 'ō'io fish
You crouch, work the knees, and you post
Where are you oh horsewoman
Beautiful blossom of Hawai'i who loves the Hawaiian cowboy

A   **E7**
Ha'ina mai ka puana ku'u lei 'o lei lehua
     A   **D**   **A** **E7** **A**
Roselani, lei 'ilima 'o nā lei, lei u'i ē

Tell the tale in the refrain my garland, lei of lehua
Roselani, lei of 'ilima, the garlands, leis of beauty

A
Roselani dandee is the pride of Maui Island
D
She can surely cut a caper on the lava by the sea
E7
When I lower my spurs to her tender little sides
A
She'll wiggle and whinny and wiggle all the way

Off to the hills and to the slopes of Polipoli
       D
We'll ramble through the bushes

Where the heifers love to play
E7   **A**
Roselani loves her Hawaiian cowboy

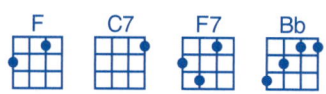

He Aloha Nō ʻO Honolulu

[F]He aloha nō ʻo Honolulu i ka ua Kū[C7]kalahale
Ka nuku aʻo Māmala ʻau aʻe nei ma ho[F]pe
Kau mai ana ma mua ka malu [F7]ʻulu aʻo Le[Bb]le
Kukui [F]ʻaʻā mau, pio [C7]ʻole i ke Kauaʻu[F]la

Dearly loved is Honolulu in the Kūkalahale rain
The entrance of Māmala Bay fares on behind
Up ahead is the breadfruit shade of Lele
The ever-blazing torch unextinguished by the Kauaʻula wind

[F]ʻAu aku i ke kai loa oni mai ana ʻo [C7]ʻUpolu
Hoʻokomo iā Mahukona i ka makani ʻĀpaʻa[F]paʻa
E wiki ʻoe ʻapa nei [F7]eia aʻe ʻo Kawai[Bb]hae
Hoʻo[F]haehae Nāulu, i ka [C7]makani kuʻehu ʻa[F]le

Faring out to the deep sea ʻUpolu Point appears
Entering Mahukona in the ʻĀpaʻapaʻa wind
Make haste, slowpoke, for here is Kawaihae
Where the Nāulu showers stir up wave gusting winds

[F]ʻO ka hao a ka Mūmuku poho pono nā peʻa he[C7]ke
ʻO ka heke nō nā Kona i ke kai māʻokiʻo[F]ki
Kiʻina ke koiʻi koi [F7]i ka piko o Hualā[Bb]lai
A la[F]ʻi wale ke kau[C7]nu ʻaʻole pahuna ha[F]la

The buffeting of the Mūmuku wind fills out the topsails
The Kona districts are foremost with their sea-patterned hues
The rush sweeps to the summit of Hualālai
And love is contented, no thrust is missed

[F]Hala ʻole nō kāua i ke kole maka ona[C7]ona
E haupā ʻoe a kena i ka piko ʻoe a lihali[F]ha
Hāliʻaliʻa mai ana [F7]kou aloha kākia i[Bb]wi
Hoʻo[F]komo iā Honuʻa[C7]po i ke kai kauha[F]ʻa

We make no error with the tender-eyed kole fish
You eat heartily, right to the rich oily belly
I'm reminded of your love holding me fast
Coming in to Honuʻapo in the restless sea

He Mele Aloha

F **C7**
Ha'alele ka Maunaloa i ka pohu la'i a'o Kona
.... **F**
Ho'okomo iā Ho'okena i ka pewa a'o ka manini
.... **F7** .... **Bb**
Ha'ina mai ka puana 'o ka heke nō nā Kona
.... **F** **C7** .... **F**
No Kona ke kai malino kaulana i ka lehulehu

The *Maunaloa* departs the quiet tranquility of Kona
Porting into Ho'okena in her bay like a manini tail
The story is told that the Kona districts are the finest
For Kona are the calm seas, famous among all people

This travel song by Lot Kauwē from around 1920 follows the sea routes of the ship Maunaloa *from Honolulu to Maui and the west coast of Hawai'i.*

He Aloha Kuʻu Ipo

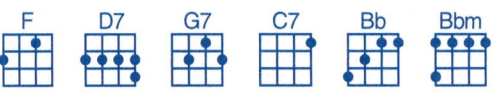

F	D7	G7

He aloha kuʻu ipo, kuʻu hoa pili
Ke kaunu mole paʻa i ka puʻuwai
(C7   Bb Bbm F)

Ua like nō ʻoe me ka lokelani
I kilipohe i ka ua kakahiaka

Hoʻoipo ke ʻala noho i ka poli
He waiwai nui ia na ka manaʻo

ʻO ʻoe a ʻo wau ka i kui like
I ka lei mae ʻole a ke aloha

Haʻina ʻia mai ana ka puana
Ke kaunu mole paʻa i ka puʻuwai

Beloved is my sweetheart, my close companion
For whom the thrill of love is deep in my heart

You are like the Hawaiian rose
Beautifully formed and dewy in the morning rain

I woo the sweetness I hold to my bosom
A great treasure to my mind

You and I are the ones who have strung together
An unfading garland of love

The story is told
The thrill of love deep in my heart

The metaphor of a single perfect blossom sparkling with dew gives an elegant sense of a special someone in this love song by Mary Kawena Pukui and Maddy Lam. Translation by Mary Kawena Pukui.

He Mele Aloha

He Hawai'i Au

   G   D7   C
I kēia pō, eia au me 'oe
  G   D7   G D7
Kēia pō, ua ho'i mai au
 G   D7   C
He loa ka helena ma ke ala hele
   G   D7   G
E huli i wahi ma kēia au

 B7   Em   G7
Maopopo a ua 'ike ho'i
 C   D7   G
Ka home i loko o ku'u pu'uwai
 B7   Em   Eb7
Ua ho'i mai au, ke 'ike nei au

  G   D7   C
'A'ole au e 'auana hou
   G   D7   G
Ke maopopo he Hawai'i au

This night, here I am with you
This night, I have returned
Long has been my journey on the road
Searching for a place in this world

I understand now, and truly know
Where home is, here in my heart
I've returned and now I know

I shall never wander again
When I understand I am a Hawaiian

Peter Moon, Ron Rosha, Alice Nāmakelua collaborated on this song of love for the land of their birth.

He Inoa No Ka'iulani

F C7 F
Lamalama i luna ka 'ōnohi lā
C7 F
Kāhiko ua koko 'ula
C7 F
Ka hō'ailona kapu o ke kama lā
C7 F
He ēwe mai nā kūpuna

🎸 *hui*

F C7 F
Ahāhā, ua nani ka wahine lā
C7 F
Ahāhā, ka nohona i ka la'i
C7 F
Ahāhā, ua hele a nohea lā
C7 F
Pua ha'aheo o ke aupuni

F C7 F
Ki'ina ka wehi o ke kama lā
C7 F
I ka mokupuni o Mano
C7 F
Ka hala o Naue i ke kai lā
C7 F
Laua'e 'a'ala o Makana

F C7 F
Kāohi 'ia iho ka mana'o lā
C7 F
A ho'i mai 'o Lilinoe
C7 F
Ka wahine noho i ke anu lā
C7 F
I ka piko o Maunakea

The display of a rainbow illuminates above
An adornment with the blood red rain
This is the sacred sign of the princess
The lineage passed down from the ancestors

chorus:
Well, now, the lady is so pretty
Here now, dwelling in tranquility
My, how she has become so beautiful
A flower that her nation embraces with pride

Fetch the adornment for the princess
On the island of Mano
The *hala* of Naue in the sea
And the fragrant *laua'e* of Makana

Any further thoughts should be repressed
Until Lilinoe returns
The woman who dwells in the chilly cold
At the summit of Maunakea

This mele inoa by Lili'uokalani acknowledges Ka'iulani's ancestors from Kaua'i. Mano is short for Manokalanipō, a famous Kaua'i chief from the Halālea district. Naue is noted for its pandanus, and the Makana cliff for its fragrant laua'e fern. 1877. Translation by Hui Hānai.

He Mele Aloha

He ʻOno

D Keu a ka ʻono ma ke alopiko lā **D7**
G Kahi momona piko ka nenue lā
D Lihaliha wale ke momoni aku lā
ʻO ka ʻōʻio halalē ke kai lā **D7**
G ʻO ka ʻōpelu e pepenu ana lā
D He ʻono toumi to hoʻi tau i tou puʻu **A7**
te momoni aku **D**

hui

A7 He ʻono a he ʻono a he ʻono ʻiʻo nō
a he ʻono nō **D**

D Mai piʻikoi ʻoe i ke akule lā **D7**
G A he iʻa ʻāhaʻi i ka hohonu lā
D Hoʻi iho ʻoe i kahi ʻanae lā
Me ka manini pūlehu ʻia lā **D7**
G ʻO ke kole ē ka iʻa maka onaona lā
D He ʻono toumi to hoʻi tau i tou puʻu **A7**
te momoni aku **D**

Oh how delicious is the belly
Rich belly of the pilot fish
Oily good to swallow
Bone fish to slurp the gravy
Scad fish to dunk with
Delicious, a treat for the throat to swallow

chorus:
Delicious, delicious, real delicious, just delicious

Don't aspire for akule
A fish that flees to the depths
Come back where the mullet is
And broiled manini
The sweet-eyed kole fish is there
Delicious, a treat for the throat to swallow

Let it suffice to say that this song by Bina Mossman has nothing to do with fish, but may speak of types of sweethearts worthy of pursuit. 1928.

He Mele Aloha

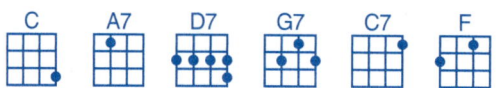

He Punahele Nō ʻOe

 C A7 D7
He punahele nō ʻoe
 G7 C G7
Na ka makua
 C A7 D7
Pūlama ʻia me ʻoe
   G7
Me ke aloha

You are one so favored
By the parents
You have been held dear
With great affection

🎸 hui

  C7 F
He wahine uʻi
 D7 F G7
A he pua nani
 C A7 D7
Ma kuʻu poli mai ʻoe
 G7 C
Kuʻu lei

chorus:
You are a beautiful woman
And a pretty blossom
Come into my embrace
Garland of mine

 C A7 D7
You are beautiful lady
 G7 C G7
Pride of my heart
 C A7 D7
You were a beautiful baby
   G7
Right from the start
 C7   F
Youʻre so sweet and lovely
 D7 F G7
Like a pretty flower
 C A7 D7
Close to my bosom Iʻll hold you
 G7 C
Baby mine

An enchanting love song from parent to child by Albert Nāhaleʻā.

He Uʻi

   F   C7   F
He uʻi nō ʻoe ke ʻike mai
            C7   F7
He pua hoʻoheno i ka lā
Bb   D7   G7
ʻO ʻoe nō kaʻu i aloha
  F   C7   F
He pua i milimili ai

You are indeed a beauty to behold
A cherished blossom in the sun
You are the one I love
A flower that I have caressed

   F   C7   F
ʻO ʻoe he pua i ʻako ʻia
           C7   F7
He mea hoʻopili i ka ʻili
Bb   D7   G7
Nou ē koʻu manaʻo
  F   C7   F
Ua ʻohu i ka lei hīnano

You are a blossom that has been plucked
One to hold close to the skin
It is about you that I am thinking
Adorned with the hīnano lei

 F   C7   F
Mai none, mai none mai ʻoe
       C7   F7
Kuʻu lei hoʻokahi nō
Bb   D7 G7
Kou maka ʻeuʻeu
  F   C7   F
He aha aʻe nei kāu hana?

Don't tease, don't you tease me
My lei, you are the only one
Your spirited looks
What are you doing to me?

 F   C7   F
Haʻina mai ka puana
       C7   F7
Haʻina he uʻi i ka lā
Bb   D7   G7
ʻO ʻoe nō kaʻu i aloha
  F   C7   F
He pua i milimili ai

The refrain is told
Told of the beauty so apparent
You are the one I love
A flower that I have caressed

Danny Kuaʻana makes only general reference to pua, or flower, while emphasizing the attractiveness and careful handling of the bloom. 1946.

Heha Waipiʻo

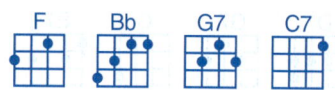

  F   Bb
Kaulana kuʻu home puni Waipiʻo
              F
Me nā peʻa nani o ka ʻāina
          G7
Kākela, he hale aliʻi
         C7
Herode kuʻu hoa like
    F
Mōʻī puni haʻakei

 F   Bb
Kukuna o ka lā koʻu kapa ia
           F
E ʻōlino nei a puni ka honua
        G7
Auē a i luna lilo
       C7
Lihi launa ʻole mai
        F
Nā aliʻi nui o ke ao

 F   Bb
E oʻu mau kini nā makamaka
         F
Me nā kupa o nei ʻāina
            G7
Me ka wailele aʻo Hiʻilawe
        C7
Koʻiawe maila i luna
        F
Koʻiawe mau i nā pali

  F   Bb
ʻAʻole pēlā ka ʻoiaʻiʻo
               F
Hakuʻepa lokoʻino a ka makamaka
       G7
Ua like nō a like
        C7
Me nā kini lehulehu
       F
Aʻo kuʻu one hānau

Famous is my home throughout Waipiʻo
And to the beautiful borders of the land
A castle, an abode of chiefs
Herod is my peer
The king who loved glory

The rays of the sun are my clothing
Glittering brilliantly around the earth
Oh, way up there above
Completely incomparable
Are the great chiefs of the world

Oh my multitude of friends
And you, the natives of this land
Along with the waterfall of Hiʻilawe
Gossamer cascade on high
Ever sparkling upon the cliffs

That is not at all true
The malicious gossip of oneʻs familiars
I am just the same
As the vast multitudes
Of my homeland

He Mele Aloha

[F] E ola māua me a'u [Bb] kini
Me a'u [F] lei o nei 'āina
Pulupē i ka [G7] hunakai
Ka i'a mili i ka [C7] lima
Heha Waipi'o i ka [F] noe

We both will live on, as will my people
And my dear lei of this land
Thoroughly drenched in sea spray
That fish caressed by hand
Sultry is Waipi'o in the mist

[F] Ha'ina 'ia mai ana ka [Bb] puana
No ka lei [F] hapa pua Sepania
He kupa no ka [G7] 'āina
E kipa mai ma [C7] loko
Hale'iwa beautiful [F] home

The refrain is told
Of the half-Spanish flower lei
A native of the land
Do come and visit
Hale'iwa, beautiful home

Said to have been written by Sam Li'a Kalāinaina Jr. & M. Smith about a home in Waipi'o, the size of which caused a stir in the district and gossip about snobbery. The song begins as a parody of self-aggrandizement and then dismisses the concerns, lauding the owner's hospitality and welcoming all. The phrase "a i luna" is a shorthand form of "aia i luna."

Henehene Kou ʻAka

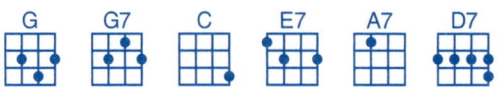

G   G7
Henehene kou ʻaka
C   G
Kou leʻaleʻa paha
E7   A7
He mea maʻa mau ia
D7   G
For you and I

          Your laughter is so teasing
          That seems to be your delight
          It's the usual thing
          For you and I

G   G7
Kaʻa uila mākēneki
C   G
Hōʻoniʻoni kou kino
E7   A7
He mea maʻa mau ia
D7   G
For you and I

          The streetcar jiggles
          And jolts your body
          It's the usual thing
          For you and I

G   G7
I Kakaʻako mākou
C   G
ʻAi ana i ka pipi stew
E7   A7
He mea maʻa mau ia
D7   G
For you and I

          We were at Kakaʻako
          Eating beef stew
          It's the usual thing
          For you and I

G   G7
I Waikīkī mākou
C   G
ʻAu ana i ke kai
E7   A7
He mea maʻa mau ia
D7   G
For you and I

          We were at Waikīkī
          Swimming in the sea
          It's the usual thing
          For you and I

G   G7
I Kapahulu mākou
C   G
ʻAi ana i ka līpoa
E7   A7
He mea maʻa mau ia
D7   G
For you and I

          We were at Kapahulu
          Eating līpoa seaweed
          It's the usual thing
          For you and I

He Mele Aloha

[G]Our eyes have [G7]met
[C]Our lips not [G]yet
[E7]But oh, you sweet [A7]thing
[D7]I'm gonna get you [G]yet

[G]Ha'ina mai ka [G7]puana   The story is told
[C]Kou le'ale'a [G]paha   It's your delight, it seems
[E7]He mea ma'a mau [A7]ia   It's the usual thing
[D7]For you and [G]I   For you and I

The delights of courtship all around town. 1930.

Hi‘ilawe

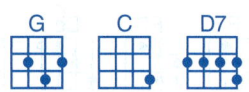

G   C   G
Kūmaka ka ‘ikena iā Hi‘ilawe
             D7   G
Ka papa lohi mai a‘o Maukele
G   C   G
Pakele mai au i ka nui manu
          D7   G
Hauwala‘au nei puni Waipi‘o
		All eyes are on Hi‘ilawe
		And the sparkling lowlands of Maukele
		I escape all the birds
		Chattering everywhere in Waipi‘o

G   C   G
Kūmaka ka ‘ikena iā Hi‘ilawe
           D7   G
Ka papa lohi mai a‘o Maukele
G   C   G
Pakele mai au i ka nui manu
        D7   G
Hauwala‘au nei puni Waipi‘o

All eyes are on Hi‘ilawe
And the sparkling lowlands of Maukele
I escape all the birds
Chattering everywhere in Waipi‘o

G   C   G
‘A‘ole nō wau e loa‘a mai
      D7   G
A he uhiwai au no ke kuahiwi
G   C   G
He hiwahiwa au na ka makua
     D7   G
A he lei ‘ā‘ī na ke kupuna

I shall not be caught
For I am the mist of the mountains
I am the darling of the parents
And a garland for the grandparents

G   C   G
No Puna ke ‘ala i hali ‘ia mai
     D7   G
Noho i ka wailele a‘o Hi‘ilawe
      C   G
I ka poli nō au o Ha‘iwahine
    D7   G
I ka poli aloha o Ha‘inakolo

From Puna the fragrance is wafted
To dwell at Hi‘ilawe waterfall
I am in the embrace of Ha‘iwahine
In the loving arms of Ha‘inakolo

G   C   G
Ho‘okolo ‘ia aku i ka nui manu
    D7   G
I like ke ka‘ina me ka ua hoa
     C   G
He hoa ‘oe no ka lā le‘ale‘a
    D7   G
Na ka nui manu iho haunaele

I am followed by flocks of birds
In succession like a clinging rain
You are a companion for days of delight
It's the birds that rabble among themselves

G   C   G
E ‘ole ko‘u nui piha akamai
   D7   G
Hala a‘e nā ‘ale o ka moana
    C   G
Hao mai ka moana kau e ka weli
   D7   G
Mea ‘ole na‘e ia i nēia ho‘okele

Thank goodness I'm big and wise
I can traverse the billows of the sea
The ocean pounds, fearsome
But it's nothing to this navigator

He Mele Aloha

G		C	G
Ho'okele 'o 'uleu pili i ka uapo
	D7		G
Honi malihini au me ku'u aloha
	C		G
He aloha ia pua ua lei 'ia
	D7		G
Ku'u pua miulana poina 'ole

The lively one steers right to the wharf
To kiss, like a newcomer, my beloved
That blossom is precious, worn as a lei
My unforgettable miulan flower

|G| |C| |G|
Ha'ina 'ia mai ana ka puana
| |D7| |G|
Kūmaka ka 'ikena iā Hi'ilawe

Tell the refrain
All eyes are on Hi'ilawe

Hi'ilawe has become a staple of slack key repertoire. Famous Hawaiian Songs, *a collection of songs arranged by Sonny Cunha and published by the Bergstrom Music Company in Honolulu in 1914, contains two versions of this song, one credited to Mrs. Kuakini entitled* Hali'a-lau-lani, *organized into four-line stanzas, and another credited to Martha K. Maui called* Ke Aloha Poina 'Ole, *arranged in two-line stanzas, and both noted as having been published in 1902. The words are mostly similiar, the music is different. Miulan is a Chinese tree whose delicate blossom has a sweet scent.*

He Mele Aloha

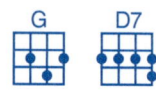

Hilo Ē

G D7 G
Aia ē, lā i Hilo ē

D7 G D7 G
ʻO ka nani ē, ʻo pua ka lehua ē

There indeed, at Hilo
Is the beauty, the lehua blossom

G D7 G
I lei ē, no ka malihini ē

D7 G D7 G
E kipa aku ai ē, i ka ʻāina ē

As a lei for the guest
When visiting this land

G D7 G
E ake au ē, a e ʻike ē

D7 G D7 G
I ka nani ē, o Waiākea ē

I so desire to witness
The beauty of Waiākea

G D7 G
Kilohi au ē, ʻo ka nani ē

D7 G D7 G
I ka ulu lehua ē, aʻo Panaʻewa ē

I gaze upon the glory
Of lehua groves in Panaʻewa

G D7 G
Haʻina ē, mai ka puana ē

D7 G D7 G
ʻO ka nani ē, pua ka lehua ē

Tell then, in the refrain
Of the beauty, the lehua blossom

Mary Heanu expresses a cheerful affection for some of the beautiful features of Hilo.

He Mele Aloha

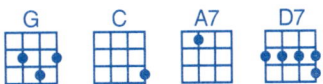

Hilo Hanakahi

   G   C   G   A7   D7 G
Hilo Hanakahi, i ka ua Kanilehua
     C   G   A7   D7 G
Puna paia 'ala, i ka paia 'ala i ka hala
    C   G   A7   D7 G
Ka'ū i ka makani, i ka makani Kuehulepo
   C   G   A7   D7 G
Kona i ke kai, i ke kai mā'oki'oki
     C   G   A7   D7 G
Kawaihae i ke kai, i ke kai hāwanawana
    C   G   A7   D7 G
Waimea i ka ua, i ka ua Kīpu'upu'u
    C   G   A7   D7 G
Kohala i ka makani, i ka makani 'Āpa'apa'a
     C   G   D7 G
Hāmākua i ka pali, i ka pali lele koa'e
    C   G   A7   D7 G
Ha'ina ka puana, i ka ua Kanilehua

        Hilo of Chief Hanakahi, in the Kanilehua rain
        Puna of fragrant bowers, bowers redolent of hala
        Ka'ū in the wind, the dust-stirring Kuehulepo
        Kona at the sea, the sea of patchwork hues
        Kawaihae by the sea, the softly whispering sea
        Waimea in the rain, the pelting Kīpu'upu'u rain
        Kohala in the wind, the buffeting 'Āpa'apa'a
        Hāmākua on the cliffs, cliffs where the tropic bird soars
        Tell the story in the refrain, of the Kanilehua rain

Keola Nālimu's song is classically Hawaiian in its passionate musical celebration of the land. From place to place around the island of Hawai'i this 1925 song praises the noted symbols of the various districts of the island. The last line is often sung "Ha'ina ka puana, no Hilo i ka ua Kanilehua."

Hilo Hula

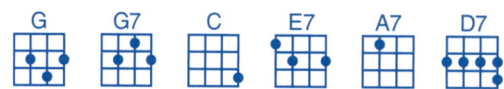

    G   G7
Kaulana mai nei 'o Hilo 'eā
  C   G
Ka ua Kanilehua 'eā
  E7   A7
Ka ua hoʻopulu ʻili 'eā
  D7   G
Ka ʻili o ka malihini 'eā

Renowned is Hilo
For the rain that sings upon the lehua
The rain that soaks the skin
The skin of the visitors

  G   G7
Nani wale hoʻi ka ʻikena 'eā
  C   G
Ka nani o Waiākea 'eā
  E7   A7
Ka wai o Waiolama 'eā
  D7   G
Mālamalama Hawaiʻi 'eā

So very beautiful is the view
Of the loveliness of Waiākea
The waters of Waiolama
All of Hawaiʻi is brightened

  G   G7
Kaulana hoʻi Mokuola 'eā
  C   G
He moku ʻau i ke kai 'eā
  E7   A7
E hoʻopulu ʻili nei 'eā
  D7   G
Ka hunehune kai 'eā

Well known is Mokuola
An island jetting out in the sea
The skin is being soaked
By the flying seaspray

  G   G7
Lei ana i ka lei nani 'eā
  C   G
Ka pua o ka lehua 'eā
  E7   A7
Haʻina mai ka puana 'eā
  D7   G
No ka ua Kanilehua 'eā

Wearing the lovely lei
The blossom of the lehua
The story is told
Of the rain that sings upon the lehua

Joe Kalima tells of the Kanilehua, the rain that sings upon the lehua trees, one of the familiar regional rains of the Hilo district. Every area on each island has a number of different and recognizable rains and winds unique to that place, and each wind and rain has a proper name to distinguish it.

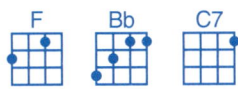

Hilo One

   F   Bb F
Aia i Hilo One
            Bb F
Ka ʻeha a ka manaʻo
         C7
ʻO sweet ʻEmalia
             F
ʻO koʻu aloha ia

There at sandy Hilo
Is what pains my thoughts
Sweet ʻEmalia
She is my love

  F   Bb F
Nāna ke kolohe
        Bb F
Kiʻina i ka liko
       C7
ʻIʻiwi pōlena
            F
ʻO ka manu o ka uka

She makes mischief
Fetching the young leaf
Like the ʻiʻiwi pōlena bird
The bird of the uplands

  F   Bb F
Kohu ʻole ʻo iala
         Bb F
I ka ʻī ʻana mai
       C7
Eia me aʻu
              F
Ka iwi aʻo Heneri

She is out of line
When she says to me
Here in my possession
Is the very essence of Henry

  F   Bb F
Haʻina ka puana
        Bb F
Aia i Hilo One
         C7
ʻO sweet ʻEmalia
            F
ʻO koʻu aloha ia

The refrain is told
There at sandy Hilo
Is sweet ʻEmalia
My own true love

This song of love written for ʻEmalia Kaihumua, a dancer in King Kalākaua's court, likens her to an ʻiʻiwi pōlena, a beautiful red forest bird, native to Hawaiʻi, tinged with gold (pōlena) tones that represent an ultimate beauty. Iwi, literally bones (of Henry), implies the core of one's being. Hilo One is the southern half of the Hilo district. Hilo Palikū, cliff-lined Hilo, is the northern half of the district. 1880s.

He Mele Aloha

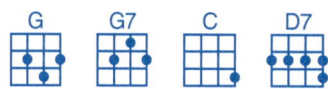

Hole Waimea

   G   G7   C   G
Hole Waimea i ka ihe a ka makani
D7   G   D7
Hao mai nā ʻale a ke Kīpuʻupuʻu
 G   G7   C   G
He lāʻau kalaʻihi ʻia na ke anu
D7   G G7
I ʻōʻō i ka nahele aʻo Mahiki

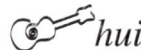*hui*

 C
Kū aku i ka pahu kū a ka ʻawaʻawa
 G
Hananeʻe ke kīkala o ko Hilo kini
D7   G
Hoʻi luʻuluʻu i ke one o Hanakahi

Waimea is stripped by the spears of the wind
And by the billowing of the cold Kīpuʻupuʻu gusts
Trees made brittle in the cold
That thrusts into the forest of Mahiki

chorus:
Hit by the thrusts, hit by the bitter cold
The hips of Hilo's throngs sag
As they return burdened to the sands of Hanakahi

This mele from the 1870s is based on a name chant for Kamehameha. Although often attributed to Leleiōhoku, George Kanahele says the consensus is that he did not compose this song. Also attributed to Lunalilo as well as to the Kawaihau Glee Club, which was founded by Leleiōhoku. Another version has it that the Kīpuʻupuʻu warriors themselves composed the original chant in honor of their leader, Kamehameha. The Kīpuʻupuʻu were young men in the Waimea district on Hawaiʻi, trained as runners and fighters. They called themselves Kīpuʻupuʻu after the icy cold rain of their homeland. To prepare for battle, they went to the forest called Mahiki and Waikā to strip (hole) the bark of saplings to be made into spears. It is said that it was heard whenever his armies moved. Waikā also derives its lyrics from the same chant.

Opposite: A charming story and lively hula about (among other things) going on a car ride and running out of gas. The story goes that composer Clarence Kinney gave this song to Johnny Almeida to settle a debt. The third line, first verse is often sung "kū aku ʻoe" but "kuʻu" shows the sense of the lyrics. While some songsheets include the line "ka pilina aʻo luna iho," Johnny Almeida and his group sang the line as "ke pilina…," highlighting a regular, but poorly documented, use of the article "ke" instead of "ka" before certain words, especially those beginning with the letter "p."

Holoholo Kaʻa

G
Kāua i ka holoholo kaʻa
A7
ʻOni ana ka huila lawe a lilo
D7
Kuʻu aku ʻoe a pau pono
G
Nā huahelu e kau ana

You and I on a joy ride
Wheels turning, carrying us far away
Just let yourself completely relax
Count the miles

G
ʻAlawa iho ʻoe ma ka ʻaoʻao
A7
Hū ana ka makani hele ulūlu
D7
Mea ʻole ka piʻina me ka ihona
G
Me nā kīkeʻe alanui

Glance to the sides
Wind whistles coming in gusts
Going up or down is easy
As are the bends in the road

G
ʻO ka pā kōnane a ka mahina
A7
Ahuwale nō i ka pae ʻōpua
D7
Eia kāua i ka palena pau
G
A huli hoʻi mai kāua

The moon shines brightly
Fair upon the towering clouds
Here we are at the road's end
Let's turn and go back

G
He manaʻo koʻu i ke kani koʻele
A7
Ua haki ka pilina aʻo luna iho
D7
He laʻi pono ke kaunu ana
G
He nanea mai hoʻi kau

I worry about the clanking sound
Springs broken top to bottom
Passion is calmed
So delightful

G
Haʻina kō wehi e kuʻu lei
A7
Ke huli hoʻi nei kāua
D7
Step on the gas, going my way
G
Ke ʻoni nei ka huila

Sing your song my beloved
We go home
Step on the gas, going my way
Wheels are turning

He Mele Aloha

Honolulu City Lights

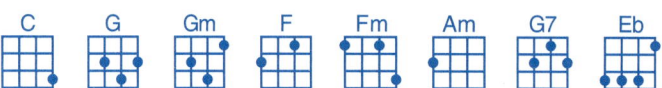

C   G
Looking out upon the city lights
Gm   F
And the stars above the ocean
Fm   C   Am
Got my tickets for the midnight plane
G   C
And it's not easy to leave again

C   G
Took my clothes and put them in my bag
Gm   F
Try not to think just yet of leaving
Fm   C Am
Looking out into the city lights
G   C
It not easy to leave again

chorus

  F G7   C   F
  Each time Honolulu city lights
       G
  Stir up memories in me
  F G7   C   F
  Each time Honolulu city lights
    G7   C
  Will bring me back again

C   G
Put on my shoes and light a cigarette
Gm   F
Wondering which of my friends will be there
Fm   C   Am
Standing with their leis around my neck
G   C
It's not easy to leave again

Eb   C
You are my island sunset
Eb   C
And you are my island rain

Keola Beamer wrote this looking down over the twinkling lights of Honolulu from his home on ʻĀlewa Heights. 1978.

Honolulu I'm Coming Back Again

[F] I seem to [Bb] hear the Pali [Bbm] calling [F] me
[Bb] I seem to hear the [Bbm] surf at Waikī[F]kī
And from Pacific [A7] Heights
I seem to see the [Dm] lights
Of a [G7] city that is very dear to [C7] me

[F] I seem to see the [Bb] waving [Bbm] sugar [F] cane
The cocoa [F7] palms all nodding in the [Bb] rain
In fancy [D7] I am led
Back to dear old [G7] Diamond Head
Hono[C7]lulu I am coming back a[F]gain

This song by F.B. Silverwood and David Lindeman was issued under the auspices of the Chamber of Commerce of Honolulu in 1919 with the intriguing subtitle, "Honolulu expects you in 1922."

Honomuni

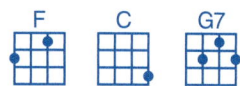

F
Kāua i ka holoholo ka'a
C
Mea 'ole ka pi'ina me ka jeep ride
G7
Aia i ka nani a'o Honomuni 'eā
Home ho'okipa malihini
        C

Here we are riding in a car
Hills are simple to climb on a jeep ride
There in the beauty of Honomuni
The home that welcomes guests

F
Kaulana wale 'oe e Moloka'i
C
Pumehana ke aloha na ka malihini
G7
'Ike 'ia i ka nani o Kalaupapa 'eā
Lei ana i ke kukui
       C

You are renowned oh Moloka'i
Warm is the affection for visitors
The beauty of Kalaupapa is seen
Garlanded in kukui trees

F
Moloka'i Nui a Hina
C
Me nā kini makamaka o ka 'āina
Ho'ohaehae ho'opoina 'eā
I leo pule nō o Pi'ilani
           C

Great Moloka'i child of Hina
With the friendly multitudes of the land
Stirred up are dim memories
The prayerful voice of chief Pi'ilani

F
Ha'ina 'ia mai ana ka puana
C
Pumehana ke aloha na ka malihini
G7
'Ike 'ia i ka nani o Kalaupapa 'eā
Lei ana i ke kukui
       C

The refrain is told
Of the warmth of affection for visitors
Seen in the beauty of Kalaupapa
Garlanded in kukui trees

This mele by John Pi'ilani Watkins is also known as Moloka'i. *Nā Hono O Pi'ilani included the islands of Maui, Moloka'i, Lāna'i and Kaho'olawe, over which the Maui chief held sway. Pi'ilani was one of Maui's greatest chiefs and during his reign there was peace.*

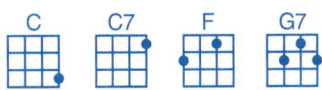

Ho‘okena

   C   C7   F   C
Kaulana mai nei a‘o Ho‘okena
 G7   F   G7
I ka hau kaomi mu‘o lau niu
               C
He niniu mai ho‘i kau
 G7   C
I ka pewa a‘o ka manini

   C   C7   F   C
Kau aku i ke ka‘a ‘oni ka huila
 G7   F   G7
Ka lalawe i ka ‘ili pili pālua
         C
Uluhua wau iā ‘oe
 G7   C
Kahi moa kani ahiahi

   C   C7   F   C
Na ke kelepona au i ha‘i mai
 G7   F   G7
I ka pō le‘ale‘a o Ka‘awaloa
              C
He loloa mai ho‘i kau
 G7   C
Ke ki‘ina a ke aloha

   C   C7   F   C
Ha‘ina ‘ia mai ana ka puana
 G7   F   G7
I ka hau kaomi mu‘o lau niu
               C
He niniu mai ho‘i kau
 G7   C
I ka pewa a‘o ka manini

Famous is Ho‘okena
For the hau that presses against the coconut leaf
Spinning dizzily about
Like the tail of the manini fish

Boarding the car, the wheels turn
A physical thrill when we two are together
But I am annoyed with you
A rooster that crows in the evening

By telephone I was told
Of the fun night at Ka‘awaloa
Such a very long way
For the workings of love to go

Tell through the refrain
Of the hau that presses against the young coconut leaf
Dizzily spinning about
Like the tail of the manini fish

Lot Kauwē extolls Ho‘okena, on Hawai‘i, for the hau that presses against the coconut leaf and the joys of sharing time with a loved one. Distance and garrulous chatter can't stop love.

Ho'okipa Pāka

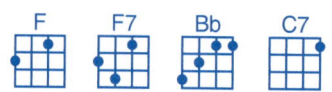

F	F7 Bb	F

Ha'aheo 'i'o nō e Ho'okipa Pāka
C7   F
Kahi o ka lehulehu
C7   F
E kipa ho'onanea
C7   F
Nanea mai ho'i kau

Truly proud is Ho'okipa Park
Place for all the public
To feel welcomed and relaxed
So very enjoyable

F   F7 Bb   F
Nanea mai ho'i kau ke noho 'oe lā
C7   F
Ma lalo o ka lau o ka hau lā
C7   F
Kahi e malu ai 'oe lā
C7   F
E malu 'olu ai 'oe

How enjoyable it is when you sit
Under the leaves of the hau
Where you'll be shaded
You'll be cool and comfortable

F   F7 Bb   F
He nani 'i'o nō ke 'ike aku lā
C7   F
I ka papa he'e nalu
C7   F
He'e ana i ka pu'eone
C7   F
He one kaulana nō

Truly beautiful it is to gaze out
To the surfers
Gliding upon the sandbars
A sandy beach so renowned

F   F7   Bb   F
Pulu au i ka huna kai, kai he'ehe'e i ka 'ili
C7   F
A me ka 'ehu kai kilikilihune
C7   F
A konikoni i ka 'ili
C7   F
Hu'i koni au ma'e'ele

I am soaked by the seaspray that runs
  off the skin
And the sea mist spray so fine
That tingles the skin
I'm chilly and tingling to numbness

F   F7 Bb   F
E ō i kou inoa e Ho'okipa Pāka
C7   F
Kahi a ka lehulehu
C7   F
E kipa ho'onanea
C7   F
Nanea mai ho'i kau

Answer to your name oh Ho'okipa
  Park
Place for all of the public
To feel welcomed and relaxed
So very relaxing

Alice B. Johnson sings of the glory of a beautiful beach day at Ho'okipa, Maui. 1930s.

Ho'onani I Ka Makua Mau

G   Bm   C D7 G
Ho'onani i ka Makua mau
       Em   C   D7
Ke Keiki me ka 'Uhane nō
  Em   Am   C   D7   Em
Ke Akua mau ho'omaika'i pū
G   C   D7   G
Ko kēia ao, ko kēlā ao

    C   Cm G
'Āmene

Glorify the eternal Father
The Son and Holy Ghost
Almighty God, praise in unison
Those of the earth and the heavenly host
   Amen

G   Bm   C   D7   G
Praise God from whom all blessings flow
          Em   C   D7
Praise him all creatures here below
  Em   Am   C   D7 Em
Praise him above ye heavenly host
G   C   D7   G
Praise Father Son and Holy Ghost

    C Cm G
Amen

The Doxology was translated into Hawaiian by Hiram Bingham in the 1820s.

He Mele Aloha

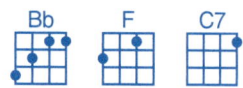

Hu'i Ē

| Bb | F | Bb | F |
Hu'i ē, hu'i koni
| C7 | F | C7 | F | C7 | F |
Hu'i koni lā, hu'i koni lā nei pu'uwai

Aching, aching with a throb
Aching and throbbing is this heart

| Bb | F | Bb | F |
He 'iniki, he 'iniki welawela lā
| C7 | F | C7 | F | C7 | F |
He 'iniki lā, he 'iniki lā kā ke aloha

A pinch, a very sharp pinch
A pinch, a pinching quality has love

| Bb | F | Bb | F |
'Eha au, me ka walania
| C7 | F | C7 | F | C7 | F |
'Eha au me ka 'eha koni, 'eha 'i'o nō

I hurt, with a burning pain
I hurt with a tingling ache, truly painful

| Bb | F | Bb | F |
'Imo ē, 'imo ko maka ē
| C7 | F | C7 | F | C7 | F |
'Imo ko maka, 'eha 'o iala, me ka 'eha koni

Wink, wink your eye
Wink, make him suffer with a tingling pain

| Bb | F | Bb | F |
'Oni ē, 'oni ko kino ē
| C7 | F | C7 | F | C7 | F |
'Oni ko kino, ko nui kino lā, he 'olu 'i'o nō

Move, move your body
Move your body, your entire body, it feels so good

| Bb | F | Bb | F |
I mua ē, kū mālie ē
| C7 | F | C7 | F | C7 | F |
Hā'awi ke aloha me ka 'eha koni, pono kēlā

Move forward, stand quietly
Give love with a throbbing ache, that's perfectly fine

| Bb | F | Bb | F |
I mua ē, kū mālie ē
| C7 | F | C7 | F | C7 | F |
Hā'awi ke aloha me ka 'eha koni, sure kēlā

Go forward, calmly pause
Give love with a tingling pain, that's for sure

Lydia Keku'ewa wrote this for the 1932 movie Bird of Paradise.

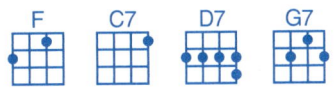

Hukilau Song

  F
Oh we're going to a hukilau
                 C7
A huki huki huki huki hukilau
Everybody loves the hukilau
Where the laulau is the kaukau at the big lūʻau

   D7
We throw our nets out into the sea
   G7
And all the ʻamaʻama come a swimming to me
        F
Oh, we're going to a hukilau
   C7   F
A huki huki huki hukilau

 F
What a beautiful day for fishing
             C7
That old Hawaiian way
Where the hukilau nets are swishing
       G7   C7
Down in old Lāʻie bay

Oh, we're going to a hukilau
  C7
A huki huki huki, huki huki huki,
            F
Huki huki huki hukilau

Countless tourists danced their very first hula to this song by Jack Owens amid great good-natured hilarity at various lūʻau or at the Kodak Hula Show in Waikīkī. 1948.

Hula Breeze

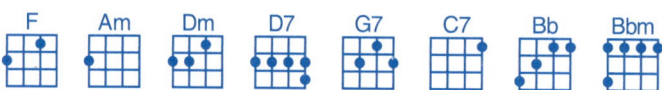

　　　　F　　　　　　Am　　　　　Dm　　　　D7
Whispering to me from a tall coco tree
　　　G7
Comes a hula breeze
　　　C7
I hear the beat of the waves
　　　　　　　　　　　　F　　C7
On the shore of Waikīkī

　F　　　　　　　　　Am　　　　　Dm　　　　　　D7
Softly through the air from a brown maiden fair
　　　G7
Comes a song to me
　　　C7
I hear the swish of her skirt
　　　　　　　　　　　　　　　F　　　Bb　F
As she dances to Liliʻu ē noho nani mai

F7　　　　Bb　　　　Bbm　　F　　　F7
Soft Hawaiian guitars are playing
　　　Bb　　　Bbm　　F
As they have a big lūʻau
　　　　　　　G7
And the moon shines bright with its tropical light
　　　C7
As kāne and wāhine raise a wela ka hao

　F　　　　　　Am　　　　　Dm　　　　D7
Whispering to me from a tall coco tree
　　　G7
Comes a hula breeze
　　　C7
It makes me wanna go back
　　　　　　　　　　　　　　F
To my little grass shack far away

Written by Bucky Henshaw while away at military school in 1935, and augmented by Harry Owens.

He Mele Aloha

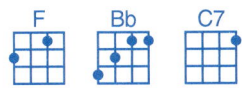

Hula O Makee

F Bb F Bb F 'Auhea iho nei lā 'o Makee? C7 Bb F A ka Malulani lā e huli hele nei	Where has the *Makee* gone? The *Malulani* looks everywhere
F Bb F Bb F Eia 'o Makee kaha i ka pa'a C7 Bb F Ka waiho kapakahi i ka 'āpapa	Here's the *Makee*, sweeping in to become stuck Left keeled over on the reef
F Bb F Bb F 'O ke kani honehone a ke oeoe C7 Bb F A e ha'i mai ana lā i ka lono	Softly sounds the alarm Telling the news to be heard
F Bb F Bb F 'O ka hola 'umi ia o ke aumoe C7 Bb F Kā'alo Malulani ma waho pono	It's ten o'clock at night The *Malulani* passes by, just outside
F Bb F Bb F Kū mai Hailama pa'a i ka hoe C7 Bb F I mua a i hope ke kūlana nei	Hailama stands and grasps the paddle The ship rocks forward and back
F Bb F Bb F A he e'e kakeke mai nei au C7 Bb F No nēia 'oneki nui ākea	And I'm a slip-sliding passenger On this great, wide deck
F Bb F Bb F Ākea ka moana nou e Makee C7 Bb F Ma ke kai holuholu o ka 'Ie'ie	The ocean is too broad for you, *Makee* And the rolling seas of 'Ie'ie channel
F Bb F Bb F Ha'ina 'ia mai ana ka puana C7 Bb F 'Auhea iho nei lā 'o Makee	Tell the refrain Where has the *Makee* gone?

This tells the true story of the foundering of the ship **Makee** (pronounced "Makī") on the reef off of Keālia, Kaua'i, discovered there by the ship **Malulani**. Alerted by the work whistle, local folk came from all around to watch and help the rescue effort. Hailama, a well-known steersman and fisherman from Hā'ena, was called to steer the **Makee** off of the reef, which he did, but the ship was mortally damaged and sunk. Hailama had a distinctive stance, usually depicted in the hula. An event like this would inspire composers, and indeed several versions and attributions exist, providing a good example of oral tradition and its influence on Hawaiian song as a collaborative process. Two versions were published in 1903, one attributed to James Ka'ōpūiki and the other, longer version, unattributed. A slightly different version in Nā Mele o Hawai'i Nei, in which the **Makee** founders off Kapa'a, is not attributed, but the Huapala website credits that version to William S. Ellis. Linda Sproat was told by her grandmother, Julia Akana, that Amy Hobbs Mahikoa from Kalihiwai wrote this song. Besides telling the story, there may also be suggestions of love, illicit love and love lost.

I Aliʻi Nō ʻOe

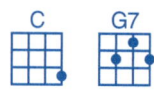

   C   G7   C
I aliʻi nō oe, i kanaka au lā
           G7   C
Ma lalo aku au a i ko leo lā

You're like a chief, I a subject
I'm under the power of your word

 C   G7   C
I noho aku au a i kuke nāu lā
        G7   C
I kuene hoʻi no ko nui kino lā

I stay and I cook for you
Like a servant for all your needs

 C   G7   C
He keu ʻoe a ke aloha ʻole lā
         G7   C
I nēia mau maka ʻimo aku nei lā

You, though are totally unaffectionate
To these eyes that wink at you

 C   G7   C
Hōʻike mai nō, a he palupalu lā
        G7   C
A he iwi haʻi wale ko ka ʻamakihi lā

Do express some softness there
The ʻamakihi has fragile bones

 C   G7   C
ʻO ka pou kaena iho kēia lā
      G7   C
E ʻuīʻuī nei ke kaula ʻili lā

This is a pillar of strength
The tether is squeaking now

 C   G7   C
Haʻina ʻia mai ana ka puana lā
       G7   C
I aliʻi nō ʻoe, i kanaka au lā

Tell the story in the refrain
You are like a chief, I a subject

I treat you like royalty and labor on your behalf. You don't appreciate my efforts, and problems are arising. Be careful.

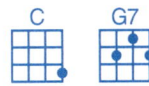

I Kona

C   G7
Aia i Kona kai ʻōpua i ka laʻi
                    C
ʻAʻohe lua e like ai me ʻoe

There at Kona is where the calm sea reflects clouds
There is no other to compare with you

C   G7
Malihini mākou iā ʻoe i Kona
                    C
I ke kono a ke aloha no mākou

We are strangers to you in Kona
At the invitation of so much love for us

C   G7
Haʻina ʻia mai ana ka puana
                  C
ʻAʻohe lua e like ai me ʻoe

Tell the story in the refrain
For there is no other to compare with you

This traditional song praises Kona, where it can be so still that the clouds are mirrored in the sea. A later version by George Kelepolo shares the title, some of the lyrics, and the intention.

I Mua Kamehameha

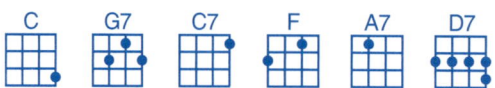

  C
I mua Kamehameha ē
      G7
A lanakila 'oe

Paio, paio like mau
     C
I ola kou inoa

Ka wā nei hō'ike a'e 'oe
 C7   F
'A'ohe lua ou
          C A7
E lawe lilo ka ha'aheo
 D7 G7 C
No Kamehameha ē

Go forward Kamehameha
Until you have gained victory
Fight, fight always
That your name may live on
Now is the time to prove
That you are incomparable
And bring pride
To Kamehameha

Charles E. King wrote this rally song for Kamehameha School in 1928. Translation from Kamehameha Schools' 2001 song contest program.

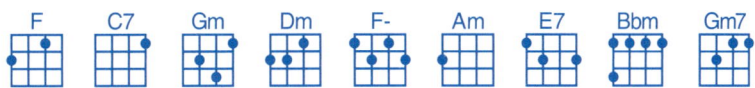

I Will Remember You

F   C7 Gm C7   F C7 Dm
The summer came we were together
     Gm   C7   F
Oh! It was heaven when summer came
         Gm   C7   F   Dm
Now dear it's over and I must leave you
     Gm   Gm7 C7
Only in memory we'll be together

F F- Gm   C7   F
I will remember you, in the silent and lonely night
           Am   Gm   C7   F
And should I be ever blue, I'll sing this song of you

F F-   Gm   C7   F
Please spare your tears for me, darling smile when I go away
        Am   Gm   C7   F
On this sunny summer day, I'll wear your ginger lei

Am   E7
When the winds of winter come crying thru the darkness
Am   Dm
Your lovely voice will come to me
Am   E7
Even tho in spirit across the mighty ocean
Bbm   C7
Crying "Hawai'i nei"

F F- Gm   C7   F
I will remember you, in the silent and lonely night
          Am   Gm   C7   F
And the memory of your smile, will bring me back the light

F F- Gm   C7   Gm   F
I will remember you, when the leaves lie upon the ground
     Gm   C7   Gm   F
With the memory of a kiss, a kiss in summer found

Am   E7
When the winds of winter come crying thru the darkness
Am   Dm
Your lovely voice will come to me
Am   E7
Even tho in spirit across the miles that part us
Bbm   C7
Crying "I love you"

F F- Gm   C7   F
I will remember you, 'till the spring of another year
      Am   Gm   C7   F
'Till I hold you close again, I will remember you

R. Alex Anderson and Carter Nott wrote this in 1941.

He Mele Aloha

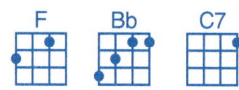

Iā ʻOe E Ka Lā E ʻAlohi Nei

    F   Bb F
Iā ʻoe e ka lā e ʻalohi nei
C7   Bb   F
Ma nā welelau aʻo ka honua

     For you, oh sun, glittering
     To the furthest reaches of the world

    F   Bb F
Hōʻike aʻe ʻoe a i kou nani
C7   Bb   F
I ka mālamalama ʻoi kelakela

     You reveal your glory
     Brilliance greater than all

    F   Bb F
Nāu i noiʻi noelo aku
C7   Bb   F
Pau nā pali paʻa i ka ʻike ʻia

     You are the one who has searched afar
     All of the wondrous sights have been seen

    F   Bb F
ʻIke ʻoe i ka nani aʻo Hīmela
C7   Bb F
I ka hene waiʻolu lawe mālie

     You've witnessed the Himalayas' grandeur
     With its beautiful slopes, rising serenely

    F   Bb F
He mauna i lohia me ke onaona
C7   Bb   F
Kaulana i ka nani me ke kiʻekiʻe

     A mountain suffused with sweet fragrance
     Famous for beauty and lofty height

    F   Bb F
Kiʻekiʻe ʻo Kalani noho mai i luna
C7   Bb F
Nāna i hehi ia kapu o Kahiki

     Lofty is the royal one, placed on high
     He who has crossed the foreign boundaries

    F   Bb F
Heihei kū ana i ka nuku ʻale
C7   Bb F
I ke kai hālaʻi lana mālie

     Having raced over the billows' crests
     And floated upon the calm seas

    F   Bb F
Haʻina ʻia mai ana ka puana
C7   Bb F
E ola e ka lani a mau loa

     Tell the story through the refrain
     May you, oh majesty, live forever

This name song was composed for Kalākaua by Nāhinu before the king left on his world tour in 1881. Visiting other nations to build alliances and bring progress to his kingdom, he became the first sovereign of any nation ever to circle the globe. Later versions contain a number of small variations, like "nāna, i ʻaʻe nā kapu o Kahiki" and "Hehihehi kū ana i ka nuku ʻale." Sometimes the song is ended with an additional verse "E ola ʻo Kalani a mau loa, a kau i ke ao mālamalama." — may the Royal One live forever, in the world of enlightenment.

He Mele Aloha

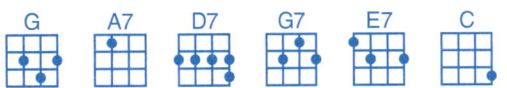

I'll Weave a Lei of Stars for You

    G
I'll weave a lei of stars for you
        A7   D7
To wear on nights like this

Each time you wear my lei of stars
    A7   D7
I'll greet you with a kiss
   G7   C
The moon is green with jealousy
 E7   A7 D7
And all the planets too
    G   E7
And when you wear my lei of stars
  C   D7   G
The fairest one is you

R. Alex Anderson and Jack Owens wrote this in 1949.

He Mele Aloha

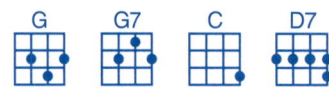

'Imi Au Iā 'Oe

G	G7 C	G

'Auhea wale 'oe e ke aloha lā
D7   G C G
E ka mea hō'eha'eha pu'uwai
    G7   C   G
Na wai e 'ole ke aloha lā
 D7   G C G
A he waiwai ua sila mua 'ia

𝄋 *hui*

 G   G7   C   G
'Imi au iā 'oe e ke aloha lā
    D7   G   C G
Ma nā paia 'a'ala o Puna
       G7   C   G
A i hea lā 'oe i nalowale iho nei
   D7   G C G
Ho'i mai nō kāua e pili

 G   G7   C   G
'A'ohe kohukohu o ka ua lā
   D7   G C G
Ke pili mai me a'u ka wahine u'i
            C   G
Aia ko'u hoa a e kohu ai
   D7   G C G
'O ka 'i'iwi hulu 'ula o ka nahele

Where are you, oh my love
The one who pains the heart
Who could deny such a love?
A treasure, already bound by promise

chorus:
I search for you, my love
Amid the fragrant bowers of Puna
And where have you disappeared to?
Let us come back together again

The rain has no attraction for me
When a beautiful woman is at my side
There is the appropriate companion for me
The red-feathered 'i'iwi of the forest

Also known as King's Serenade, *this Charles E. King song tells about a young man searching for his beloved lost in the Puna district. It was featured in the operetta* Prince of Hawai'i *and was also the theme song of the movie* Bird of Paradise *in 1932 and 1951. It provides yet another example of the overlapping of Hawaiian songs, as Lili'uokalani wrote a similiar song entitled* Ka 'Imina A Ke Aloha, *dated 1874, which Charles King published in 1916 as* 'Imi Au Ke Aloha.

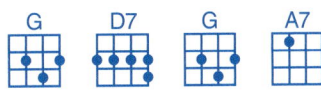

'Iniki Mālie

|G   D7   G G7|
Waikapū, makani kokololio
|C   G A7|
Makani houhou 'ili
| D7   G|
'Īnikiniki mālie

Waikapū, wind in gusts
Wind that presses the skin
Gently pinching

|G   D7   G G7|
Wailuku, makani lawe mālie
|C   G A7|
Makani houhou 'ili
| D7   G|
'Īnikiniki mālie

Wailuku, wind that comes softly
Wind that presses the skin
Gently pinching

|G   D7   G G7|
Waiehu, makani hō'eha 'ili
|C   G A7|
Makani houhou 'ili
| D7   G|
'Īnikiniki mālie

Waiehu, wind stinging the skin
Wind that presses the skin
Gently pinching

|G   D7   G G7|
Waihe'e, makani kili'o'opu
|C   G A7|
Makani houhou 'ili
| D7   G|
'Īnikiniki mālie

Waihe'e, wind so graceful
Wind that presses the skin
Gently pinching

|G   D7   G G7|
Ha'ina 'ia mai ana ka puana
|C   G A7|
Makani houhou 'ili
| D7   G|
'Īnikiniki mālie

Let the refrain be told
Wind that presses the skin
Gently pinching

This 1917 mele by James Kahale tells of the winds of Nā Wai 'Ehā, the four adjoining areas on the eastern slopes of the West Maui Mountains. The importance of knowing the winds was perpetuated in chant and song. Historian Samuel Kamakau helps to illustrate this in his description of Pāka'a, Keawenuia'umi's personal attendant, "Pāka'a was a learned man who was trained in several arts until he became an expert in them... He was familiar with all the winds from Hawai'i to Kaua'i, the direction they blew, and the way they affected the ocean. He knew each ahupua'a and things pertaining to the land." (Kamakau 36).

He Mele Aloha

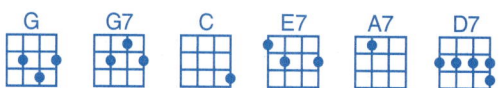

Island Medley

G G7 C G			

  G   G7   C   G
'Ike hou ana i ka nani a'o Hilo
  C   G   A7   D7
I ka uluwehiwehi o ka lehua
 G   G7   C   G   G7
Lei ho'ohihi a ka malihini
   C   E7 A7   D7   G
Mea 'ole i ke kono a ke aloha

Hawai'i:
Witnessing again the beauty of Hilo
Amid the flourishing growth of the lehua
The lei that charms visitors
All becomes naught as love beckons

 G   D7   G
'A'ohe lua e like ai
     D7   G
Māhiehie launa 'ole
    D7   G
Hia'ai wale Haleakalā
       D7   G
A 'o Maui nō e ka 'oi

Maui:
There's no other that can compare
Unmatched splendor
So delightful, Haleakalā
And Maui indeed is the best

 G   G7   C   G
Aloha O'ahu, lei ka 'ilima
          A7   D7   G
Kohu manu 'ō'ō, hulu melemele

O'ahu:
Beloved is O'ahu, adorned with 'ilima
Like an 'ō'ō bird, of golden feather

 G   G7
Maika'i wale nō Kaua'i
C
Hemolele wale i ka mālie
D7
Kuahiwi nani Wai'ale'ale
               G
Lei ana i ka mokihana

Kaua'i:
Fine indeed is Kaua'i
Flawless in the calm
Beautiful mountain, Wai'ale'ale
Adorned with a lei of mokihana

 G   G7
Ua like nō a like lā
   C
Me ku'u one hānau
     D7
Ke po'okela i ka piko o nā kuahiwi
    G   G7
Me Moloka'i Nui a Hina
  C
'Āina i ka wehiwehi
  G   D7   G
E ho'i nō au e pili, 'ae, 'ae, 'ae

Moloka'i:
So alike, so very like
The land of my birth
The finest at the heart of mountains
Like Great Moloka'i, child of Hina
Land of beauty and verdure
I shall return to stay

Hui are plucked from five different songs, each one lauding one of the islands, and strung together in a lei of loving pride for all of Hawai'i's lands.

He Mele Aloha

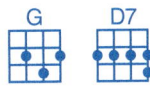

Ka ʻAnoʻi

G	D7		

Aia i Alakaʻi ka ʻanoʻi
Nā pua keu a ke aloha

There at Alakaʻi is the desirable one
The flowers overjoyed with love

Ke aloha ka i hiki mau loa
Noʻu a no iala kekahi

Love is forever forthcoming
For me, and for that one too

ʻO iala ka pua i poni ʻia
I kukuni paʻa ʻia ka ʻiʻini

She's the blossom that is anointed
Desire is branded permanently

He ʻiʻini kau nō ka manaʻo
ʻO haliʻa hana mau i ke kino

Wanting takes over my thoughts
Good memories endlessly run through my being

Kuʻu kino ua lono i ka leo
I ke kani a nā manu o uka

My person is attentive to the voices
That are sounded by the birds of the upland

ʻAneʻane hiki mai ʻo Uila
Ke āiwaiwa o luna

Uila soon will be arriving
The amazing one of the heights

Nāna e kaomi nā mano
Hakukoʻi ka wai i nā pali

It was she who will dam up the springs and wells
Water shall rush over the cliffs

Haʻina ʻia mai ka puana
Nā pua keu a ke aloha

The story is told
About the flowers overjoyed with love

This song by Kamealoha was published in Holstein's Ka Buke Mele o nā Hīmeni Hawaiʻi *in 1897.*

Ka Beauty A'o Mānoa

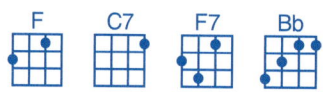

[F] Nani wale ke 'ike i kakahiaka lā
[C7] Ke kuahiwi o [F] Mānoa [F7]
[Bb] Ke noenoe [F] mai nei
[C7] Ho'opulu ana i ke [F] one
[C7] Pulu pē i ka [F] 'ilihia

[F] He beauty i ka ua Tuahine o Mānoa
[C7] Pā aheahe ka [F] makani [F7]
[Bb] I ke 'ala o ka [F] laua'e
[C7] Ke onaona o nā [F] pua
[C7] Māhiehie i ka [F] wao

[F] I ka waokele i pali uliuli lā
[C7] Honehone i ka [F] Puakea [F7]
[Bb] Ke pā wai a inu a [F] kena
[C7] Heha i ka ho'oluliluli [F]
[C7] He mana'o pono [F] kēia

[F] Puana e ka u'i i ka uka o Mānoa
[C7] I ka 'ehu [F] kakahiaka [F7]
[Bb] Pulu pē i ka [F] 'ilihia
[C7] Ho'opulu ana i ke [F] one
[C7] Ke pili mai i [F] 'ane'i
[C7] Ka beauty a'o [F] Mānoa

Beautiful to behold in the morning
The uplands of Mānoa
With a gentle mist
Quenching the land
I am drenched with awe

A beauty is the Tuahine rain of Mānoa
Engulfed in the breeze
Bringing the sweet scent of the laua'e
And the fragrance of the flowers
Elegance in the forest

In the forest and on the lush green cliffs
Sweetly kissed by the Puakea rain
One can drink 'til satisfied
To the hilt of pleasure
Ah! Such a good idea!

So shall the uplands of Mānoa
Remain beautiful in the morning
Drenched in awe
The land is quenched
Here we shall be together
In the beauty of Mānoa

Tony Conjugacion received the Nā Hōkū Hanohano Award for Song of the Year in 1986 for this song. Translation by Tony Conjugacion.

He Mele Aloha

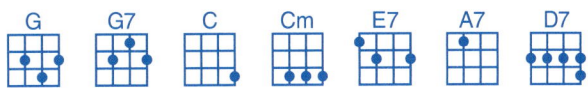

Ka Lehua I Milia

```
G         G7      C    Cm G E7
'Ike maka i ka nani o uka
   A7        D7       G
Ka lehua i milia e ka ua noe
```
I have seen the beauty of the uplands
A lehua blossom caressed by the misty rain

```
G              G7      C     Cm    G    E7
He welina, na ke aloha e ho'onipo nei
    A7         D7           G
E hō'oni nei iā loko o ka pu'uwai
```
A token from the loved one
That creates a stir in the heart

```
G           G7       C    Cm    G  E7
Ku'u lei, ku'u pua nani mae 'ole
      A7        D7        G
Nohenohea i ka maka a ka ipo
```
My darling, my never fading flower
Ever lovely in the eyes of the lover

```
G            G7    C    Cm    G  E7
E ho'olale mai ana e naue aku
    A7        D7         G
E kui a lei i ko aloha makamae
```
An urge has now come to me
To string and wear your pure love as a lei

```
G          G7     C    Cm    G  E7
Ha'ina 'ia mai ana ka puana
   A7        D7       G
Ka lehua i milia e ka ua noe
```
My story is told
Of the lehua blossom caressed by the misty rain

One of six songs included in this collection which emanate from the long and creative collaboration between Mary Kawena Pukui and Maddy Lam. Translation by Mary Kawena Pukui.

He Mele Aloha

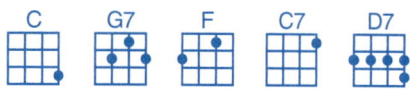

Ka Makani Kāʻili Aloha

   C   G7
E aloha aʻe ana nō au
                      C G7
I ka makani kaulana o ka ʻāina
  C   C7   F
Aʻu e hoʻoheno nei
      C   G7   C C7
Ka makani kāʻili aloha

🎸 *hui*

      F   C
Kuʻu pua, kuʻu lei, kuʻu milimili ē
     D7   G7
Kuʻu lei kau i ka wēkiu
     C   C7   F   D7
A he milimili ʻoe, a he hiwahiwa naʻu
     C   G7   C
A he lei mau no kuʻu kino

 C   G7
I aloha ʻia nō ia home
                  C G7
Ia home luakaha a ka malihini
 C   C7   F
Aʻu i noho ai a kupa
     C   G7   C C7
Ka makani kāʻili aloha

I express my love
For the famous wind of this land
Which I hold dear to me
The love-snatching wind

chorus:
My flower, my lei, mine to cherish
My lei that I adore above all others
You are a precious thing, a treasure
A lei to adorn my person

Beloved is that home
That home so delightful to visitors
Where I stayed and came to know well
The love-snatching wind

This song recalls the story of a Kīpahulu man whose wife left and went off to Oʻahu. A priest chanted love prayers into a favorite calabash which was then set afloat, drifting to Waikīkī. The wife, stirred by love magic to gather līpoa, spotted the calabash and on opening it was struck by the churning energy therein and made her way home. There are many versions and attributions for this beloved song, including being often credited to Matthew H. Kāne. 1916.

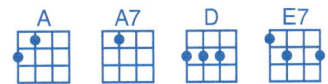

Ka Naʻi Aupuni

| A | A7 | D |
E Hawaiʻi nui kuauli
| A | | E7 |
E nā hono aʻo Piʻilani
| A | A7 | D |
Oʻahu o Kākuhihewa
| A | E7 | A |
Kauaʻi o Manokalanipō
| E7 | A | A7 |
Kauaʻi o Manokalanipō

🎸 *hui*

| D | | A |
E naʻi wale nō ʻoukou
| | E7 | |
I kuʻu pono, ʻaʻole pau
| A | A7 | D |
I ke kumu pono o Hawaiʻi
| A | E7 | A |
E mau ke ea o ka ʻāina i ka pono
| | E7 | A |
E mau ke ea o ka ʻāina i ka pono

| A | A7 | D |
I hoʻokahi, kahi ka manaʻo
| A | E7 | |
I hoʻokahi, kahi puʻuwai
| A | A7 | D |
I hoʻokahi, kahi ke aloha
| A | E7 | A |
E mau ke ea o ka ʻāina i ka pono
| E7 | A | A7 |
E mau ke ea o ka ʻāina i ka pono

Oh great green-backed Hawaiʻi
Oh many bays of chief Piʻilani
Oʻahu of Kākuhihewa
Kauaʻi of Manokalanipō

chorus:
Strive indeed, all of you
Toward the good I've done, boundless
Toward the solid foundation of Hawaiʻi
The land shall live on through righteousness

Let the minds be as one
Let the hearts be united
Let the same love be shared
The land shall live on through righteousness

The last words uttered by King Kamehameha on his deathbed in 1819, according to the first published account, were "E ʻoni wale nō ʻoukou i kuʻu pono. (ʻAʻole pau)" with the last two words in parentheses. In later published accounts, ʻoni changed to naʻi, the parentheses were omitted, and "ʻaʻole pau" has been added into the quote itself, as in this song. Because that historical event lived on in published works and in the oral legacy, variations become valuable parts of the whole. The last line is said to have originally been "E mālama i ka maluhia," later replaced by "E mau ke ea o ka ʻāina i ka pono," the famous saying attributed to Kamehameha III in 1843. Another variation is in the first line, which is often sung "E Hawaiʻi moku o Keawe."

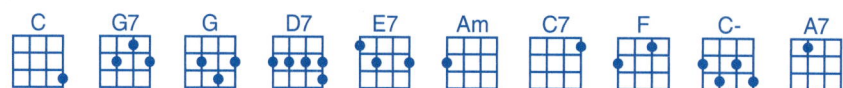

Ka Ua Loku

   C   G7
Kaulana wale e ka ua o Hanalei
                C   G7
E nihi aʻe nei i nā pali
   C   G
E hoʻopili ʻia me ka lauaʻe
       D7   G7
Me he ipo hoʻoheno nei i ka poli
                     C
Ka hoene mai nō a ke kai
     E7   Am C7
Me he ala e ʻī mai ana
   F   C-   C   A7
E hoʻi mai nō kāua lā e pili
  D7   G7   C
Ka ua loku kaulana aʻo Hanalei

       Famous indeed is the rain of Hanalei
       Sweeping along the cliffs
       To be joined with the lauaʻe fern
       Like a sweetheart cuddling in embrace
       The sea murmurs softly
       As though it were saying
       You and I should be together again
       Like the famous pouring rains of Hanalei

Alfred ʻAlohikea was able to capture the magnificence of Hanalei in his songs. "Ka ua loku" is the famous drenching rain of Hanalei. 1920s.

He Mele Aloha

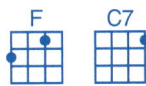

Ka Wai Māpuna

F
Ka wai māpunapuna lā
C7   **F**
E naue mālie nei i ka la'i

Lipolipo launa 'ole lā
C7   **F**
Kauwahi 'ale 'ole iho

From sparkling spring the waters clear
Glide on so smoothly o'er the lee
Of deepest blue without compare
Roll on without a ripple wave

🎸 *hui*

    F
    Kokōhi (ehehehe) i ka 'ono (ehehehe)
       C7
      unahe i ka poli
    F
    Ka wai o Lohia

    Pahe'e (ehehehe) ka momoni (ehehehe)
       C7   **F**
    A he 'olu ka ihona iho

chorus:
Then tarry, I pray thee
Thou waters of Lohia, to cool this
    fevered brow
I'd quaff thee and sip thee
Thou sparkling waters of the lee

F
Lei ana Hiku i ka noe lā
C7   **F**
Ho'ohihi Līhau ka lipo lā

Anahe 'o ia ala e inu lā
C7   **F**
Ka wai 'ula 'iliahi

As Hiku with snowy wreath reclined
From Līhau's heights espied the spring
Forth hastened down her thirst to lave
From the sparkling waters of the lee

F
Iā 'oe ka 'uhene i ka wai
C7   **F**
Ka nēnē li'ili'i i ke kulu aumoe

Ho'ola'i Kaua'ula lā
C7   **F**
Kālele nu'a i ka palai

This flirting tune is to you, O water
Slowly being allured in the late night
Kaua'ula reposes peacefully
Upon a bed of thick ferns

Written by Lili'uokalani in 1876. *The Queen's Songbook includes an excellent discussion of the ambiguities in this song, for instance the intent of "Ka wai o Lohia," with a discussion of the possibilities in "wai olohia," "Kaiolohia," and "wai lohia." The third stanza comes from a different version of this song known as* Kokōhi, *published later by Charles E. King. Translation by Lili'uokalani and Hui Hānai.*

Ka Wai O Nāmolokama

[G] Kaulana wale hoʻi ʻoe
Ka wai o Nā[D7]molokama
ʻUʻiʻuʻiʻuʻina nei
Nākolokolo i nā [G] pali
ʻUheʻuheʻuhene ana
[D] [A7] I ka nani o ke kua[D7]hiwi
[G] He hiwahiwa hoʻi ʻoe
A he mili[D7]mili hoʻi
Kilakila wale ʻoe
Kau ana i ke kiʻe[G]kiʻe
ʻO ʻoe a [G7] ʻo wau i [C] laila [Cm]
[D7] Ka wai kaulana o Nāmolo[G]kama

You are so famous
O waters of Nāmolokama
Splashing and splashing
Rumbling on the cliffs
Making a merry sound
In the mountainous beauty
You are indeed precious
A favorite one
You are majestic
Placed on high
There you will be with me
The famous waters of Nāmolokama

Alfred U. ʻAlohikea describes Nāmolokama, the majestic mountain which defines the back of Hanalei valley and gives name to the waterfall that scores it. 1920s.

He Mele Aloha

Ka Wiliwiliwai

Bb
E ka wiliwiliwai
F7 **Bb**
Koʻiawe i ka laʻi

A he aha kāu hana
F7 **Bb**
E naue mālie nei?

hui
Bb **Cm** **F7**
Ei nei, ei nei, e poahi mai nei
Bb **Cm Bb F F7 Bb**
Āhea, āhea ʻoe kāohi mai?

Bb
Oki pau ʻo ia ala
F7 **Bb**
Ua ninihi ka lawena

Kuʻu iki iho ʻoe
F7 **Bb**
I inu aku wau

O whirley water
Gentle rain shower on the move
What do you think you're up to
Circling, twirling so quietly

chorus:
There! Yea yea coming up! As you revolve
Will you, will you hold still?

Amazing the way you take over
Irresistable
Come, slow down a little
So I can take a drink

The introduction of Western inventions, such as electricity, radio and telephone, was memorialized in Hawaiian mele. In this case the lawn sprinkler, introduced in Honolulu in 1890, becomes the central character as Liliʻuokalani puts words to an older melody. Translation by Mary Kawena Pukui.

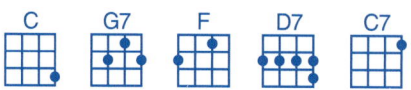

Ka'ahumanu

    C   G7
Lei Ka'ahumanu i ke aloha
              C
Lei ha'aheo i ka lanakila
                  G7
Lei i ka mamo hulu melemele
             C
Lei Hawai'i i kou inoa

Ka'ahumanu is wreathed in love
Pride's wreath in victory
Lei of yellow mamo feathers
Hawai'i's crown your name

hui

     F   C
E ola e ka 'Ī a me ka Mahi
    D7   G7
E ala nā kini o ka 'āina
      C   C7   F
Ho'okahi pu'uwai me ka lōkahi
    C   D7   G7 C
I ola ka inoa 'o Ka'ahumanu

chorus:
Long live the 'Ī and the Mahi, warrior class
Arise, kinsmen of the land
One heart in unity
To perpetuate the name Ka'ahumanu

   C   G7
Eia ko lei e lei ai
                C
Na ke aloha i lawe mai nei
              G7
I lei ho'oheno mau ia nou
              C
I ola ka inoa 'o Ka'ahumanu

Here is your lei to wear
By love brought here
An expression of continuing affection for you
To perpetuate the name of Ka'ahumanu

Written by Helen Desha Beamer in 1916 for 'Ahahui Ka'ahumanu, a Hawaiian women's benevolent society. Translation by Mahi'ai Beamer.

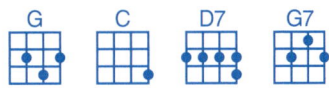

Kaimana Hila

  G   C   G
I waho mākou i ka pō nei
 D7   G G7
A ʻike i ka nani o Kaimana Hila
 C   G   D7   G
Kaimana Hila, kau mai i luna

We were all out last night
And saw the beauty of Diamond Head
Diamond Head, set high above

  C   G
I waho mākou i Waikīkī
 D7   G G7
A ʻike i ka nani o papa heʻe nalu
 C   G   D7   G
Papa heʻe nalu, heʻeheʻe malie

We were all out at Waikīkī
And saw the beauty of board surfing
Board surfing, gently gliding

  C   G
I waho mākou Kapiʻolani Pāka
 D7   G G7
A ʻike i ka nani o lina poepoe
 C   G   D7   G
Lina poepoe, hoʻoluhi kino

We were all out at Kapiʻolani Park
And saw the beauty of the race track
Race track, that tires the body

  C   G
Haʻina ʻia mai ana ka puana
 D7   G G7
A ʻike i ka nani o Kaimana Hila
 C   G   D7   G
Kaimana Hila, kau mai i luna

The refrain is told
We saw the beauty of Diamond Head
Diamond Head, set high above

This is a ramble through Waikīkī popularized by Andy Cummings. An earlier version published by Charles E. King in 1916 has verses that commemorate Makee ʻAilana (an island in Kapiʻolani Park), the horse racing track, the Seaside Hotel, and ʻĀinahau, all of which exist today only in memory and song.

He Mele Aloha

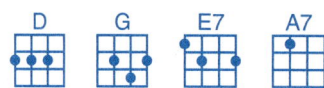

Kaimukī Hula

```
   D
'O ka'u nō ia e 'ī aku ai lā
   G                D
Hū ana ka makani ē
               E7
'U'umi ke aloha me ka waimaka lā
   A7           D
Hū ana ka makani ē

   D
Mālama pono 'oe i ko lei hulu lā
   G                D
Hū ana ka makani ē
            E7
O pulu i ka ua, mae kona nani lā
   A7           D
Hū ana ka makani ē

   D
Mea 'ole ē ka loa o Kaimukī lā
   G                D
Hū ana ka makani ē
            E7
Ke ana 'iliwai ko'u makemake lā
   A7           D
Hū ana ka makani ē

   D
He aha nei hana a ke kelepona lā
   G                D
Hū ana ka makani ē
            E7
Ke kapalulu nei o ke aumoe la
   A7           D
Hū ana ka makani ē

   D
Ha'ina 'ia mai ana ka puana lā
   G                D
Hū ana ka makani ē
            E7
'O 'oe a 'o wau, nalo ia mea lā
   A7           D
Hū ana ka makani ē
```

It is for me to say
The wind whistles along
Love tugs at the heart and bring tears
The wind whistles along

Take good care of your feather lei
The wind whistles along
Or it'll be drenched in rain, fading its beauty
The wind whistles along

The expanse of Kaimukī is nothing to me
The wind whistles along
The pressure on the steam gauge is what I care about
The wind whistles along

What is the telephone doing
The wind whistles along
Ringing so late at night
The wind whistles along

Tell the refrain
The wind whistles along
You and I together, all else becomes naught
The wind whistles along

This mele by Alice M. Rickard hints of a secret love for a cherished one, the lei hulu, that was possibly not so secret, gossip spread by whistling wind. 1940.

He Mele Aloha

Chords: C C7 F A7 D7 G7

Kalama'ula

    C   C7   F C
A he sure maoli nō, 'eā
      A7   D7
Me ke onaona, ē
   C   G7   C
Me ka nani o Kalama'ula

Surely and truly indeed
Filled with sweet fragrance
The beauty of Kalama'ula

  C   C7 F C
E kapa 'ia nei, 'eā
        A7   D7
He u'i mai ho'i kau, ē
   C   G7   C
Me ka nani o Kalama'ula

Referred to by name
As a remarkable beauty
The beauty of Kalama'ula

  C   C7   F C
'Āina ua kaulana, 'eā
     A7   D7
I ka ho'opulapula, ē
   C   G7   C
Me ka nani o Kalama'ula

Land that is renowned
For nurturing the people
The beauty of Kalama'ula

  C   C7 F C
E ho'i kāua, 'eā
        A7   D7
E noho i ka 'āina, ē
   C   G7   C
Me ka nani o Kalama'ula

Let us two return
To dwell upon the land
The beauty of Kalama'ula

  C   G7   F C
Ha'ina mai ka puana, 'eā
       A7   D7
E ho'i mai kāua, ē
   C   G7   C
Me ka nani o Kalama'ula

Let the tale be told
You and I shall return
To the beauty of Kalama'ula

This beloved song of Moloka'i is credited to Hannah Dudoit, although, like many other songs, it is variously attributed. Kalama'ula, literally the red torch or red lama tree, is a land division on South Moloka'i and site of the first Hawaiian homestead area.

Kaleleonālani

     F   C7
Welo ana ē ka hae Hawaiʻi
          F   F7
Hāliʻi lua i ka ʻili kai
 Bb   F
E haʻi mai ana i ka lono
     C7   F   F7
Ke Kuini ʻEmalani ko luna

hui

       Bb   F
Kaleleonālani kou inoa
      C7   F   F7
A he hiwahiwa ʻoe na ka lāhui
      Bb   F
A he lani ʻo iala no ʻoukou
      C7   F
A he milimili hoʻi na mākou

  F   C7
A waho o nā nalu o Kolea
                     F   F7
ʻIke ʻia ē ka nani o Kahului
      Bb   F
ʻAʻohe mea nani ʻole o laila
     C7   F
Ua nuʻa ka lehua ʻau i ke kai

The Hawaiian flag is waving
Spread wide over the sea
Telling the news
That Queen Emma is there on board

chorus:
Kaleleonālani is your name
You're a precious one for the nation
The true sacred one for all of you
And cherished by all of us

Outside the surf of Kolea
The beauty of Kahului is seen
There is nothing not beautiful there
Lehua blossoms fill the sea in welcome

Nuʻuanu wrote this for Queen Emma, who took the name Kaleleonālani (flight of the royal ones) after the death of her son, Prince Albert, and then her husband, Alexander Liholiho, King Kamehameha IV. 1870s.

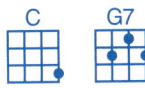

Kalena Kai

   C   G7   C
'O Kalena Kai, Hale'au'au
G7   C   G7   C
'O Līhu'e i Mālamanui

     C   G7   C
'O ka 'ehu'ehu o ke kai
G7   C   G7   C
Ka moena pāwehe o Mokulē'ia

    C   G7   C
'O ka lae 'o Ka'ena ka'a ma mua
G7   C   G7   C
Kū ana Pu'ukoa me Pu'uhulu

   C   G7   C
'O ke kula loa ia o Mailehuna
G7   C   G7   C
'O ka wai pa'ihi i ka pu'uwai

    C   G7   C
'O ka wai iho ia pono kāua
G7   C   G7   C
'O Ka'ala kau mai i luna

  C   G7   C
Hao ka makani lūlū ka lehua
G7   C   G7   C
'O Halemano me Pu'ukoa

  C   G7   C
Ha'ina mai ana ka puana
G7   C   G7   C
Ka lua o nā lani kou inoa

Kalena Kai, Hale'au'au
And the plain of Līhu'e to Mālamanui

The misty spray of the sea
Mokulē'ia, spread like a patterned mat

The point of Ka'ena rolls on ahead
And there's Pu'ukoa and Pu'uhulu

The great plain spreads before Mailehuna
The water dear to the heart

That is the water that comforts us
And Ka'ala stands proudly above

The wind blows scattering the lehua
There stand Halemano and Pu'ukoa

Tell the story in the refrain
For the second of the royal ones here is your name song

This song for Liholiho tells us not only about a place, but about the love of place. Kalena Kai is a mountain area on O'ahu above Mokulē'ia. Līhu'e and Mālamanui are land areas in the Wahiawā plain, Ka'ena Point and Mailehuna are in the Wai'anae side of the mountain range, all visible from atop Ka'ala. The verse order differs in various versions. This order makes geographic sense as one journeys around the Wai'anae mountains.

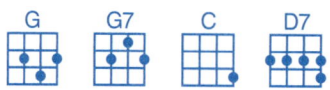

Kaleponi

   G
Hele au i Kaleponi
            G7
Hoʻi mai male kāua
C   G
A he aha kou makemake
D7   G
A pane maila ʻo iala
D7   G
Pāpale ipu kapakahi
D7   G
Kāmaʻa hila lauliʻi
D7   G
Kīhei suʻu weluwelu
D7   G
Pelekoki hapa nihoniho
D7   G
Me ka lole mūʻekekeʻi

   G
I'm going to California
               G7
When I come back we'll be married
C   G
What would you like me to bring you?
D7   G
And she answered shyly
D7   G
A hat with a crooked crown
D7   G
A pair of high heel shoes
D7   G
A shawl with some fringe
D7   G
A petticoat with half scallops
D7   G
And a tight short dress

Both the Hawaiian and English lyrics are intended to be sung in this perky song from the 1930s by Bina Mossman. This song was later attributed to K. Kaʻapuni in Charles King's songbook of 1950.

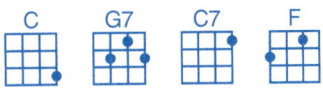

Kalua

C
'O wai ka hali'a ka 'ano'i a loko   Who is the dream, the heart's desire?

C
'O nēia ka pō
Nou ka hali'a, e Kalua
G7
Nou nō ka 'i'ini
A ka pu'uwai
'O wai lā ka hali'a
　　　　　　C
Aloha a Kalua

This is the night
The dream is of you, Kalua
For you is the desire
There in the heart
Who shall be the dream
Love of Kalua

C
Ho'oheno nei ka ipo
　　C7　　F
Iā 'oe, e Kalua
C
Ka pua i mōhala i ke aumoe
G7
Hi'ipoi ke aloha makamae
C
No nā kau a kau
G7　　　　　C
Nou ka 'i'ini e Kalua

The sweetheart cherishes
Only you Kalua
The perfect blossom of the night
Hold precious the love so pure
Now and forever
For you is the desire, oh Kalua

C
This is my night of love, this is the hour of Kalua
G7
My arms are open now, my heart has spoken now
　　　　　　　　　　　C
Who will be Kalua's only love?

C   C7   F
Before the night is old my arms will hold Kalua
C
My beating heart is true, wanting you
G7
Your beating heart I see, wanting me
C   G7   F C
And now my song is through, I give to you, Kalua

Written in 1952 for the movie Bird of Paradise *by Ken Darby, although he probably did not write the Hawaiian lyrics. The English, not a translation, is intended to be sung.*

He Mele Aloha

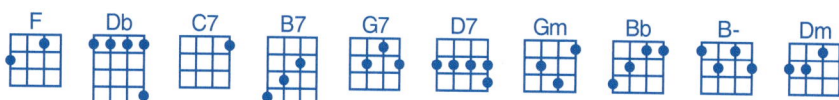

Kamehameha Waltz

   F   Db   F
Kū kilakila ʻo Kamehameha
       C7   B7 C7
Kuʻu home hoʻonaʻauao
I ka laʻi o Kaiwiʻula
        F G7 C7
Uluwehi i ka lau kiawe
       F   Db F
A he home naʻu i aloha
        D7   Gm
A e haʻaheo mau loa ai
Bb   F D7   G7   C7 F
E ola mau ʻo Kamehameha

Majestic stands Kamehameha
My home of education
In the calm of Kaiwiʻula
Adorned by kiawe trees
It is a home that I love
And of which I'm always proud
Long may Kamehameha live

 F   C7
Nou, e Pauahi lani nui
             F
Ka manaʻo e hoʻōho hauʻoli nei
B7   C7
Ola iā ʻoe nā kini pua
 F   C7
O Hawaiʻi kulāiwi
Nā hana lua ʻole
           F
A ka puʻuwai o ke aliʻi aloha
    B-   C7   Dm
Kau kou inoa i ka wēkiu
Bb   G7 C7 F
A nou kuʻu mele nei

For you, oh great Pauahi lani
Our exclamations of joy
Life is granted by you to the
   multitudes of descendants
Of Hawaiʻi the homeland
The unequaled efforts
From the heart of the loving chiefess
May your name be highly honored
And for you is this my song

Charles E. King, one of the most prolific of Hawaiʻi's songwriters, didn't start composing until he was in his 40s, his first hit being Na Lei O Hawaiʻi *written in 1913. Two years later he wrote this song and dedicated it to his alma mater, Kamehameha Schools (class of 1891). Of all the Hawaiian composers, he was among the most formally trained in musical theory and liked royal music — this song reflects those preferences.*

He Mele Aloha

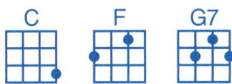

Kananaka

   C   F   C
'O ka pā mai a ka Ma'a'a
 G7   C   G7   C
Halihali mai ana lā i ke 'ala
               F   C
Ke 'ala onaona o ka līpoa
 G7   C
Hana 'oe a kani pono

hui

   C   F   C
Nani wale ia pu'e one
 G7   C   G7   C
I ka nalu he'e mai a'o Kananaka
              F   C
Kahi a mākou i he'e ai
 G7   C
I ka 'ehu'ehu o ke kai

   C   F   C
'O ka mahina hiki aloalo
 G7   C   G7   C
Ho'ola'ila'i ana lā i nā pali
                 F   C
Pōhina wehiwehi i ke onaona
 G7   C
Koni ma'e'ele i ke kino

The blowing of the Ma'a'a wind
Bears with it a fragrance
A sweet scent of the līpoa seaweed
Get it until you are satisfied

chorus:
Beautiful is that stretch of sand
With the surf break of Kananaka
Where we have ridden the waves
There amid the spray of the sea

The moon rises to its zenith in the sky
Poised aloft here above the cliffs
A silvery gleam, lush with fragrance
Bringing a throb and a tingle to the body

This hula often performed as a hula noho, or sitting dance, is about the mermaid Kananaka who lived in the surf outside of Lahaina. Mermaids did not exist in traditional Hawaiian lore, and Kananaka may be an innovation inspired by the whalers' tales in Lahaina. Maui elders credit this song to Kauhailikua, a court dancer for Kalākaua and grandmother of Eddie Kamae. Kauhailikua taught hula to Emma Sharpe and Pua Lindsey. 1915.

Kanaka Waiwai

    F   F7
Ma ke ala hele ʻo Iesū
  Bb   F
I hālāwai aku ai
 C7   F   Dm
Me ke kanaka, ʻōpio hanohano
 G7   C7
Kaulana i ka waiwai
 F   F7
Pane mai ē ka ʻōpio
  Bb   A7
"E kuʻu haku maikaʻi
  Bb   F
He aha hoʻi kaʻu e hana aku ai
G7   C7   F
I loaʻa ē ke ola mau?"

It was on the path that Jesus
Chanced to meet
With a young man of position
Renowned for his wealth
The youth spoke, saying
"O my good lord
What, indeed, must I do
To gain eternal life?"

🎸hui

  Bb
"E hāʻawi, e hāʻawi lilo
  F
I kou mau waiwai
 C7
Huli a hahai mai iaʻu
  F   Bb   F
I loaʻa ē ke ola mau"

chorus:
"Give away, give away completely
All of your many riches
Turn and follow me
To gain eternal life"

 F   F7
Minamina ē ka ʻōpio
  Bb   F
I kona mau waiwai
 C7   F   Dm
I ke kūʻai a hāʻawi lilo aku
 G7   C7
I ka poʻe nele a hune
 F   F7
Huli aʻe ʻo Iesū lā
  Bb   A7
Pane aku i ka ʻōpio
  Bb   F
"'Aʻole aʻe hiki ke kanaka waiwai
G7   C7   F
I ke aupuni o ka lani"

The youth regretted parting
With his many riches
To be sold and given away
To the poor and the destitute
Jesus then turned
Responding to the youth
"The rich man shall never reach
The kingdom of heaven"

[F]Let me walk through Paradise with [F7]you Lord
[Bb]Take my hand and lead me [F]there
[C7]All my earthly treasures [F]I will gladly [Dm]give
[G7]Teach me how to love and how to [C7]share
[F]Greed and lust and vanity were [F7]mine Lord
[Bb]Then I found your love [A7]divine
[Bb]Now on my knees I pray that I can find the [F]way
[G7]Let me walk [C7]through Paradise with [F]you   ([F7]Iā ʻoe)

Originally known as Iesū Me Ke Kanaka Waiwai, *its message is founded in the Bible, "It is easier for a camel to go through the needle's eye than for a rich man to enter into the kingdom of God." George Kanahele explained that, although there is some controversy regarding authorship, he believed it to be written by Johnny Almeida. The English lyrics, which are often inserted between the chorus and the second verse, were not part of the original composition. 1915.*

He Mele Aloha

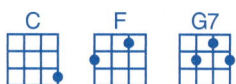

Kāneʻohe

     C   F   C
ʻŌlapa ka uila i Kāneʻohe
F   C   G7   C
Ka hui laulima o ʻĪlaniwai

hui
      F   C
   Me ka ua ʻĀpuakea
      G7   C
   Ka laʻi aʻo Malulani
     G7   C
   Me ke anu o ke Koʻolau

C   F   C
Kaulana mai nei Koʻolaupoko
F   C   G7   C
Ua ʻā ka uila a i Kāneʻohe

C   F   C
Walea ana ʻoe me ke onaona
F   C   G7   C
Kuʻu lei hulu mamo pili i ke anu

C   F   C
Hanohano Mōkapu i ka ʻehu kai
F   C   G7   C
Te tua motumotu aʻo Heʻeia

C   F   C
Hoʻokahi mea hou ma Heʻeia
F   C   G7   C
Ka uea kelekalepa leo nahenahe

C   F   C
Aia ʻike lihi o ka ʻāina
F   C   G7   C
Kahi a ke aloha i walea ai

C   F   C
Ua ana hoʻi au a i ko leo
F   C   G7   C
Ko pane ʻana mai pehea au

C   F   C
Haʻina ʻia mai ana ka puana
F   C   G7   C
Ua ʻā ka uila a i Kāneʻohe

chorus:
With the ʻĀpuakea rain
The calm of Malulani
And the coolness of the Koʻolau

The lightening flashes at Kāneʻohe
The working team of ʻĪlaniwai

Koʻolaupoko is famous
And lights go on at Kāneʻohe

You delight with the sweetness
My mamo feather lei with me in the cold

The glory of Mōkapu is the sea spray
And the jagged ridge of Heʻeia

A new thing at Heʻeia
Is the sweet-voiced telegraph wire

Glimpses of the land
Where love finds delight

I am fulfilled by your voice
You asking how I am

Tell the refrain
Lights go on at Kāneʻohe

The installation of electricity at Kāneʻohe in the late 1920s was celebrated in this song by Abbie Kong and Johnny Noble. This version, from Nā Mele o Hawaiʻi Nei, *is longer and a little different from the one published by Noble in 1937. In that one the hui ended with "Ka laʻi o ke Koʻolau, Me ke anu o ke kuahiwi."*

Kāua I Ka Huahuaʻi

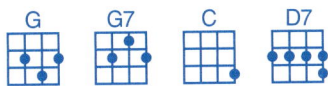

G
'Auhea wale ana 'oe
　　　　　　　G7
E kaʻu mea e liʻa nei
C　　　　　　G
Mai hōʻapaʻapa mai 'oe
D7　　　　　G
O loaʻa pono kāua

Oh do pay heed
Desire of my heart
Don't you procastinate
Lest we be discovered

hui

G
Kāua i ka huahuaʻi
　　　　　　　　G7
E ʻuhene lā i pili koʻolua
C　　G
Pukukuʻi lua i ke koʻekoʻe
D7　　　　　G
Hanu lipo o ka palai

chorus:
You and I in the upwelling rush
Teasing and clinging as
　　companions
Cuddling together in the chill
Deeply inhaling the scent of fern

tag

C G   D7 G   G7
Auē tāua
C G   D7 G
Auē tāua

tag:
Oh my, you and I
Oh my, you and I

G
He aloha au iā 'oe
　　　　　　G7
I kāu hanahana pono
C　　　　　G
Laʻi aʻe ke kaunu me iala
D7　　　　　G
Hōʻapaʻapa i ka manawa

I do love you
For the perfect warmth you exude
Romance is a delight with that one
Causing the heart to tarry

Composed by Leleiōhoku as a love song around 1860, it was revised by Johnny Noble in 1936 and again several years later with the addition of silly English lyrics and a nonsense "Hawaiian" version and renamed the Hawaiian War Chant.

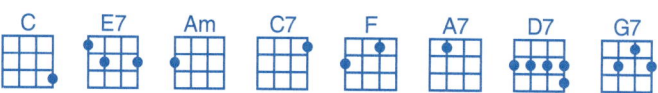

Kaua'i Beauty

    C   E7 Am   C7   F A7   D7
Hanohano Kaua'i, Manokalanipō
   C   D7   G7   C
Kīhāpai pua, ua kaulana

     C   E7 Am   C7   F   A7 D7
'Ohu'ohu i ka maile a'o ka nahele
  C   D7   G7   C
I ke 'ala onaona o ka mokihana

  C   E7 Am C7   F   A7 D7
I wili 'ia me maile lauli'i
  C   D7   G7   C
Ke 'ala ho'oheno o ka malihini

C   E7 Am   C7   F   A7 D7
Ha'ina 'ia mai ana ka puana
    C   D7   G7   C
Ku'u lei mokihana e moani nei

  C   E7 Am C7   F   A7 D7
Ha'ina 'ia mai ana ka puana
    C   D7   G7   C
Ku'u lei mokihana poina 'ole

Glorious is Kaua'i of chief Manokalanipō
A flower garden that is renowned

Adorned with maile of the forest
And the sweet fragrance of mokihana

Entwined with dainty leafed maile
A fragrance cherished by visitors

May the story be told in the refrain
My mokihana lei whose fragrance is wind-borne

Tell the refrain
My unforgettable mokihana lei

This is a mele pana, a song that celebrates a special place and often starts with 'hanohano' or 'kaulana.' Composer Henry Waia'u pays special tribute to Kaua'i of Manokalanipō, an ancient Kaua'i chief. 1929.

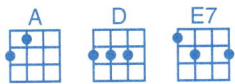

Kauanoeanuhea

A	D
'Auhea wale ana 'oe
| E7 | D A |
E Kauanoeanuhea
| | D |
Huli au i ke onaona
| E7 | D A |
'A'ole i loa'a mai

Where could you be
Oh cool, fragrant mist?
I search for your sweet fragrance
But it isn't found

| A | D |
Aia paha 'oe i luna
| E7 | D A |
I ka malu o Maunaleo
| | D |
He wehi no ia uka
| E7 | D A |
Ka uka o Kānehoa

Perhaps you are high above
In the shelter of Maunaleo
An adornment of that upland
The high reaches of Kānehoa

| A | D |
Na ke ahe a ka Mālie
| E7 | D A |
E hali mai i ku'u aloha
| | D |
He aloha i hi'ipoi 'ia
| E7 | D A |
No nā kau a kau

It is the gentle Mālie wind
That will bring my love to me
A love so cherished
From season to season

| A | D |
Eia ho'i ke aloha
| E7 | D A |
No Kauanoeanuhea
| | D |
He wehi no ia uka
| E7 | D A |
Ka uka o Kānehoa

Here indeed is the love
For the cool, fragrant mist
An adornment of that upland
The upland of Kānehoa

Keali'i Reichel writes of the mist of 'Īao that cannot be gained by chasing after it, but, if one waits patiently, it will come down and gently embrace you. Such is love — elusive when sought after. 1994.

He Mele Aloha

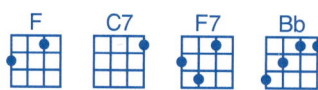

Kaula ʻIli

    F   C7   F   F7
ʻO ʻoe ka i hui ihola
  Bb   C7   F   C7
Ka manaʻo e puapuaʻi ala
  F   C7   F
Eia aʻe ʻo Puʻuohulu
  C7   F
Ulu nō au iā ʻoe, ua hiki nō

     F   C7   F F7
Hoʻomākaukau kou kaula ʻili
  Bb   C7   F C7
I luna o ka puʻu Kanakaleonui
  F   C7   F
E hoʻolohe i ke kani a nā manu
         C7   F
Oh never mind, ke hina pū, ua hiki nō

You are the one who brought together
These thoughts that well up in me
Puʻuohulu hill draws near
And I'm inspired by you, which is fine

Prepare your lariat
Atop the hill Kanakaleonui
Listen to the song of the birds
Oh never mind, if we tumble together, it is fine

The hui of this song is the same as the hui in Eliza Holt's Puʻuohulu. It is unclear as to which is the earlier song. In this song the allusion to Puʻu Kanakaleonui, a prominent hill located high up the slopes of Maunakea, places the geographical reference on Waimea, on Hawaiʻi Island, whereas in Puʻuohulu the reference to Māʻili places the reference in Waiʻanae, Oʻahu.

He Mele Aloha

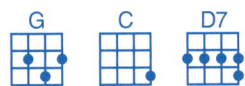

Kaulana Nā Pua

G   C   G
Kaulana nā pua aʻo Hawaiʻi
                     C   G
Kūpaʻa ma hope o ka ʻāina
                          D7
Hiki mai ka ʻelele o ka loko ʻino
                              G
Palapala ʻānunu me ka pākaha
	Famous are the children of Hawaiʻi
	Loyal to the land
	The evil hearted messenger comes
	With a document of extortion and greed

G   C   G
Pane mai Hawaiʻi moku o Keawe
                     C   G
Kōkua nā hono aʻo Piʻilani
                       D7
Kākoʻo mai Kauaʻi o Mano
                              G
Paʻa pū me ke one o Kākuhihewa
	Hawaiʻi, island of Keawe, answers
	The bays of Piʻilani help
	Kauaʻi of Mano lends support
	Firmly united with the sands of Kākuhihewa

G   C   G
ʻAʻole aʻe kau i ka pūlima
                      C G
Ma luna o ka pepa o ka ʻenemi
                  D7
Hoʻohui ʻāina kūʻai hewa
                          G
I ka pono sivila aʻo ke kanaka
	Do not fix a signature
	To the paper of the enemy
	With its sin of annexation and sale
	Of the civil rights of the people

G   C G
ʻAʻole mākou aʻe minamina
                  C G
I ka puʻu kālā o ke aupuni
                       D7
Ua lawa mākou i ka pōhaku
                         G
I ka ʻai kamahaʻo o ka ʻāina
	We do not value
	The heaps of money of the government
	We have enough with stones
	The remarkable food of the land

G   C   G
Ma hope mākou o Liliʻulani
                         C G
A loaʻa ʻē ka pono o ka ʻāina
                         D7
Haʻina ʻia mai ana ka puana
                          G
ʻO ka poʻe i aloha i ka ʻāina
	We support Liliʻuokalani
	Until we gain the rights of the land
	The story is to be told
	Of the people who love the land

Ellen Wright Prendergast wrote this "stone-eating song" in 1893 at the urging of members of the Royal Hawaiian Band to express their bitter opposition to annexation of Hawaiʻi to the United States. Declaring loyalty to the Queen, it says "we will not sign the paper, but will be satisfied with all that is left to us, the stones, the ʻai kamahaʻo (mystic, astounding, sustaining, remarkable food) of our native land." Also known as *Mele ʻAi Pōhaku* and *He Lei No Nā Poʻe Aloha ʻĀina*. Translation by Hui Hānai.

Kaulana ʻO Waimānalo

G	A7

Kaulana ʻo Waimānalo
I ka pali o Makapuʻu
I ke kai hāwanawana
Hoʻopuni ʻia e nā pali

Famous is Waimānalo
For the sea cliffs of Makapuʻu
For the whispering sea
A land encircled by cliffs

Hiehie aʻo Mānana
Kū kilakila i ke kai
Pōʻai mau ʻia ana
E ke kai hānupanupa

Mānana is distinguished
Rising majestically in the sea
Ever encircled
By the pounding sea

ʻAlawa iho ʻoe
I nā papa heʻenalu
Hiehie ke kūlana
I ka heʻe mālie mai

You glance down
Toward those on surf boards
A proud stance
As they gently skim the waves

Ua nani nā home
Aʻo Waimānalo
Ua piha me ke aloha
A me ka nui hauʻoli

The homes are beautiful
There in Waimānalo
Filled with affectionate welcome
And great joy

Haʻina mai ka puana
Kaulana ʻo Waimānalo
I ka pali o Makapuʻu
I ke kai hāwanawana

Tell, then, the story
That Waimānalo is renowned
For the sea cliffs of Makapuʻu
And for the whispering sea

Many know Mānana better as Rabbit Island, included in this song about Waimānalo and Makapuʻu by Sam Kamuela Naeʻole.

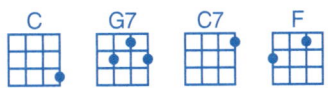

Kawaihau Medley
Lanakila Kawaihau, Kalalea, Moikeha

C **G7** **C**
Inu i ka wai māpuna
G7 **C**
Ha'aheo i kou lei lehua
G7 **C**
A he leo no pūpū kani oe
C7 **F** **G7** **C**
Ua lanakila 'o Kawaihau

(from Lanakila Kawaihau)

Drink of the spring water
Proud in your lehua lei
The voice of the singing land-shells
Kawaihau is victorious!

C **C7** **F**
Ki'eki'e Kalalea i ka makani
G7 **C**
'O ka pali kaulana o Anahola
C7 **F**
Noho iho e ka 'ohu noe i nā pali
G7 **C**
A he nani maoli nō mai 'ō a 'ō

(from Kalalea)

Kalalea is majestic in the wind
The famous precipice of Anahola
The mist settles softly on the cliffs
True beauty everywhere

C **C7** **F**
E aha ana Moikeha
C **C7**
I ka 'ili kai a'o Puna
C **C7** **F**
E ana paha i ka loa
G7 **C**
Me ka laulā o Kapa'a

(from Moikeha)

What is *Moikeha* doing
There on the sea in Puna?
Maybe it's measuring the length
And breadth of Kapa'a?

Kawaihau Glee Club, which sang this medley, was a men's choral group founded in 1876 by Leleiōhoku, and dissolved after his death a year later. Musical competition happened at the highest levels of Hawaiian society. Choral groups, patronized or led by various chiefs, competed with each other for prizes and honors. Translation by Dixon Stroup.

He Mele Aloha

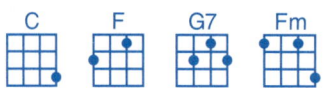

Kawaipunahele

C   F C
Nou e Kawaipunahele
F   C G7
Kuʻu lei aloha mae ʻole
F   Fm
Pili hemo ʻole, pili paʻa pono
G7   C
E huli hoʻi kāua
G7   C
E Kawaipunahele

For you Kawaipunahele
My beloved never-fading lei
Secure together, solidly joined
Come, let us reunite
O Kawaipunahele

C   F C
Kū ʻoe me ke kiʻekiʻe
F   C G7
I ka nani aʻo Wailuku
F   Fm
Kuʻu ipo henoheno, kuʻu wehi o ka pō
G7   C
E huli hoʻi kāua
G7   C
E Kawaipunahele

You stand majestically
In the splendor of Wailuku
My cherished sweetheart
My adornment of the night
Come, let us reunite
O Kawaipunahele

C   F C
Eia hoʻi ʻo Kealiʻi
F   C G7
Kali ana i ka mehameha
F   Fm
Mehameha hoʻi au, ʻehaʻeha hoʻi au
G7   C
E huli hoʻi kāua
G7   C
E Kawaipunahele

Here is Kealiʻi
Waiting in loneliness
I am lonely, and I am hurt
Come, let us reunite
O Kawaipunahele

C   F C
Puana ʻia ke aloha
F   C G7
Kuʻu lei aloha mae ʻole
F   Fm
Pili hemo ʻole, pili paʻa pono
G7   C
Ke pono hoʻi kāua
G7   C
E Kawaipunahele

Tell of the love
Of my beloved never-fading lei
Secure together, solidly joined
When it's right, for you and I
O Kawaipunahele

This song by Kealiʻi Reichel beckons to the loved one to return to the relationship. Such songs employ a prescriptive magic that is often quite effective. 1994.

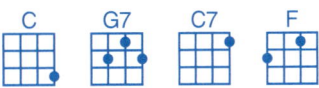

Kawohikūkapulani

C	G7	C
He lei ʻāʻī ʻoe na ke kupuna
C7	F	C
A he milimili ʻoe na ka makua
	G7	C
Pūlama ʻia ʻoe me ke aloha
	G7	C
Hiʻipoi ʻia ʻoe ma kuʻu poli

| C | G7 | C |
He lei aloha ʻoe, ua kaulana
| C7 | F | C |
I paukū ʻia me ka ʻāhihi
| | G7 | C |
Hoʻohihi nō wau, naʻu ʻoe
| | G7 | C |
ʻO koʻu kuleana paʻa nō ia

| C | G7 | C |
Haʻina ʻia mai ana ka puana
| C7 | F | C |
Kuʻu lei nani ʻoe poina ʻole
| | G7 | C |
Hea aku mākou, e ō mai ʻoe
| | G7 | C |
ʻO Kawohikūkapulani, he inoa

You are an adornment for the grandparents
And a darling for your parents
Cherished with love
You are cradled on my bosom

You are a beloved lei, renowned
Linked with the dainty ʻāhihi lehua
I too am involved, for you are mine
This is my right, permanently

The story is told
You are my beautiful child, unforgettable
We call, you answer
Kawohikūkapulani, a name song for you

Helen Desha Beamer wrote this enduring musical gift of love from parent to child for her daughter on her wedding day. 1941. Translation by Mahiʻai Beamer.

Ke ʻAla O Ka Rose

D　　　　　　A7　　　D　D7
Ke ʻala o ka rose ua hā pā mai
G　　　D　　A7　　　D
Ka maile lauliʻi o ke kuahiwi

The perfume of the rose comes to me
The delicate leaved maile of the mountain

D　　　　　　A7　　　D　D7
Ka hala o kai, maile aʻo uka
G　　　D　A7　　　　D
Kui aʻe kāua a lawa kuʻu lei

Pandanus from the shore, maile from the heights
Let us combine them, and my lei is done

D　　　　　　A7　　　D　D7
Mea ʻole ē ke kula me ke kaimana
G　　　　D　A7　　　D
Ke kumu manakō hoʻoluliluli

Gold and diamonds are not important to me
The mango tree, bending to the breeze, is

D　　　　　　A7　　　D　D7
Hāwele pono iho i ke kaula ʻili
G　　　D　　A7　　D
Makuʻu o ka noho ʻItalia

Properly secure the reins
On the pummel of the Italian saddle

D　　　　　　A7　　　D　D7
Ua kani ē ka pio, hone i ke kula
G　　　D　A7　　D
Manaʻo iho oe, ʻo wau ia

A whistle sounds, sweet on the plains
And you think that it's me

D　　　　　　A7　　　D　D7
Haʻina ʻia mai ana ka puana
G　　　　D　　A7　　　D
Ke ʻala o ka rose, ua hā pā mai

Tell the story in the refrain
The perfume of the rose comes to me

Danny Kaʻōpio, from the island of Niʻihau, composed this in 1932, at age of 17, when he was courting a beauty named Loke.

Ke Aloha

G	D7
Ma ku'u poli mai 'oe
G	
E ku'u ipo aloha
A7	
He 'ala onaona kou
D7	G
No ke ano ahiahi

Come into my embrace
Oh my beloved sweetheart
You have a sweet and lovely fragrance
For the peacefulness of twilight

| G | D7 |
Mamuli a'o ko leo
| G |
Ua malu nēia kino
| A7 |
He kino palupalu kou
| D7 | G |
I ka hana a ke aloha

At the sound of your voice
My body is at ease
Your body is so soft and gentle
At the endeavors of love

| G | D7 |
Ua la'i nō ho'i au
| G |
I ka hanu o ka ipo
| A7 |
E ho'oipoipo nei
| D7 | G |
Nanea pū kāua

So serene am I
In the perfume of a lover's breath
As we make love
And share in the delight

| G | D7 |
Ha'ina mai ka puana
| G |
E ku'u ipo aloha
| A7 |
He 'ala onaona kou
| D7 | G |
No ke ano ahiahi

The refrain tells the story
Oh my beloved sweetheart
You have a sweet and lovely fragrance
For the peacefulness of twilight

A romantic invitation, beckoning to a loved one to share the sensual delight of an evening together, by Lei Collins and Maddy Lam.

Ke Kali Nei Au

```
    C  G7   C C7 F            C
    Eia au ke kali nei
       G7    E7    Am    D7      G7
    Aia lā i hea kuʻu aloha
    C   D7  G7           C
    Eia au ke huli nei
                        G7
    A loaʻa ʻoe, e ka ipo
                              C
    Maha ka ʻiʻini a ka puʻuwai
    C  A7 D7   G7          C
    Ua sila paʻa ʻia me ʻoe
                         Dm
    Ko aloha makamae, e ipo
    G7                  C
    Kaʻu ia e lei aʻe nei lā
    C              C7       F
    Nou nō ka ʻiʻini (Noʻu ka ʻiʻini)
    D7              G7
    A nou wale nō (Wale nō)
    C  A7  D7          G7       C   G7
    A ʻo ko aloha kaʻu e hiʻipoi mau
       C              A7             D7 G7  C
    Naʻu ʻoe, (naʻu ʻoe) e lei (e lei) naʻu ʻoe, e lei
```

Here I am, awaiting
Where indeed could my love be?
Here I've been searching
And found you my beloved
The desire of the heart is appeased
We are ever sealed
Your precious love, my dear
I shall always wear like a lei
For you alone is my desire (your desire is for me)
And only for you (only me)
And your love is mine to forever cherish
You are mine to hold dear
You are mine like a precious lei

```
    C    G7     C   C7     F            C
    This is the moment I've waited for
       G7       E7      Am       D7             G7
    I can hear my heart singing, soon bells will be ringing
    C      D7    G7             C
    This is the moment of sweet "Aloha"
                             Dm
    I will love you longer than forever
    G7                              C
    Promise me that you will leave me never
             D7         G7             C
    Here and now dear, all my love I vow dear
    C                               Dm
    Promise me that you will leave me never
    G7                        C
    I will love you longer than forever
               C7        F
    Now that we are one (my darling)
    D7                 G7
    Clouds won't hide the sun (my love)
       C    A7    D7               G7          C   G7
    Blue skies of Hawaiʻi smile on this our wedding day
       C      A7      D7 G7  C
    I do love you with all my heart
```

Ke Kaʻupu

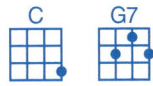

C
Iā māua i hoʻolaʻi iho ai
G7   **C**
Kaha ana ke kaʻupu i ka laʻi
I laila ke aloha haʻanipo
G7   **C**
Haʻalipo i ka poli pumehana

hui

    C
    Inā pēlā kāu hana
    G7   **C**
    Pākela ʻoi aku ka pipiʻi
    I kāu hana ʻolu noʻeau
    G7   **C**
    Kohu like me Waiʻaleʻale

C
Kuhi au ua like me ia nei
G7   **C**
Ka lalawe ninihi launa ʻole
ʻAkahi a ʻike i ka noe
G7   **C**
Ua loha i ka wai hoʻolana

C
ʻO ka hana nipo kāu e ke anu
G7   **C**
Ua māewa poniponi i ka noe
Pōahiahi wale ka ʻikena
G7   **C**
Ke koni iho, koni aku, koni aʻe

As we sat together
An albatross appeared in the calm
It was then that love grew ardent
Warming the heart with affection

chorus:
If that is the way you behave
It becomes ever so difficult
Your deeds so gentle and clever
Reminds one of Waiʻaleʻale

I thought it was like this
The most careful and gentlest touch
Then saw the mist for the first time
Hanging low over the tranquil water

You like to woo, oh crisp chill
As you spread in a lavender mist
Making visibility obscure
Causing a throbbing here, there and beyond

Kamehameha died on the night of Hoku, and the name Leleiōhoku, or "Flight to the presence of Hoku," became a lineage name. This song was composed by Leleiōhoku, younger brother of Kalākaua and adopted son of Ruth Keʻelikōlani. 1888.

Opposite: *Known also as the* **Hawaiian Wedding Song,** *this beautiful duet is by Charles E. King, the English lyrics are by Al Hoffman and Dick Manning. 1925.*

Keaukaha

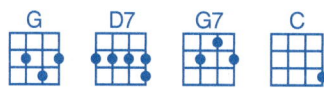

    G   D7
'Ike 'ia i ka nani o Keaukaha
                                G
'Āina ho'opulapula no nā Hawai'i
                G7   C
Home uluwehiwehi i ka ulu hala
         D7   G
He nohea i ka maka o ka lehulehu

hui

    G   D7
He makana kēia mai ke ali'i
                            G
Nou, e nā kini pua, no nā Hawai'i
                G7   C
Mālama pono iho a he waiwai nui
        D7   G
'O ke ola nō ia, ka pu'uhonua

    G   D7
Mahalo iā 'oe, e ke ali'i
                        G
'O Kalaniana'ole nō kou inoa
              G7   C
E hana like kākou me ke aloha
      D7   G
I mau ke ea o ka 'āina i ka pono
C   D7   G
I mau ke ea o ka 'āina i ka pono

Well known in the beauty of Keaukaha
Is the homestead land for the Hawaiians
Verdant home in the hala groves
Admirable in the eyes of the people

chorus:
This is a gift from the Chief
For you, the many descendants, the Hawaiians
Take good care, this is a great treasure
It is life — a place of refuge

Thanks goes to you, Chief
Kalaniana'ole indeed, is your name
Let us all work together with love
So that the life of the land will be perpetuated in righteousness

Albert Nāhale'ā received a homestead in Keaukaha. He wrote this song in thanks to Prince Kūhiō for creating the Hawaiian Homestead program, also referred to as "'Āina Ho'opulapula." Originally named Ku'u Home 'O Keaukaha, *but generally known by the shorter title.*

He Mele Aloha

Keawaiki

    C   D7
Eia lā he kono ua loa'a mai Keawaiki
  G7   C   F   C
E kipa e nanea e ho'olaukanaka
               D7
E pā'ina ai ho'i me ia kini
  G7   C
Keiki aloha na Hawai'i
      G7   C
He punahele ho'i 'oe na mākou

  C   A7   D7
He nani a he 'olu'olu 'i'o nō
  G7   C
Ia home i ka 'ae kai
     A7   D7
I laila 'oe e ola ai
  G7   C
Keiki aloha a Hawai'i
      G7   C
He punahele ho'i 'oe na mākou

Here is an invitation received from Keawaiki
To visit, relax, to get together
And lunch with friends
Beloved son of Hawai'i
You are our favorite indeed

Truly beautiful, cool and comfortable
This home by the sea
You live there
Beloved son of Hawai'i
You are our favorite indeed

Helen Desha Beamer wrote this for Francis 'Ī'ī Brown, named after his home on the Big Island. 1942. Translation by Mahi'ai Beamer.

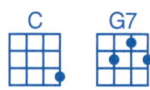

Kilakila ʻO Haleakalā

C
Kauhale o Kaʻaoʻao
G7
ʻIke aku iā Kilohana
Kāua i ke one heʻeheʻe
C
Me nā alanui kīkeʻekeʻe

Kaʻaoʻao is our home
That looks upon Kilohana
You and I on the sliding sands
And zigzagging pathways

C
Kau ana lā kau ana
G7
Kau ana ko ia ala maka
ʻO ua lio holo peki!
C
Mea ʻole ko ia ala holo!

Settling there, settling there
That one's gaze is fixed
Oh, that prancing horse!
Its gait is of no importance

🎸 *hui*

C
Kilakila ʻo Haleakalā
G7
Kuahiwi nani o Maui
Haʻaheo ʻoe Hawaiʻi
C
Hanohano ʻo Maui nō ka ʻoi

chorus:
Majestic Haleakalā
Beautiful mountain of Maui
Prized by you, Hawaiʻi
Glorious Maui is the very best.

This song appears to be of mixed origins, the second stanza being from the 1870 song Kau Ana, *the hui may be by Charles E. King. The stanzas are often sung slowly, the hui quite fast.*

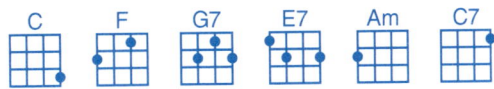

Kimo Hula

C   F G7   F   C
Aia i ka uka o Piʻihonua
  E7   Am C7
Ke kīhāpai pua ulumāhiehie
       F   C
I laila au lā ʻike i ka nani
    G7   C
O nā pua ʻala a he nui wale

In the uplands of Piʻihonua
A flower garden in beautiful array
There I see the beauty
Of the flowers, fragrant, in great profusion

C   F G7   F C
Hoʻohihi nā manu o ke kuahiwi
 E7   Am C7
Nā ʻiʻiwi maka pōlena
   F   C
I ka ʻono o ka wai o nā pua
     G7   C
O Moanikeʻala i ka uluwehiwehi

The birds of the forest are attracted here
The yellow-eyed ʻiʻiwi
At the sweet nectar of the flowers
Of Moanikeʻalaʻs beautiful garden

C   F G7   F C
Mahalo iā ʻoe, e ka hoa aloha
   E7   Am C7
I ka hoʻokipa i nā malihini
   F   C
Eia ko lei poina ʻole
 G7   C
ʻO Leimakani, Leionaona

Thank you, dear friend
For the gracious hospitality to visitors
Here is your unforgettable beloved
Leimakani, Leionaona

C   F G7   F C
Haʻina ʻia mai ana ka puana
  E7   Am C7
Moanikeʻala i ka uluwehiwehi
       F   C
Hea aku mākou, e ō mai ʻoe
   G7   C
Kimo o ka uka ʻiuʻiu he inoa

The story is told
Moanikeʻala, beautifully verdant
We call, you answer
Kimo of the highlands, your name song

Moanikeʻala, in Piʻihonua, high above Hilo, was the home of Kimo and Leimakani Henderson. This mele was written by Helen Desha Beamer as she journeyed to Piʻihonua, completed by the time of her arrival and performed as a gift of thanks to her hosts. 1953. Translation by Mahiʻai Beamer.

He Mele Aloha

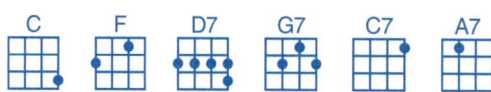

Kinuē

   C   F   C
Hanohano Pauahi i ka uhiwai
  A7   D7 G7   C   C7
Me ka ua kilihune o ke kuahiwi
         F   C7   F
Hone ana ē ka leo o ke kelepona
    C   G7   C
E kono mai ana iaʻu e kipa aku

Glorious Pauahi in the mist
And fine rain of the mountain
Sweet soft voice on the telephone
Inviting me to visit

   C   F   C
Launa pū me nā hoa aloha
 A7   D7 G7   C   C7
Ia home hoʻokipa pumehana
        F   C7   F
Hoʻohihi nā manu i ka laʻi
      C   G7   C
Hoʻolaʻi nā malihini i ka nani

Enjoying together with dear friends
The warm hospitality of this home
The birds are lured by the quiet calm
The guests content in beautiful surroundings

  C   F C
E ake ana e ʻike iā Papaloa
 A7   D7 G7   C   C7
A he loa, a he loa mai hoʻi kau
         F   C7   F
Ia home kaulana o ia uka
       C   G7   C
Moani ana ke ʻala o nā pua

Longing to see Papaloa
So far away, so distant
This home well known in these uplands
Wafting sweet fragrance of the flowers

 C   F   C
Mea ʻole ke alanui kīkeʻekeʻe
 A7   D7 G7   C   C7
I ka holu mālie hoʻi a ka jeep
        F   C7   F
Hea aku nō au, ō mai ʻoukou
      C   G7   C
Nā pua lei aloha a Kinuē

The crooked road is as nothing
To the easy swaying of the jeep
I call, you answer
Beloved children of Kinuē

Written by Lilinoe Wall for the Arthur Greenwell family of Kona, and put to music by Helen Desha Beamer. 1948. Translation by Mahiʻai Beamer.

He Mele Aloha

Kīpū Kai

[F] No Kīpū Kai ke aloha [C7]
Home i ka pili kahakai [F]
[F7] I laila au e ʻike ai [Bb] [G7]
[C7] I ka nui lokomaikaʻi [F]

For Kīpū Kai is my affection
Where there's a home at the
　water's edge
It was there I found
Such unbounded hospitality

[F] Pau ʻole koʻu hoʻohihi [C7]
I ka nani aʻo Hāʻupu [F]
[F7] Mauna kiʻekiʻe i luna [Bb] [G7]
[C7] Hanohano ke ʻike aku [F]

Endless is my admiration
For the beauty of Hāʻupu
A hill so high above
Majestic to my sight

[F] Nanea i ka hoʻolohe [C7]
I ka halulu mai o ke kai [F]
[F7] Ka nalu nui e holu ana [Bb] [G7]
[C7] I ka lae aʻo Kuahonu [F]

I enjoy listening quietly
To the roar of the sea
As large waves come rushing in
To Kuahonu Point

[F] Makemake wale ka ʻikena [C7]
I nā manu pīkake nani [F]
[F7] E kakaʻi e haʻaheo ana [Bb] [G7]
[C7] I ka malu aʻo ke kiawe [F]

It is delightful to see
The pretty peacocks
Strutting by together
In the shade of the kiawe trees

[F] Puana ʻia me ke aloha [C7]
No ka nani aʻo Hāʻupu [F]
[F7] Me Keaka lokomaikaʻi [Bb] [G7]
[C7] Ka haku aʻo Kīpū Kai [F]

Thus ends my song with
　affection
For the beauty of Hāʻupu
And to Jack the kind-hearted
The owner of Kīpū Kai

Composed in the 1950s by Mary Kawena Pukui and Maddy K. Lam for Jack Waterhouse and his Kīpū Kai Ranch on Kauaʻi. Hāʻupu, a ridge on Kauaʻi that separates Kīpū Kai from the main part of the island, is dominated by a peak of the same name. Hāʻupu, also called Hoary Head, is a wahi pana of great significance to Hawaiians, as its peak can be used as a predictor of weather for the surrounding area. Translation by Mary Kawena Pukui.

Kōke'e

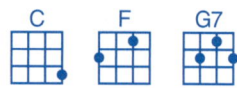

    C   F   C
'Upu a'e, he mana'o
 F   C   G7
I ka wēkiu o Kōke'e
     C   F   C
I ka nani o ka 'āina
 F   C   G7 C
O ka noe pō'ai'ai

Thoughts well up in me
Of the highlands of Kōke'e
Of the beauty of the land
And the swirling mists

🎸 *hui*

      C   G7   F
'O Kalalau he 'āina la'a
    C   G7
I ka ua li'ili'i
       C   F   C
'O Waimea ku'u lei aloha
 F   C   G7   C
Never more to say goodbye

chorus:
Kalalau, a sacred land
In the fine, passing rains
Waimea is my lei of love
Never more to say goodbye

  C   F   C
E ho'i mai ana i ka hikina
 F   C   G7
I ka lā welawela
    C   F   C
I ke kai hāwanawana
 F   C G7   C
I Po'ipū ma Kōloa

Returning to the east
In the sun, clear and hot
To the whispering seas
At Po'ipū and Kōloa

  C   F   C
Mele au no ka beauty
 F   C   G7
I ka uka 'iu'iu
    C   F   C
I Kōke'e ua 'ike au
 F   C G7   C
I ka noe pō'ai'ai

I sing of the beauty
In the far highlands
At Kōke'e I have seen
The mists that swirl about

Composed by Dennis Kamakahi in 1979 for Kōke'e, the forested heights above Waimea and Kekaha, overlooking the valleys of the Nā Pali coast.

Kona Kai ʻŌpua

F   **F7**   **Bb**   **D7**   **G7**
Hanohano ʻo Kona kai ʻōpua i ka laʻi
C7
ʻŌpua hīnano kau i ka mālie
F   **C7**
Puaʻi nā wai i ka maka o ka ʻōpua
F   **F7**   **Bb**   **D7**   **G7**
ʻAʻole nō ʻelua aʻe like aku ai
C7
Me Kona kai ʻōpua (Kona kai ʻōpua)

Ke kai māʻokiʻoki (kai māʻokiʻoki)
                    F
Ke kai malino aʻo Kona

hui

  F   **Bb**   **F**
Haʻaheo i ka mālie
              C7
ʻO Kona kai ʻōpua i ka laʻi

Kilakila ʻo Hualālai
                F
I ke kai malino aʻo Kona

F
Haʻaheo Hawaiʻi i nā Kona
                    C7
Ka wai kau i ka maka o ka ʻōpua

Hualālai kau mai i luna
        F
Ka heke ia o nā Kona

He ʻāina wela ʻiʻo nō nā Kona
                  C7
He ʻEka ka makani aʻe ʻolu ai

ʻO ka pā kolonahe a ke Kēhau
      F
I ka ʻili o ka malihini

Grand is Kona of the clouds mirrored in the sea
Puffy white clouds nestled in the calm
Waters spill forth from the cloud banks
There's no other that can compare
With Kona of the mirrored seas
A sea of mingling hues
The calm seas of Kona

chorus:
Proud indeed in the tranquility
Kona of mirrored seas in the calm
Majestic is Hualālai
The calm seas of Kona

Hawaiʻi island is proud of the Kona district
The water in the face of the clouds
Hualālai stands there above
The finest of the Kona District
Kona is truly a sweltering land
The ʻEka breeze brings sweet relief
The gentle touch of the Kēhau breeze
Cooling on the visitor's skin

Henry Waiaʻu composed this for his son's graduation from Kamehameha School in 1941. This hui was not a part of the original composition.

He Mele Aloha

Koni Au I Ka Wai

G
Hoʻohihi kahi manaʻo
D7
I ka ʻehu kai o Puaʻena
G   **G7**   **C**   **A7**
Kai hāwanawana i ka laʻi lā
D7   **G**
I ka laʻi wale aʻo Waialua

In me springs a desire
For the ocean spray of Puaʻena
The whispering waters that lap the shore
Of beautiful Waialua

hui

G
Koni au, koni au i ka wai
                    D7
Koni au i ka wai huʻihuʻi
G   **G7**   **C**   **A7**
I ka wai aliʻi, ʻo ke kini lā
D7   **G**
ʻOlu ai ka nohona o ka laʻi

chorus:
I yearn, yearn for the water
Yearn for a cool refreshing drink
Royal liquid, gin
That makes life so pleasant

G
Alia ʻoe e ka ʻehu kai
D7
E lelehune nei i ke one
G   **G7**   **C**   **A7**
One hānau o ke kupuna lā
D7   **G**
Pūʻili lau liʻi o ka uka

Wait a bit, oh sea spray
Splashing upon the sand
Homeland of the ancestors
And the dainty fruits of the shore

G
ʻAkahi hoʻi au lā ʻike
D7
I nā laʻi ʻelua
G   **G7**   **C**   **A7**
ʻElua māua i ka laʻi lā
D7   **G**
Wai kāpīpī i ka pali

Finally I have witnessed
Both of the pleasures
We were two in the calm
Where water sprayed on the cliffs

C   **F**   **C**   **G7**   **C**
Kiss me my darling honi kāua la ē, ʻo kou chance pono kēia
                F   **C**
ʻAuhea wale ana ʻoe e ka ipo lauaʻe lā ē
G7   **C** **D7**
Down by the pūnāwai with me

Kalākaua wrote this under his pen name "Figgs" in 1888. The "Kiss me my darling..." verse is from a different song, but so often added as a medley that we've included it here.

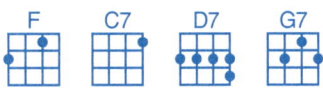

Kō'ula

     F   C7   F   D7   G7
Nani wale ē ka ua a'o Kō'ula
   C7   F
Kilihune nei i ka ua li'ili'i

How beautiful is the rain of Kō'ula
Showering down in misty droplets

    F   C7 F   D7   G7
'O ka pi'o ana mai o ke ānuenue
   C7   F
Ho'oheno ana i ka lau lā'au

The arching of the rainbow above
Caresses the leaves of the trees

    F   C7   F   D7   G7
Kaulana manowai, wai a'o Puna
   C7   F
Ke kumu o ka wai a'o Manuahi

Famous this spring, the water of Puna
The source of the waters of Manuahi

    F   C7   F   D7   G7
Kūmaka ka 'ikena i ia wai lewa
   C7   F
Ko'iaweawe i ka welelau pali

All eyes gaze at this water on high
Spraying and dancing over the cliffs

   F   C7   F D7   G7
E ola ka 'ōpua kū kilakila
   C7   F
Ma ke kihi o ke ao a'o Mālama

Cottony clouds rise majestically
At the beginning of daylight in Mālama

   F   C7 F D7   G7
Ha'ina ka inoa poina 'ole
   C7   F
Kaulana nā manowai o Puna

Told is the unforgettable name
Renowned are the great springs of Puna

This song by Alvin Isaacs, Sr. was originally entitled **Manowaiopuna**. *It honors the waters that grace the Puna district of Kaua'i.*

Kūhiō Bay

'Akahi ho'i a 'ike ku'u maka
I ka nani a'o Waiākea
'A'ohe lua e like ai
Me ka nani a me ka nani a'o Kūhiō Bay

Finally my eyes have seen
The beauty of Waiākea
There is no other to compare
With its beauty and the beauty of Kūhiō Bay

Mahalo a'e au i ka nani a'o Hilo
Me ka ua a e ho'opulu nei
Oni ana Mokuola 'au i ke kai
'O ua 'āina e kaulana nei

I admire the beauty of Hilo
And its drenching rains
Mokuola appears in the sea
A land indeed renowned

Waiānuenue a he wai kaulana
Wai māka'ika'i a ka malihini
Wai kamaha'o i ka'u 'ike
E pāpahi e ho'opē nei i ka nahele

Waiānuenue, a noted falls
A sight enjoyed by visitors
A cascade, wondrous in my sight
Adorning and perfuming the forest

Composed by Keliana Bishaw, this song speaks of the beauty of Hilo and of the landmarks of that fine city.

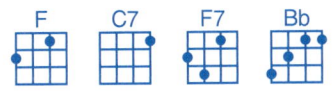

Kupa Landing

F
Hoʻokena i ka laʻi
C7
Honumū aʻo nā manu
F7   Bb
ʻIke ʻia ʻo ka lihi
F   C7   F
Alia ʻoe a pūlale mai

Bb
ʻO Kupa Landing
F
Hanohano i ka laʻi
C7   F   F7
Hōʻolu ʻia nō, Hoʻokena
Bb
Hoʻoheno ka manaʻo
F
Nā kupa o ka ʻāina
C7   F
Hōʻolu i ka maka o ka malihini

🎸hui
F
Kani nei, kani nei, kani nei
Aʻo nā manu
C7   F C7
ʻŪ lā, lāē, ʻū lā lāē ū
F
Hone nei, hone nei, hone nei
I Hoʻokena
C7   F
ʻU lā, lāē, ʻū lā lāē ū

Hoʻokena is peaceful
And the birds flock to Honumū
And glance about shyly
But don't you rush

Kupa Landing
Its glorious solace
Hoʻokena, charming
Cherished in the thoughts
Of the natives of the land
Charming, too, in the eyes of visitors

chorus:
Singing, singing, singing
Birds
Teasing, teasing and bantering
Trilling, trilling, trilling
At Hoʻokena
Teasing, teasing and bantering

Lot Kauwē's song from the 1890s commemorates Kupa Landing, at Kupa Bay, on Hawaiʻi at Hoʻokena — cattle-raising country. When it came time to ship the cattle out the cowboys swam them to the ships. In 1926 Kupa Bay was swallowed by lava. Whether or not Kupa is the Hawaiianization of Cooper, or was in fact the original Hawaiian place name, is unclear. In any event, this is a great yodelling song, a favorite of Hawaiian falsetto singers.

He Mele Aloha

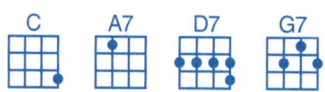

Ku'u Hoa

   C   A7   D7
He aloha ku'u ipo
C   G7   C
Ku'u hoa maka onaona noho i ke kuahiwi

Beloved is my sweetheart
My sweet-faced companion of the forest

   C   A7   D7
Ho'i mai nō kāua
C   G7   C
Me a'u e pili, e ku'u i'ini a ka pu'uwai

Let us two come back together
Cling to me, oh desire of my heart

   C   A7   D7
'O ka pā kōnane
C   G7   C
A ka mahina lā, ahu wale nō ka pae 'ōpua

The clear light shimmers
From the moon, over banks of clouds

   C   A7   D7
Ha'ina mai ka puana
C   G7   C
Ku'u hoa maka onaona noho i ke kuahiwi

Tell the refrain
Of my sweet-faced companion of the forest

Composed by Francis Keali'inohopono (Pono) Beamer for his wife, this song entices a sweetheart to enjoy a moonlit night together. 1937.

He Mele Aloha

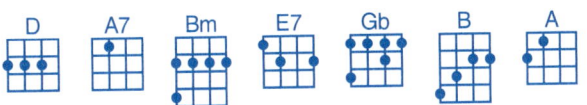

Ku'u 'I'ini

    D   A7
'Auhea wale ana 'oe
                  D
He hali'a ka i hiki mai
            A
Me he lā e 'ī mai ana
Bm   E7   A
Aia i laila ke aloha
A7 D   A7
Eia me a'u ka 'i'ini
                Gb
Nou, e ku'u lei poina 'ole
  B   E7
I walea ka nohona iho
              A E7 A7
Me 'oe, ku'u ipo nohea

Oh, do pay heed
A remembrance has come upon me
As though saying to me
There, indeed, is the beloved
The desire is here with me
For you, my unforgettable garland
That makes life so pleasant
With you, my beautiful love

🎸 *hui*

   A7   D
Ho'i mai, ho'i mai ke aloha
A   E7   A7
'Oiai ka manawa kūpono
  D   B   E7
Na wai e 'ole ka 'i'ini
D   A7   D
I ka pua nani mae 'ole

chorus:
Return, let love return
While the time is right
Who could deny the desire
For such a blossom of unfading beauty

D   A7
Puapua'i mai ana ke 'ala
                D
I ho'opē 'ia e ka liko lehua
           A
Aia i laila ku'u 'i'ini
Bm   E7   A
Me 'oe ke aloha niponipo
A7 D   A7
Ko aloha ka'u e hi'ipoi nei
            Gb
He aloha 'oe no nā kau a kau
B   E7
Ho'i mai, ho'i mai kāua e pili
           A E7 A7
E lei e ku'u lei poina 'ole

The perfume pours forth
Moistened with leafbuds of lehua
It's there my desire dwells
The yearning love is with you
You are beloved forever
Return, let us come back together
To don my unforgettable garland

Charles E. King reminds us that it's all about desire. 1921.

Ku'u Ipo I Ka He'e Pu'e One

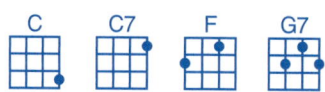

    C C7   F   C
Ku'u ipo i ka he'e pu'e one
   G7   C
Me ke kai nehe i ka 'ili'ili
     C7 F   C
Nipo aku i laila ka mana'o
  G7   C C7
Ua kili'opu māua i ka nahele

hui
    F   C
E iala, e maliu mai
   G7   C C7
Eia ko aloha i 'ane'i
   F   C
Hiki mai ana i ka pō nei
  G7   C
Ua kili'opu māua i ka nahele

   C C7 F   C
Ka 'oē nenehe a ke kai
   G7   C
Hone ana i ka piko wai'olu
  C7 F   C
I laila au lā 'ike
 G7   C C7
Kili'opu māua i ka nahele

   C C7 F   C
Hiki 'ē mai ana ka makani
  G7   C
Ua hala 'ē aku ē ka Pu'ulena
    C7 F   C
Ua lose kou chance e ke hoa
  G7   C C7
Ua kili'opu māua i ka nahele

My lover who glides over the sandbars
Like the sea nestles among the pebbles
Thoughts yearn for that moment
We two shared delight in the forest

chorus:
Oh you, please listen to me
Here is your love, right here
Having appeared last night
We two shared delight in the forest

The whispering murmur of the sea
Teasing at the center of pleasure
There I came to know
We two shared delight in the forest

The breeze has already blown
It's too late, the Pu'ulena wind has passed
You've lost your chance, my friend
We two shared delight in the forest

Likelike sings of her love, gentle as the sea gliding over the sand dunes, in this best known of her compositions. The Hawaiian text clearly shows that the "we" who delight in the forest does not refer to the one being addressed and asked to listen. The poet expresses that love came too late, for passion arrived the night before. Princess Likelike died in 1887, when she was only 36 years old.

He Mele Aloha

Kuʻu Ipo Pua Rose

C		C7	F	Db	C

He aloha kuʻu ipo pua rose

A7		Dm		D7 G7	C

Kuʻu lei o ke ano ahiahi

Beloved is my sweetheart, the rose
My darling of the evening hours

A he lei naʻu i haku a lawa
I kāhiko no kuʻu kino

Made by me into a lei
To adorn my person

He nohea i ka maka ke ʻike
I ka milimili a kuʻu lima

You are fair indeed to see
A flower fondled by my hands

He uʻi hoʻoheno puʻuwai
He aloha honehone i ka poli

A beauty that appeals to my heart
A loved one to cherish in my bosom

Aloha ē ka leo o ka moa
E kāhea mai ē ua ao

I love the voice of the cock
That proclaims that day is here

Puana ka inoa o kuʻu lei
Lei aloha o ke kakahiaka

This ends the song for my loved one
My beloved one of the morning

John Kameaaloha Almeida tells us through the crow of the rooster that the lovers have spent the night and will celebrate the dawn together. 1946. Translation by Mary Kawena Pukui.

Ku'u Lei Aloha

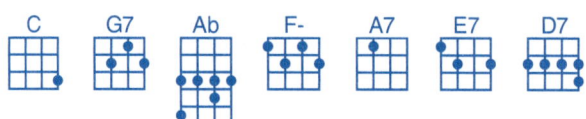

    C   G7
Ā 'o ke 'ala
   C
Ka i hiki mai
             G7
Na ke ahe lau makani
        C
Hali mai i o'u nei
    G7
Hiki ko aloha
          C
Kau mai ka hali'a
Ab   C   A7
Nou ho'okahi
D7   G7
E ku'u ipo nohea

Ah, the fragrance
Is what has come
The gentle touch of the breeze
Carries it to me
Your love arrives
And fond memory is evoked
For you alone
Oh my beautiful sweetheart

hui

  C   A7   D7
Ku'u lei aloha
  G7   C   C7
E ku'u lei makamae
F   F-   C   A7
Aia me 'oe ka hali'a, ka 'ano'i
D7   G7
A nēia pu'uwai
C   A7   D7
Ho'okahi mea nui
G7   E7
'O ka leo o ke aloha
A7   D7
Ke pane mai, 'olu au
F   G7   C
Maha nei pu'uwai

chorus:
My beloved lei
Lei so precious to me
With you, there's sweet memory and desire
In this heart of mine
Only one thing is important
The voice of the beloved
When you respond, I'm comforted
This heart of mine is at ease

The touch of the breeze, like a gentle voice, evokes loving thoughts of one's sweetheart, says composer Charles E. King. 1925.

He Mele Aloha

Ku'u Lei 'Awapuhi

     G   D7
'Auhea lā 'oe, e ke aloha
                      G
'Awapuhi pala o ka ua noe
          D7
A eia no me a'u
              G
I ka poli o ke aloha

🎸 *hui*
  G   G7
E ku'u aloha ē (e ō)
             C
'Auhea lā 'oe (eia nō au)
          D7   G
A huli aku au iā 'oe

Where are you, my beloved
Sweet ginger blossom of the misty rain
Ah, here you are with me
In the embrace of love

chorus:
O my love (I respond)
Where can you be? (Here I am)
I turn, then, to you

Composed by Emily Taylor for the movie Bird of Paradise. *The melody is taken from an old song* Ku'u Lei Pūpū, *the original words of which appear to have been lost to time. 1950s.*

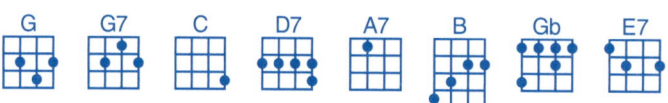

Kuʻu Lei Poina ʻOle

     G   G7
Kuʻu ipo, kuʻu lei
  C   G
I ka laʻi a ʻEhu
   D7
Hiʻipoi ʻia iho
  G   C   G   D7
Ke aloha makamae
  G   G7
Nou nō nā hāʻupu ʻana
    C   B
A ka manaʻo e nū nei
  E7   A7
Hoʻi mai kāua e pili
G   Gb   G D7 G
E lei kuʻu lei poina ʻole

    G   G7
ʻO ka pā kolonahe a ka ʻEka
    C   G
Makani kupa o ka ʻāina
    D7
Lawe mai ana i ke aloha
 G   C   G   D7
A hāʻale i kuʻu maka
    G   G7
A he makamaka ke aloha
  C   B
Hoa pili no ia uka
  E7   A7
Ua kama ʻia a paʻa
G   Gb G D7 G
A paʻa ma koʻu puʻuwai

My sweetheart, my dear garland
In peaceful Kona of chief ʻEhu
Held near in fond embrace
Is the precious love
For you are the fond recollections
That stir here in the mind
Let us come back together
To share my unforgettable lei

The soft caress of the ʻEka breeze
Familiar wind of the land
Bringing with it the affection
And my eyes brim with tears
Love is a dear friend
A close companion of that upland
Bound together securely
Held fast here in my heart

Matthew H. Kāne wrote the lyrics and Charles E. King the music about the ʻEka, the daily sea breeze that cools the Kona district of Hawaiʻi island, and which is often mentioned in songs for that area. 1917.

He Mele Aloha

Ku'u Pua I Paoakalani

E ka gentle breeze e waft mai nei
Ho'ohāli'ali'a mai ana ia'u
E ku'u sweet never fading flower
I bloom i ka uka o Paoakalani

O ye gentle breeze that wafts to me
Sweet cherished memories of thee
Of that sweet never fading flower
That blooms in the fields of Paoakalani

hui

'Ike mau i ka nani o nā pua
O ka uka o Uluhaimalama
'A'ole na'e ho'i e like
Me ku'u pua i ka la'i o Paoakalani

chorus:
Tho' I've often seen those beauteous flow'rs
That grew at Uluhaimalama
But none of those could be compared
To my flower that blooms in the fields of Paoakalani

Lahilahi kona mau hi'ona
With soft eyes as black as jet
Pink cheeks so delicate of hue
I ulu i ka uka o Paoakalani

Her face is fair to behold
With softest eyes as black as jet
Pink cheeks so delicate of hue
That grew in the fields of Paoakalani

Nane 'ia mai ana ku'u aloha
E ka gentle breeze e waft mai nei
Oh come to me ka'u mea e li'a nei
I ulu i ka uka o Paoakalani

Now name to me the one I love
Ye gentle breezes passing by
And bring to me that blossom fair
That bloometh in the fields of Paoakalani

Lili'uokalani composed this in 1895, writing on the cover of her sheet music "During her Imprisonment in the 'Iolani Palace by the Republican Government of Hawai'i." During her eight months of house arrest she was not allowed visitors, but she did receive flowers. Usually they came from her gardens in Pauoa, but in March, Johnny Wilson, the boy who brought her the flowers, later mayor of Honolulu, brought some which she recognized as having come from her home Hamohamo in Waikīkī. She wrote this song about those flowers, employing a traditional Hawaiian riddling device by challenging the singer to guess their name, and dedicated it to Johnny Wilson. (Hui 64). Translation by Lili'uokalani.

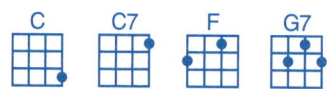

Laimana

C	C7
'Ike aku i ka nani

F

Ka home a'o Laimana

G7

Home kau i ka nu'u

C

Home piha hau'oli

G7   C

Home piha hau'oli

Look and see the beauty
The home of Lyman
Home on high complete with love
Home filled with love
Home filled with love

C   C7

Nanea me nā hoa aloha

F

Ma ka lihi kai a'o Kona

G7

No Kona ke kai malino

C

No Hualālai kou makua

G7   C

No Hualālai kou makua

Relaxing with many friends
By the edge of the sea of Kona
Kona of the calm seas
Hualālai is your parent
Hualālai your parent

C   C7

He kohu kula kaimana

F

'Alohi nei i ka lā

G7

Ua 'ohu 'oe a kūpa'a

C

Nā keiki aloha o ka 'āina

G7   C

Nā keiki aloha o ka 'āina

It is like a diamond ring
Sparkling in the sun
You've worn your loyalty
To the beloved children of the land
The beloved children of the land

C   C7

E ō mai kou inoa

F

Ka home a'o Laimana

G7

Home kau i ka nu'u

C

Home piha hau'oli

G7   C

Home piha hau'oli

Answer to your name
Home of Lyman
Home on the heights
Home filled with joy
Home filled with joy

Lei Collins writes of the Lyman's house and hospitality in Kona. 1960s.

145
He Mele Aloha

Lanakila Kawaihau

   F   C7   B- F
Ke lei nei ko lei nani
     C7   B- F
A ke onaona e hea mai nei
    C7   B- F
Walea ana i ka inu wai
  D7   G7   C7   F
A he ʻai haʻaheo no Kawaihau

hui

     C7   F
Inu i ka wai māpuna
    C7   F
Haʻaheo i ko lei lehua
      C7   F
A he leo no pūpū kani oe
 F7   Bb   G7   C7 F
Ua lanakila ʻo Kawaihau

 F   C7   B-   F
Nohenohea ia mau pua
    C7   B- F
A he kumu o ke ʻala
    C7   B- F
A naʻu na ke onaona
 D7   G7   C7 F
I hoʻokani ke kaula kia

Your beautiful lei adorns you
Whose sweetness beckons
Delighting in a sip of water
And it's a proud win for Kawaihau

chorus:
Drink of the spring water
Proud in your lehua lei
Land shells trill the refrain
Kawaihau is victorious

Those blossoms are so handsome
And a source of sweet perfume
And it was I, the charming one
Who made the reins sing

Mekia Kealakaʻi was noted for being able to compose extemporaneously. He wrote this song on the spot to celebrate the political victory of Colonel Samuel Parker and Prince Jonah Kūhiō Kalanianaʻole. 1903.

He Mele Aloha

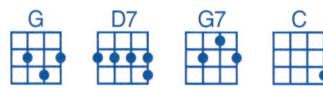

Latitū

hui

    G   D7   G
Kainō a ʻo au wale nō ka i ʻike
 D7   G
I nā latitū aʻo ia aupuni
       G7   C
A eia kā he nui loa a he lehulehu
      D7   G
Nā pailaka o ia awa kū moku ē

chorus:
It seemed that I alone knew
The latitudes of that kingdom
But here it is that many and numerous
Are the pilots of that port

 G   G7   C
Loko ʻino maoli nō hoʻi ʻoe e ke hoa
 D7   G
Ko lilo ʻana i ka ulaia
              G7   C
Aloha ʻole nō hoʻi ʻoe i nei kupuʻeu
 D7   G
E ʻau kū hele nei i ka moana

You my friend are really cruel
With your willful craziness
You have no love for this upstart
Who travels all over the ocean

 G   G7   C
E kuhi ana paha ʻoe a e nalo ana
 D7   G
Kāu hana hōʻehaʻeha naʻau
           G7   C
I ka nalo ʻana aʻe o kuʻu maka
 D7   G
Lawa pono iho ai ko makemake

You are maybe guessing it'll go away
Your actions that pain the heart
Once my face disappears from sight
Your desires will have been satisfied

 G   G7   C
Aia i mua kuʻu nui kino
 D7   G
Aia i hope kuʻu hoʻoilina
         G7   C
I ʻaneʻi hoʻi au ʻeha ka manaʻo
 D7   G
I ka lohe ʻana mai ua heo ʻoe

There, up ahead is the essence of me
There, behind is my legacy
Right here am I, with hurt feelings
Having heard that you've departed

Harry Swinton's famously kolohe kaona as a sailor laments his lover's fickle nature—many and numerous are the pilots of her port. A good example of the Hawaiianization of English, as latitude became latitū.

He Mele Aloha

Laupāhoehoe Hula

[D] Eia mai au 'o ka boy lā
[A7] A'o Laupāhoehoe [D] lā
[G] Kihikihi nā po'ohiwi lā
[A7] Pūkonakona ke kino [D] lā

Here am I, a boy
Of Laupāhoehoe
Broad are my shoulders
Husky is my body

[D] Mea 'ole ka pi'ina pali lā
[A7] Ka ihona me nā 'alu [D] lā
[G] I ke kahawai aku au lā
[A7] I ka 'o'opu nāwao [D] lā

I don't mind climbing hills
Going down the slopes
I go to the river
For 'o'opu nāwao

[D] A he hoe wa'a ia hana lā
[A7] I ke kai hānupanupa [D] lā
[G] 'A'ohe a'u mea hopo lā
[A7] I nā 'ale o ke kai [D] lā

Canoe paddling I also do
Over the rising waves
I have no fears
Of the billows of the sea

[D] Ho'i mai au i ka hale lā
[A7] Nunui nā miki'ai [D] lā
[G] Kū'ono'ono 'o loko lā
[A7] Pūkonakona ke kino [D] lā

I come home
And eat big fingers of poi
Fill my insides well
And keep my body husky

[D] Ha'ina mai ka puana lā
[A7] Eia mai au 'o ka boy [D] lā
[G] A'o Laupāhoehoe [D] lā
[A7] Kihikihi nā po'ohiwi [D] lā

This is the end of my story
Here am I, a boy
Of Laupāhoehoe
With broad shoulders

Irmgard Aluli and Mary Kawena Pukui composed this together. Although Aluli's music and inspiration was quintessentially Hawaiian, English was her primary language, so she partnered with Pukui to ensure correct poetry in the Hawaiian language. Translation by Mary Kawena Pukui.

He Mele Aloha

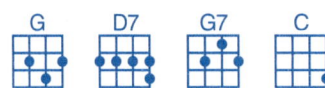

Lē'ahi

  G   D7
Lē'ahi, 'uhe'uhene
          G   G7
Kaimana Hila, 'uhe'uhene
      C   G   D7   G
Hōkū o ka 'ale kai Māmala, 'uhe'uhene

   G   D7
Mālama 'oe, 'uhe'uhene
        G   G7
I ka poe pele, 'uhe'uhene
  C   G   D7   G
O ili kāua i ka pūko'a, 'uhe'uhene

     G   D7
'O ka poe kaulana, 'uhe'uhene
       G   G7
Kau i ka nuku, 'uhe'uhene
    C   G   D7   G
Nāna e ho'owale nei i ka moana, 'uhe'uhene

   G   D7
Hā'awi ke aloha, 'uhe'uhene
    G   G7
Lūlū lima, 'uhe'uhene
     C   G   D7   G
Me nā huapala maka onaona, 'uhe'uhene

   G   D7
Ha'ina 'ia mai, 'uhe'uhene
    G   G7
Ana ka puana, 'uhe'uhene
      C   G   D7 G
Goodbye kāua, e ke aloha, 'uhe'uhene

Lē'ahi
Diamond Head
Star of the billows of Māmala

Be careful
About the buoy with the bell
Lest we go aground on the reef

The famous buoy
Placed at the harbor mouth
Which entices one to the open sea

Give fond greetings
A shaking of hands
With the sweet-faced young beauties

And so it shall be told
Through this story
Goodbye for us, my love

Mary Pūla'a Robins wrote about Lē'ahi, Diamond Head, which marks the eastern boundary of Māmala Bay. Mary Robins' husband was a lighthouse keeper, so she had a special awareness of things like buoys, reefs and bays, but more than simple maritime observation may be at hand in this mele. 1895.

Lei Aloha, Lei Makamae

    F   G7 C7   F
E kuʻu lei, e kuʻu lei
     C7   F
Lei aloha naʻu, lei makamae
   A7   Dm
Eia au ke kali nei
          G7   C7
Hoʻi mai kāua, hoʻi mai e pili

hui

 C7
Ko aloha kaʻu
   F
E hiʻipoi nei
         C7   A7
No nā kau a kau, nā kau a kau
     D7   G7
Nou hoʻokahi nā liʻa a loko
    Bb C7   F
Āhea lā ʻoe, maliu mai
  F7 Bb D7 G7
E kuʻu lei makamae
        C7   F
Hoʻi mai kāua e pili

Beloved one, beloved of mine
To me you're precious, a precious lei
Here I wait, my heart yearning
Oh come my love with me abide

chorus:
Your love is the thing
That I cherish always
For all time, all time
For you alone does the heart yearn
When will you heed my plea?
Oh beloved one, my precious
Let us be together again

One of Charles King's most beautiful love songs, a favorite at weddings. 1934.

Lei Hali‘a

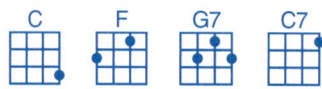

    C   F   C
He ahu a‘o Lanihuli
   G7   C G7
No ka noe o Nu‘uanu
    C   F   C
Nu‘alia i ka pō‘ai pali
    G7   C C7
I ka pā iki mai o ke Kona ē

hui

    C7   F   C
He ‘ohu i ka lei hali‘a
    G7   C G7
‘Ala māpu i ke anuhea
     F   C
Hea mai i ke aumoe
        G7   C
Moemoeā, moe mālie i ka poli ē

Lanihuli is laden like an altar
For the mists of Nu‘uanu
Amassed there in the circle of cliffs
By the sultry buffeting of the Kona wind

chorus:
Adorned with a lei of fond recollection
A permeating fragrance that comes sweetly
Beckoning to me in the deep of the night
Dream, sleep gently, there in the heart

  C   F   C
Luhiehu ka lau o ka palai
    G7   C G7
Pāpālua i ke kilihuna
  C   F   C
Kilihea ka liko ‘āhihi
    G7   C C7
Hīhīmanu, hihipe‘a me ka maile ē

The fronds of palai are luxuriant
Double so in the fine misty rain
Bedewed are the young shoots of the ‘āhihi
Elegant, entwined in an abundance of maile

 C   F   C
‘Auamo ‘o Konahuanui
    G7   C G7
I ke ao hākumakuma
   C   F   C
Kū māhiehie Kilohana
   G7   C C7
Ua pō i ke ‘ala hīnano ē

Konahuanui shoulders the burden
Lifting the dark, heavy clouds
That Kilohana, in its glory, may rise
Mantled in the heady fragrance of hīnano

Puakea Nogelmeier compares a sultry Kona-wind day in Nu‘uanu to a heart that's heavy with emotion and thought. Recognizing the small beauties at hand is like enjoying pleasant memories from our own lei of recollections — empowering the heart and uplifting the spirit. The wafting of hīnano, the perfume of the male hala, implies the return of the refreshing tradewinds. Lanihuli, Konahuanui and Kilohana are peaks in the Ko‘olau mountains overlooking Nu‘uanu Pali. 1994.

He Mele Aloha

Lei 'Ilima

'O ka 'ilima nō koʻu lei (G, Am)
Ka liʻa ia a nei puʻuwai (D7, G)
He wehi ia no kuʻu kino (E7, A7)
Lei hoʻohihi a ka manaʻo (D7)
ʻIʻini au lā i kou nani (G, Am)
He hiwahiwa i kaʻu ʻike (D7, B7)
ʻO wau kou hoa e kohu ai (E7, A7)
E lei ʻilima ē, lei ʻilima (D7, G)

The ʻilima is my lei of choice
The thing my heart longs for
Adornment for my person
A garland that entrances the mind
I yearn for the beauty of you
A thing so precious to my sight
I am the companion to suit you
Oh lei ʻilima, lei ʻilima

Flower songs such as this one by Charles E. King are often strung together with others, such as Pua Carnation, Maile Lei, *and* Pua Mae ʻOle, *into a mele lei of love. 1926.*

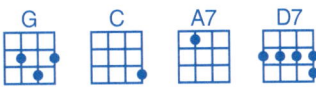

Lei Nani

ʻAuhea wale ʻoe kuʻu lei nani (G, C, G)
Hoʻi mai nō kāua a e pili (A7, D7, G)

Where are you my beautiful lei
Let us two come back and be together

Kou aloha kaʻu aʻe hiʻipoi nei (G, C, G)
Hākuʻikuʻi ʻeha i koʻu manaʻo (A7, D7, G)

Your love is what I cherish
Drumming away in my thoughts

ʻAnoʻai ka pilina poina ʻole (G, C, G)
E lei aʻe ʻoe me kuʻu lei (A7, D7, G)

The memorable union was good fortune
You'll always be adorned with my affection

Haʻina ʻia mai ana ka puana (G, C, G)
Hoʻi mai nō kāua a e pili (A7, D7, G)

The story shall be told
Let us two come back and be together

Credited to Charles Nāmāhoe who first recorded this song, said to be based on Lei Lani *by Joseph Solomon Kuni, in 1929.*

He Mele Aloha

Lei No Ka'iulani

G
'O ua mau pua lehua
C   **G**
I lawe 'ia mai no ku'u lani
C   **G**   **A7**
I wili 'ia me maile lauli'i
D   **A7**   **D7**
I 'ohu, i wehi no Ka'iulani
G
Me he pūnohu 'ula lā i ke kai
G7   **C**
Ka nohea nohea ke 'ike aku
Eb   **G**
I ku'u wehi lani
A7   **D7**   **G**
E ola mau 'o Ka'iuonālani

  🎸 *hui*

G   **C**
E ki'i mai ho'i e lei
G   **D7**
E Ka'iulani i ka 'iu o luna
G   **C**
I ko lei lehua puakea
A7   **D7**   **G**
I wili 'ia me maile lauli'i

       Those blossoms of lehua
       Brought here for my chiefess
       Entwined with dainty-leafed maile
       As an adornment, beauty for Ka'iulani
       Like a rising red mist over the sea
       The fine appearance is handsome to behold
       My beloved royal beauty
       Long live Ka'iuonālani

chorus:
Come take and wear as a garland
Oh Ka'iulani of the lofty reaches
This, your rare white lehua lei
Entwined with dainty leaved maile

G
Makamaka ka 'ōnohi o kāu kama
C   **G**
Kāhiko maila i ka pae 'ōpua
C   **G**
E hō'ike mai ana ku'u lani
D   **A7**   **D7**
Ua mau lei lehua puakea nei
G
I haku 'ia me ka mikioi
G7   **C**
Me ka hala o Naue i ke kai
Eb   **G**
Laua'e 'a'ala o Makana
A7   **D7**   **G**
He makana nou no Kawaihau mai

The rainbow fragment, your subject, takes
   pleasure
Your beauty adorning the cloud banks
My chiefess shall display
Those rare lei of white lehua
Crafted so very skillfully
With the pandanus of Naue at the sea
The fragrant laua'e of Makana
A gift offered to you from Kawaihau

Charles Hopkins attributed this to John Edwards when he published it in 1899. It is elsewhere attributed to Moki.

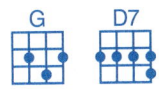

Lei ʻOhu

Lei ʻohuʻohu ʻoe e Hilo Hanakahi (G)
Ka lehua makanoe aʻo Panaʻewa (D7)
Lei kaulana aʻo Hilo (G)

Lei ʻohuʻohu ʻoe Maui nui a Kama (G)
Ka roselani onaona o ke ʻala hola (D7)
Lei kaulana aʻo Maui (G)

Lei ʻohuʻohu ʻoe Kākuhihewa (G)
Ka ʻilima melemele kau poʻohiwi (D7)
Lei kaulana o Oʻahu (G)

Lei ʻohuʻohu ʻoe Manokalanipō (G)
Ka mokihana hua liʻiliʻi o Waiʻaleʻale (D7)
Lei kaulana o Kauaʻi (G)

Haʻina ē ka wehi o nā mokupuni (G)
Ka lehua, ka roselani, ʻilima, mokihana (D7)
O nā moku ʻehā (G)

You, Hilo Hanakāhi, are festooned
With the misty-laden lehua of Panaʻewa
Famous garland of Hilo

You, great Maui of Kama are festooned
With sweet roselani whose fragrance fills the air
Famous garland of Maui

You, Kākuhihewa, are festooned
With golden ʻilima upon your shoulders
Famous lei of Oʻahu

You Manokalanipō, are festooned
With the small mokihana berries of Waiʻaleʻale
Famous garland of Kauaʻi

Tell of the adornments of the islands
The lehua, roselani, ʻilima, and mokihana
Of the four islands

Composer George E. Akiu makes reference to a great historical chief of each island, each of whose rule was characterized by peace, prosperity and great works, coupled with the flower lei of that island. 1930.

He Mele Aloha

Lei Pīkake

A E7 D   A   E7   A
Māpu 'ia ke 'ala o ka pīkake

E7   D   A   E7   A
I ka ō aheahe a ka makani

The fragrance of the pīkake is wafted
By a gentle blowing of the wind

hui:

D A   E7   A   D A   E7   A
Aloha a'e au i ka pua 'ume'ume mau

chorus:
I love the flower that constantly attracts

A   E7 D   A   E7   A
'Ako au i nēia pua aloha

E7   D   A   E7   A
I poina 'ole 'ia ai a he launa 'ole

I pluck this flower of my attraction
It will never be forgotten, it is second to none

A   E7   D   A   E7   A
'Ohu'ohu ho'i pili i ka pu'uwai

E7   D   A   E7   A
He lei ho'olei a'e pūlama

Elegant and close to my heart
A lei to wear and cherish

A   E7 D   A   E7   A
Puana 'ia mai ko'u mana'o

E7   D A   E7   A
He lei pīkake ku'u aloha

An echo of my thoughts
A pīkake lei is my love

C   G7 F   C   G7   C
Puana hou 'ia mai ko'u mana'o

G7   F C   C7   C
He lei pīkake ku'u aloha

Echoing again
A pīkake lei is my love

Barry Flanagan was entranced by the connection between Ka'iulani, her love of peacocks (pīkake), and the renaming of the little Arabian jasmine flower to honor her. The last verse is transposed from the key of A to the key of C — a frequently used device in Hawaiian music. (See "Chord Transpositions" in front of book.) 1984. Hawaiian translation by Kī'ope Raymond.

He Mele Aloha

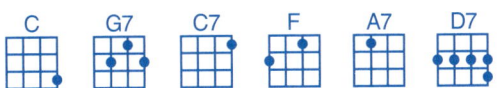

Lovely Hula Hands

C
Lovely hula hands
                   G7
Graceful as the birds in motion
Gliding like the gulls o'er the ocean
          C
Lovely hula hands
G7   **C**
Kou lima nani ē

C
Lovely hula hands
                   G7
Telling of the rain in the valley
And the swirling winds on the pali
         C
Lovely hula hands
G7   **C**
Kou lima nani ē

C   **C7**
I can feel the soft caresses
          F   **C7**   **F**
Of your lovely hands, your lovely hula hands
A7   **D7**
Every little move expresses, so I'll understand
G7   **C**
All the tender meaning of your hula hands
                  G7
Fingertips that say "Aloha"
Say to me again "I love you"
          C
Lovely hula hands
G7   **C**
Kou lima nani ē

George Kanahele felt that of all the hapa haole songwriters, R. Alex Anderson probably came closest to instinctively capturing a Hawaiian sound. 1940.

Mahina ʻO Hoku

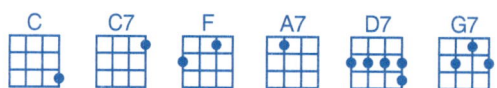

C   C7 F   C
ʻAuhea wale ʻoe mahina ʻo Hoku
A7   D7   G7   F   C
Hōʻike aʻe ʻoe i kou nani

                         Where are you, oh full moon
                         Do reveal your beauty

C   C7 F   C
Ua laʻi nā kai, mehameha nā pali
A7   D7   G7   F   C
ʻO ʻoe a ʻo au e hoʻoipoipo nei

                         The seas are still, the cliffs are in solitude
                         Itʻs just you and I, making love

C   C7 F   C
He moani ke ʻala o ka pua hīnano
A7   D7   G7   F   C
E apo mai ʻoe me kou aloha

                         The fragrance of hīnano drifts in the air
                         Wonʻt you embrace me with your love

C   C7 F   C
Haʻina kou inoa mahina ʻo Hoku
A7   D7   G7   F   C
Ke noho nani maila ma nā lani kiʻekiʻe

                         Your praise is sung, oh full moon
                         In beautiful repose among the highest heavens

In this song "Mahina ʻo Hoku" refers to the moon the night before its fullest phase, Māhealani. Circa 1940s.

Mai Poina ʻOe Iaʻu

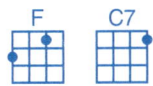

| F | C7 |

      F   C7
ʻO ʻoe kaʻu i hāʻupu aʻe nei
               F
E ka ʻōpua hiki ahiahi
              C7
Hiki maila nō hoʻi ʻoe
              F
Maha aʻela nei puʻuwai

It's you I've been thinking of
Oh billowing cloud of the evening
As soon as you appear
This heart is at ease

🎸 *hui*

     F   C7
Mai poina ʻoe iaʻu
                F
E kaʻu mea e liʻa nei
               C7
E hoʻomaumau ka ʻikena
                   F
I mau ai ke koʻiʻi koi a loko

chorus:
Do not forget me
Oh desire of my heart
Our association should continue forever
So the passion within may endure

F   C7
Ohaoha wale hoʻi
          F
Ko aloha iaʻu nei
                C7
Me ʻoe pū aku nō ia ʻupu
            F
I lei mau no nā kau a kau

Simply delightful indeed
Is your affection for me
May that thought always be with you
As an adorning lei forever

Originally published in 1897 by Holstein without attribution, a copy published by C.K. Hopkins in 1899 has a penciled notation on its front piece, "composed by prof J.S. Libornio, Director Royal Court Orchestra, for her majesty Queen Liliʻuokalani of Hawaiʻi." There is a slight variation in the chorus, "I mau ai ke koʻiʻi koi a loko" in Holstein. It was republished in 1907 with Lizzie Doiron identified as the composer.

Maika'i Ka Makani O Kohala

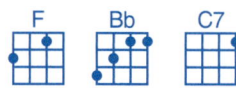

    F   Bb   F
Maika'i ka makani o Kohala
  C7   F
'Ike 'ia e ka Inuwai
           Bb   F
'O ka wai nō ia pono kāua
  C7   F
Wai kaulana o ka 'āina

How fine is the wind of Kohala
Known as the Inuwai
The water that brings life to you and I
Famous water of the land

hui

        C7   F
    Ko aloha, ko aloha ka'u mea nui
                C7   F
    He makana, he makana na ka pu'uwai

chorus:
Your love, your love is what I cherish
A gift, a gift from the heart

  F   Bb   F
Nani wale Niuli'i kāhela i ka la'i
  C7   F
'Ekolu 'ōpua i hiki mai
         Bb   F
Ālai 'ia mai e ka ulu hala
  C7   F
Nalowale ka luna o Hāpu'u

Beautiful indeed is Niuli'i expansive in the calm
Three billowing clouds have appeared
Blocked from view by the pandanas grove
The heights of Hāpu'u are obscured

  F   Bb   F
'Elua māua i ka holo o ka lio
  C7   F
Kāohi 'ia mai e Pololū
          Bb   F
Mea 'ole ka pi'ina a'o Kupehau
  C7   F
Ahuwale nā lehua o 'Āwini

We two went horseback riding
Slowed by the travel to Pololū
The ascent to Kupehau was made effortless
By the sight of the lehua of 'Āwini

| F   Bb   F
Ha'aheo ka hau i ka mauna
| C7   F
Kāhiko i ka 'ohu o ka nahele
| Bb   F
Ke kāohi mai nei Lilinoe
| C7   F
I ka 'ohu noe i ke kuahiwi

| F   Bb   F
Nē hone ka leo o ka wai
| C7   F
Hone ana i ka 'iwa
| Bb   F
Ku'u 'iwa ku'u lei kāhiko ia
| C7   F
Nā pua lehua o 'Āwini

How proud is the snow on the mountain
Adorning the fog of the forest
Lilinoe is holding back
The mists that settle on the slopes

The voice of the water sings softly
Appealing to the 'iwa fern
My 'iwa is my lei to wear
With the lehua blossoms of 'Āwini

Four verses of this song by William Sheldon were published in 1897 by Holstein under the title Ka Inu Wai — Kohala's Breezes. *The first two verses were again published by Charles Hopkins in 1899. Over time the third verse was added, contributed by the Sproat family — Pololū is the land of their birth. Well known was Niuli'i valley wall for its hanging hala forest, as was the view of the lehua of 'Āwini from the rise at Kupehau. Also known as* **Kohala March**.

Maika'i Kaua'i

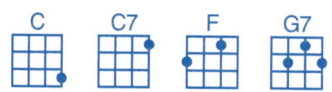

hui

    [C] Maika'i nō Kaua'i [C7]
    [F] Hemolele i ka mālie
    [G7] Kuahiwi Wai'ale'ale
    Lei ana i ka mokihana [C]

chorus:
Fine indeed is Kaua'i
So perfect in the calm
Beautiful mountain, Wai'ale'ale
Wears the mokihana lei

    [C] Hanohano wale 'o Hanalei [C7]
    [F] I ka ua nui hō'eha 'ili
    [G7] I ka wai 'u'inakolo
    I ka poli o Nāmolokama [C]

So glorious is Hanalei
With pounding rain that stings the skin
And the rustling water
In the heart of Nāmolokama

    [C] Ua nani wale 'o Līhu'e [C7]
    [F] I ka ua pa'ū pili hale
    [G7] I ka wai hu'ihu'i anu
    Kahi wai a'o Kēmamo [C]

So very beautiful is Līhu'e
In the drenching rain that clings to the house
With the cold refreshing waters
From the springs of Kēmamo

    [C] Kaulana wale 'o Waimea [C7]
    [F] I ke one kani o Nohili
    [G7] I ka wai 'ula 'iliahi
    A he wai na ka malihini [C]

So renowned is Waimea
With the roaring sands of Nohili
Amidst the red tinged waters
Water that visitors enjoy

hui

    [C] Maika'i wale nō Kaua'i [C7]
    [F] Hemolele wale i ka mālie
    [G7] Kuahiwi nani Wai'ale'ale
    Lei ana i ka mokihana [C]

chorus:
So very fine is Kaua'i
So perfect in the calm
Beautiful mountain, Wai'ale'ale
Wears the mokihana lei

Maile Lauli'i

G   **A7**
Maile lauli'ili'i ē
G   **D7 G**
Hoa pili o ka palai

Dainty-leafed maile
Close companion of the fern

G   **A7**
Lau o ka 'iwa'iwa
G   **D7 G**
Hoa pili o ka 'ie'ie

Leaf of the maidenhair fern
Close companion to the 'ie'ie

G   **A7**
Lau o ka 'awapuhi
G   **D7 G**
Ho'oheno me ke kahawai

Leaf of the ginger
Romances with the stream

G   **A7**
Ha'ina mai ka puana
G   **D7 G**
Kau mai Kīlauea

Tell the story
Kīlauea on high

G   **A7**
Ha'ina mai ka puana
G   **D7 G**
Pāpālina kikokiko

Tell the story
Of freckled cheeks

As the maile vine entwines its companion and the fern accompanies the 'ie'ie, so is my love for you, say composers Ray Kinney and David Burrows. 1928.

Opposite: This song, originally called Ku'u Lei Mokihana, *was written for the Kalawina (Congregational) Church annual 'aha (conference) on O'ahu, which traditionally included a song competition, a "sing off" of sorts. This song from Kaua'i was the winner. These words, taken from an old chant attributed to Kapa'akea, father of Kalākaua, were put to music by Henry Waia'u. Wai 'ula 'iliahi, literally sandalwood red waters, refers to the red shoots and buds of the native sandalwood tree, which is the color of the water of Waimea River during heavy rains. The two hui are often sung together at the same time, with one group singing the "Maika'i nō..." and the other the "Maika'i wale...."*

162
He Mele Aloha

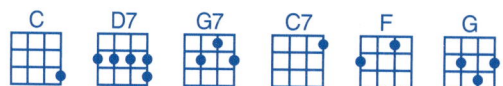

Maile Lei

    C   D7
Maile lei, lovely maile lei
              G7
You weave your magic charms
      C   G7
Around Hawai'i nei
C   D7
Every day in your subtle way
          G7
You tease the tradewinds
With your fragrance
    C
Maile lei

   C7   F
You lure the sunbeams
 C7
To shine down
      F
And hula just for you
    D7   G
And then you flirt with
  D7
All the flowers
    G   G7
Of every colored hue
       C
Where e'er you go
  D7
I will always know
      G7
My lovely maile lei
              C
Oh how I love you so

Originally entitled Lovely Maile Lei, *Maddy Lam wrote this for a Kahauanu Lake Trio concert at the Honolulu Shell in 1963. Several days before the concert President John F. Kennedy was assassinated and the concert became a memorial to him.*

163
He Mele Aloha

Maile Swing

   F   Bb   Bbm   F
Sweet and lovely ke onaona o ka maile
        C7   F
Ho'oipo ke 'ala ho'oheno sure i ka pili poli
               Bb   Bbm   F
Nanea, e walea, e luana kāua i laila
     C7   F
Mikioi ke ki'ina hei ko pu'uwai kapalili
    C#   F   C#   F
Nani ua kō ka 'i'ini a i hoa pili mau 'oe no'u
 Am
Ko'i'i ke aloha, e noelo, e 'uleu
 G7   C7
He hene wai'olu a loko, hey! hey!
 F   Bb   Bbm   F
Ha'ina ka puana ke onaona o ka maile
    C7   F
'Ano'ai ka pilina e lei a'e au me ku'u lei

     Sweet and lovely is the maile's fragrance
     A delightful scent that clings to the bosom
     You and I may linger happily
     With the sweetness that captivates your fluttering heart
     Surely I have won you for my own
     Love endures with us, stirring, animating
     A soothing sensation within, hey! hey!
     This ends my song of the maile's fragrance
     Rejoice in the tie, I wear my love as a lei

John Kameaaloha Almeida tells of the lei of maile, turned and knotted, carrying the significance of personal ties and relationships. In modern opening ceremonies, the maile often replaces the ribbon, but it is separated, never cut, for that would symbolically sever desirable relationships. 1946. Translation by Mary Kawena Pukui.

Makalapua

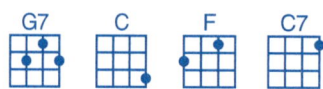

|G7   C   G7|
'O Makalapua ulumāhiehie
| C |
'O ka lei o Kamaka'eha
|G7   C   G7|
No Kamaka'eha ka lei na Li'awahine
| C   C7 |
Nā wāhine kīhene pua

🎸 *hui*

| F G7 C   G7   C C7|
E lei ho'i, E Lili'ulani ē
| F G7 C   G7   C |
E lei ho'i, E Lili'ulani ē

|G7   C   G7|
Ha'iha'i pua kamani paukū pua kīkī
| C |
I lei ho'owehiwehi no ka wahine
|G7   C   G7 |
E walea ai ka waokele
| C   C7 |
I ka liko i Omaunahale

|G7   C   G7|
Lei Ka'ala i ka ua a ka Nāulu
| C |
Ho'olu'e ihola i lalo o Hale'au'au
|G7   C   G7 |
Ka ua lei koko 'ula i ke pili
| C   C7 |
I pilia ka mau'u nēnē me ke kupukupu

|G7   C   G7|
Lei akula i ka hala o Kekele
| C |
I nā hala moe ipo o Malailua
|G7   C   G7|
Ua māewa wale i ke oho o ke kāwelu
| C   C7 |
Nā lei kāmakahala o ka ua Wa'ahila

chorus:
Beautiful, flourishing delightfully
Is the wreath of Kamaka'eha
For Kamaka'eha is the lei made by Li'awahine
And by the women with baskets of flowers

chorus:
Wear the lei, O Lili'ulani
Wear the lei, O Lili'ulani

Kamani blossoms plucked to link with ti flowers
As a lei to adorn the woman
To be at ease in the cool forest
In the leafbuds at Omaunahale

Ka'ala is wreathed by the rain of the Nāulu
That then pours down upon Hale'au'au
The rainbow-wreath rain on the pili grass
That draws the nēnē grass next to the kupukupu fern

Wear the pandanus of Kekele
And the sweetheart-pairing pandanus of Malailua
In the kāwelu grass sways
The kāmakahala wreaths of the Wa'ahila rain

Makee ʻAilana

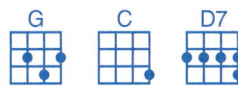

    G   C   G
Makee ʻAilana ke aloha lā
    D7   G
ʻĀina i ka ehuehu o ke kai

Makee Island is beloved
Land in the spray of the sea

   G   C   G
ʻElua, ʻekolu nō mākou
     D7   G
I ka ʻailana māhiehie

There were two, three of us
On this delightful island

 G   C G
Ka leo o ka wai kaʻu aloha
     D7   G
I ka ʻī mai he anu kāua

The voice of the water is what I love
Letting us know we're chilly

 G   C   G
Inā ʻo iū me mī nei
     D7   G
Noho ʻoe i ka noho paipai

If you were with me
You'd be sitting on a rocking chair

 G   C   G
Haʻina ʻia mai ana ka puana
     D7   G
Makee ʻAilana huʻe ka manaʻo

The story is told
Makee Island arouses such thoughts

Kapiʻolani Park once included a waterway in which rested Makee Island, about where the zoo entrance is now. Accessed by a footbridge, it was a favorite retreat for young lovers, as is suggested in this song by James ʻĪʻī. In the 1920s the Ala Wai Canal was constructed, draining the park along with the rest of Waikīkī, which had been taro and rice loʻi and duck ponds. As far as we know, there were no rocking chairs on the island.

Opposite: This mele from the 1800s honors Liliʻuokalani and Oʻahu, the island of her birth. It has various attributions, including David Nape as well as Konia, the queen's hānai mother. Another account says the words are from a chant composed by Naha Harbottle Hakuole, Mary Adams Lucas and Mrs. Auld and placed to music adapted from the hymn Would I Were With Thee, *composed by Carlo Bosetti.*

Hawaiian names often reflect some aspect of the time of birth, be it an historical note, a prophesy, the physical or social setting, or perhaps a lineage connotation. While the literal translation of such names doesn't always appeal to modern aesthetics, their beauty lies in the cultural network to which they connect. At her birth Liliʻuokalani was given the name Kamakaʻeha, which translates as "sore eyes," to commemorate the fact that Kīnaʻu, her foster mother's aunt, was confined to her home with an eye infection at the time of her birth. She was later renamed Liliʻuokalani by her brother, Kalākaua. "Liliʻu" means "scorching, burning, smarting, as salt in a raw wound or pain in the eyes." Translation by Hui Hānai.

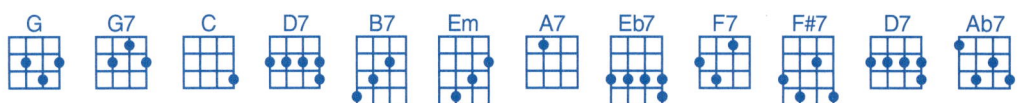

Malihini Mele

    G   G7
As I strolled along the shore
   C   G
In a muʻumuʻu made of koa
                         D7   G
While I played a tune on my sweet ʻokolehau

    G   G7
And I sang a pretty song
   C   G
As she danced her sweet kapu
                        D7   G
With a wikiwiki smile and a nuinui holokū

     B7
Pretty soon by the light of the tropical moon
  Em   B7   Em
A malihini did appear
  A7
And he strolled hand in hand on the beautiful sand
   D7
With a lovely pilikia

    G   G7
Then he softly told her how
  C   G
He'd seen a great big bad lūʻau
                D7   G
With a red ʻōpū and a great big hukilau

D7   Eb7   E7   F7   F#7   F7
Humu-humu-nuku-nuku-apu-ʻa-ʻa
E7   Eb7   G
Swim along singing a song
E7   F7   F#7   G7   Ab7 G7   F7   E7
Kānes and wahines and even little keikis kissing
  A7   D7
A hoʻomalimali and a wela ka hao

This cute song by R. Alex Anderson in 1934 is pure nonsense. Common practice is to have those keiki singing, not kissing, as the original score has it; we encourage you to mark up this workbook to suit your own style and needs.

Manu ʻŌʻō

     F   Bb   F
ʻO ka manu ʻōʻō i Mālama
     C7   F
A he nani kou hulu ke lei ʻia
       Bb   F
Mūkīkī ana ʻoe i ka pua lehua
   C7   F
Kāhea ana ʻoe i ka nui manu

hui
   F
   Hō mai, ʻoni mai
      C7   F
   Ko aloha ma nēia kīhene lehua

 F   Bb   F
No Hilo ē ka ua Kanilehua
  C7   F
Popohe lehua a i Hanakahi
         Bb   F
Hoʻokahi aʻu mea nui aia ʻoe
  C7   F
ʻO kou aloha ka i hiki mai

The ʻōʻō bird is at Mālama
And your feathers are lovely worn as a lei
You sip the nectar of lehua flowers
You beckon to the flocks of birds

chorus:
Share with me, come to me
Bestow your love on this cluster of lehua

Hilo the home of Kanilehua rain
Lehua bloom to perfection at Hanakahi's land
There's only one thing I treasure, it is you
For your love has come here to me

The Kanilehua rain is a symbol of chatter and gossip. Yet, says the composer, no matter what people say or do, I still love you. In the last verse "a i Hanakahi" is a short form for "aia i Hanakahi," there at Hanakahi's land (Hilo).

Maui Girl

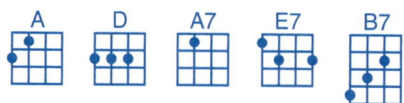

   A   D   A
I love a pretty Maui Girl
  A7   D
She lives at Waikapū
  E7
With rosy cheeks and pearly teeth
                  A   E7
And lovely nut brown hair
  A   D   A
Her waist is oh so slender
  A7   D
Her ʻōpū too much nuinui
  E7
Of all the wahine I ever did aloha
                    A
Sweet Mariah beats them all

🎸 *hui*
  A   E7
My love for you, ua hiki aku nō
                   A
Your love for me, ua pēlā nō
           A7
Don't tell Māmā, a kulikuli
        D B7
She'll tell Pāpā, a luliluli
  E7   A
Nuinui pilikia with me now

Who would have thought that this modern sounding hapa-haole song by Sylvester Thomas Kalama was published in 1892!

169
He Mele Aloha

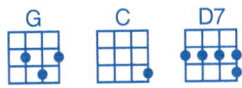

Maunaloa

'Auhea wale 'oe Maunaloa lā *(G)*
Kīkala nui *(C G)*
Ho'iho'i mai 'oe i ku'u aloha lā *(D7)*
Ē, ē, ē, Ka'awaloa nei *(G)*

Where are you, great steamer *Maunaloa*
With your broad beam
Bring back the one I love
O, here to Ka'awaloa

Ua hiki nō 'oe a e hele ana lā *(G)*
Me ka ipo manuahi *(C G)*
A na'u nō ia honi ho'okahi lā *(D7)*
Ē, ē, ē, kahi pela a'o kāua *(G)*

You've just come and now you're going
Like a casual sweetheart
And that one kiss shall be mine
O, one bed is enough for us to share

Ko hainakā popopo lā *(G)*
'Ai 'ia e ka 'elelū *(C G)*
A na'u nō ia kāwele nei lā *(D7)*
Ē, ē, ē, ko kāma'a miomio *(G)*

Your hanky, all worn and rotten
Chewed up by the roaches
And I shall take that rag
O, and shine your pointed shoe

Ha'ina 'ia mai ana ka puana lā *(G)*
Kū 'oe hele pēlā *(C G)*
A na'u nō ia honi ho'okahi lā *(D7)*
Ē, ē, ē, kahi pela a'o kāua *(G)*

Tell the tale in the refrain
Just go on, then
And that one kiss shall be mine
O, one bed is enough for us to share

Broad beamed ships ply many ports in this song attributed to Helen Lindsey Parker. This is a good example of "nā kani hoene" in Hawaiian music, tra-la-la sounds written into the song which have no direct meaning, such as "'uhe'uhene" or "'eā 'eā" or "lā."

May Day Is Lei Day in Hawai'i

F / C7
May day is Lei Day in Hawai'i
  F
Garlands of flowers everywhere
A7 D7   G7
Oh, all of the colors in the rainbow
                     C7
Maidens with blossoms in their hair
F   C7
Flowers that mean we should be happy
                     F
Throwing aside our load of care
A7 D7   G7
Oh, May Day is Lei Day in Hawai'i
C7   F
Lei Day is happy day out here

Composed by Leonard "Red" Hawk. 1928.

Me Moloka'i

🎸 *hui*

C   F C   G7
Ka mana'o nō ia e ka 'upu 'ana a'e
    C   C
Nā hono a'o Pi'ilani kū kilakila
    F   C   F
'O ka 'oi nō na'e ku'u one hānau
            C   G7
Me Moloka'i nui 'āina uluwehi
          C
'O ka heke nō ia

chorus:
It is the thought
Welling up within
The bays of Pi'ilani
Standing majestically
The best, however
Is my birth place
Great Moloka'i
Verdant land
It is unsurpassed

The hui of this song by Solomon Fuller, originally known as Ka Mana'o Nō Ia, *is all that remains in kanikapila.*

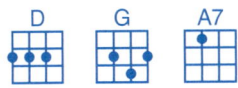

Mele O Lāna'i

D	G	D

He mele kēia 'āina o Lāna'i
              A7   D
Ka huina li'ili'i o nā mokupuni
G   D
Li'ili'i ka mana'o me ka 'ōlelo
A7   D
Mea nui o nā moku 'āina

This is a song for Lāna'i
The smallest one of the islands
Little thought or spoken of
But important in the island chain

D   G   D
Kona pua pono'ī ke kauna'oa
            A7   D
Ua 'oi kona u'i mua ka lehua
G   D
Ka waiho'olu'u like me ke gula
A7   D
Pili me kukuna o ka lā

Its own flower is the kauna'oa
Its beauty greater than the lehua
The color is like that of gold
Like the shimmering rays of the sun

D   G   D
Ka mea nui o kēia 'ailana
            A7   D
Ka hala kahiki e ho'owaiwai
G   D
E ho'okaulana 'oe i kou inoa
A7   D
'Imi ola no ka lehulehu

The important thing of this island
Pineapple that brings prosperity
You shall make your name famous
Gaining a living for the populace

D   G   D
Ha'ina 'ia mai ana ka puana
            A7   D
Pumehana kou inoa a'o Lāna'i
G   D
Li'ili'i oe ke aloha nui
A7   D
He mana'o poina 'ole

The story is told in the refrain
Warm affection for your name Lāna'i
You are little but much loved
And never to be forgotten

Val Kepilino wrote this for his sisters, who were to ride on the Lāna'i float in the 1948 Kamehameha Day Parade and needed a song for the occasion.

He Mele Aloha

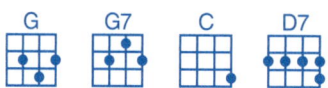

Meleana Ē

G	G7 C	G
Meleana ē, Meleana hoʻi
         D7   G
Meleana ka wahine lomilomi ʻia
           Meleana, oh Meleana
           Meleana is the woman who is massaged

Meleana ē, Meleana hoʻi
ʻO ka ulu sakamu o Kapunahou
           Meleana, oh Meleana
           In the sakamu grove of Punahou

Meleana ē, Meleana hoʻi
ʻO ʻoe ka i pono o kāua
           Meleana, oh Meleana
           You're the good one of us two

Meleana ē, Meleana hoʻi
ʻO ka ipu kukui mālamalama
           Meleana, oh Meleana
           In the bright light shining

Meleana ē, Meleana hoʻi
ʻO ka lepo ʻulaʻula o Kapahulu
           Meleana, oh Meleana
           In the red dirt of Kapahulu

Meleana ē, Meleana hoʻi
Ka hale inu pia kāhiōhiō
           Meleana, oh Meleana
           At the tavern where one gets tipsy

Meleana ē, Meleana hoʻi
ʻO ka ulu lāʻī o nakeke mai
           Meleana, oh Meleana
           In the rustling ti-leaf thicket

Meleana ē, Meleana hoʻi
E ala mai ʻoe moe loa nei
           Meleana, oh Meleana
           Wake up, you've overslept

Meleana ē, Meleana hoʻi
Meleana ka wahine pahu laholio
           Meleana, oh Meleana
           Meleana who punctures tires

Haʻina ʻia mai ana ka puana
Meleana ka wahine lomilomi ʻia
           The refrain is told
           Meleana is a woman who is massaged

He Mele Aloha

Mī Nei

C   G7   C
Ke huli hele aʻe nei ʻoe
        G7   C
E ake ana e kō ka ʻanoʻi a loko
      C7   F
Ma uka ma kai, i ʻō, i ʻaneʻi
      D7   G7
Kāu huli ʻana i kō ka ʻiʻini
                        C
Pehea nō hoʻi inā ma ʻaneʻi
            G7   C
Kilohi mai ʻoe i nēia uʻi

You are searching all about
Wanting to fulfill the desire within
Toward the mountains towards the sea, here and there
You search to fill the desire
How would it be if it were right here
You should gaze at this beauty

C   G7   C
Nā pāpālina aʻo mī nei
       G7   C
Nāu e ʻike mai noho ē ke onaona
      C7   F
Pali ē ke kua, mahina ē ke alo
      D7   G7
Ma nei poli ʻoe, pumehana kāua
                     C
Nā maka nei, kāʻili puʻuwai
         G7   C
Ke honi nei ihu, ʻolu ʻoe, ʻolu wau

These cheeks of mine
Are for you to see how very fragrant
Back straight like the cliffs, front round like the moon
Into these arms you come, we will be warm
These eyes seize the heart
When we kiss, youʻre at ease, Iʻm at ease

C   G7   C
Nēia mau lima, nēia poʻohiwi
       G7   C
ʻAlawa mai ʻoe, aia i lalo ia nani
        C7   F
Ke kiʻina nei lā a ka lawe mālie
      D7   G7
Hoʻohihi ʻoe ke ʻike mai
                          C
Haʻina ka puana pili kaʻu kēpau
              G7   C
ʻAhahana lilo ʻoe, lilo iā mī nei

These arms these shoulders of mine
Glance this way, below is the beauty
Brought forth and handled gently
You will surely fancy what youʻll see
Tell the refrain, my glue has caught you
Aha! Youʻre taken, taken by me

While you are searching all over, consider Mī nei — Me, right here. The offer is extended, with a careful listing of virtues and features. 1928.

Opposite: This song was around in the 1920s, but may be from as early as the 1870s. The first line is often tagged with "Sure a he hana lā, ʻeā."

Miloliʻi

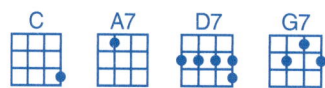

    C   A7   D7
Miloliʻi aku nei au lā
       C
I ke kau ʻēkake lā
G7   C
Nuha i ke alanui

I've been to Miloliʻi
Riding a donkey
So stubborn on the road

    C   A7   D7
Waikīkī aku nei au lā
       C
I ke kau ʻelepani lā
G7   C
Ihu peleleu

I've been to Waikīkī
Mounted on an elephant
With a very long trunk

    C   A7   D7
Calafrisco aku nei au lā
       C
I ke kau mokulele lā
G7   C
A lewa i ka lewa

I've been to San Francisco
On board an airplane
Flying in the sky

    C   A7   D7
Haʻina mai ka puana lā
       C
I ke kau ʻēkake lā
G7   C
Nuha i ke alanui

Tell the story
About being up on a donkey
So stubborn on the road

This is a fun dance for the kāne by, appropriately enough, Makuakāne. Sometimes a newer fourth verse is added in: Honolulu aku nei au lā, I ke kau steam a rola lā, Holo i ke alanui — I was just in Honolulu, riding on a steamroller that cruised the streets.

175
He Mele Aloha

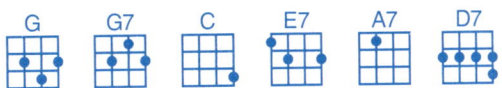

Moanalua

      G G7 C   G
I Moanalua ha'i ke 'au
E7   A7   D7   G
I Kahauiki hemo ka 'umoki

At Moanalua the axle snapped
At Kahauiki the bottle is uncorked

        G G7 C   G
'O ke kula loa ho'i o Kalihi
E7   A7   D7   G
'O Kaiwi'ula kīki'i pau

The broad plain of Kalihi
At Kaiwi'ula leaning and tilting

     G G7   C   G
'O Kapālama lo'i laiki
E7   A7   D7   G
I Keone'ula malu ke kiawe

Kapālama terraces of rice
At Keone'ula the kiawe gives shade

   G G7 C   G
'O Leleo a he loko wai
E7   A7   D7   G
Ha'aliliamanu honi kāua

Leleo, a freshwater pool
At Ha'aliliamanu we share a kiss

     G G7 C   G
'O Kapu'ukolo i Kanēkina
E7   A7   D7   G
Holo lio lā'au me ka ulua

Kapu'ukolo at Kanēkina
Riding merry-go-round horses with the sweetheart

    G G7 C   G
'O Kamanuwai moa li'ili'i
E7   A7   D7   G
Hauna ke kai, 'eha 'oe ia'u

Kamanuwai, there were little chicks
Strong-smelling sea and I hurt you

     G G G7   C   G
He aha ē ke kumu o ka 'eha 'ana?
E7   A7   D7   G
'Ōno'onou 'ia i ka hua noni

What is the reason for the pain?
Pushed into the noni fruit

    G G7 C   G
Auē 'eha 'ino i ku'u kīkala
E7   A7   D7   G
Pehea lā ia e lewa hou ai?

Ouch, there's a pain in my hip
How will it ever sway again?

David Nape re-arranged this traditional song from the 1890s that tells of car trouble leading to a long walk home with a sweetheart. The last two verses, found in Nā Mele o Hawai'i Nei, *are more modern additions.*

Moanike'ala

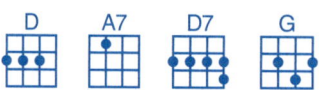

'Auhea 'o Moanike'ala (D A7 D D7)
Hoa pili o mī nei (G D)
A he aha kāu hana e pāweo nei? (A7 D)
E ka makani Pu'ulena (A7 D)

hui

Kuhi au a he pono kēia (D A7 D D7)
Āu e 'apa'apa mai nei (G D)
E wiki mai 'oe i pono kāua (A7 D)
I 'olu ho'i au e ke hoa (A7 D)

Ho'ohihi aku au e 'ike (D A7 D D7)
Ia wai māpunapuna (G D)
Ua Kuahine pi'o ānuenue (A7 D)
O ia uka 'iu'iu (A7 D)

Eia ho'i au ua wehi (D A7 D D7)
Ua li'a i ke onaona (G D)
Ia wai 'ono a ka lehua (A7 D)
Wai mūkīkī a ka manu (A7 D)

Where are you Moanike'ala
Dear companion of mine
And what are you doing turning away
Oh sulphurous Pu'ulena breeze

chorus:
I thought this was the right thing
Over which you now hesitate
Do hurry, for both our sakes
To bring me comfort, my dear

I am entranced to see
That bubbling well spring
Kuahine rain with its arching rainbow
Of those lofty heights

Here indeed am I, adorned
Desirous of the sweet perfume
That sweet nectar of lehua
Nectar sipped by the birds

This song by Leleiōhoku was published in 1888. A later version, published by Holstein in 1897, contains slight variations in a few lines. We mention this here to show the difficulty in determining the "correct" lyrics, and how easily, over time, there can be subtle shifts in the poetry, which sometimes result in significant shifts in meaning. Pu'ulena is a Kīlauea volcano breeze known for its scent of sulphur, and Kuahine, or Tuahine, is the misty curtain of rain of Mānoa Valley.

He Mele Aloha

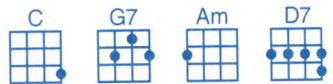

Moku O Keawe

C G7 C He aloha moku o Keawe Am D7 G7 C 'Āina i ka nani me ka maluhia	Beloved is the island of chief Keawe Land of beauty and peace
C G7 C Hoʻokūkū wau me Kaleponi Am D7 G7 C Hawaiʻi nō ka ʻoi o nā ʻailana	I compare it with California And find Hawaiʻi the best of all islands
C G7 C Na ka ʻAukekulia i kono mai iaʻu Am D7 G7 C E naue i ka ʻāina malihini	It was the ship *Australia* that drew me To visit this foreign land
C G7 C 'Āina kamahaʻo i kaʻu ʻike Am D7 G7 C Ua uhi paʻapū ʻia e ka ua noe	This is a wonderful land in my opinion Ever enveloped by fogs
C G7 C ʻIke i ka hau hoʻokuakea ʻili Am D7 G7 C Hoʻopumehana i kahi kapuahi	I know the snow that bleaches the skin That makes one warm oneself at a fireplace
C G7 C Ka ʻiniki a ke anu me he ipo ala Am D7 G7 C E koi mai ana iaʻu e hoʻi	The cold pinches like a lover And urges me to go home
C G7 C I laila huli hope koʻu manaʻo Am D7 G7 C A he kaukani mile koʻu mamao	Then my mind goes wandering back Though I am thousands of miles away
C G7 C Hū mai ke aloha no ka ʻāina Am D7 G7 C No ka poi ʻuoʻuo kāohi puʻu	Love wells up for my homeland And the smooth poi that soothes the throat
C G7 C Haʻina ʻia mai ana ka puana Am D7 G7 C Ke aloha ʻāina kuʻu lei ia	This ends my song with the refrain Patriotism and love of my homeland is my lei

ʻEmalia Kaihumua, *court dancer for King Kalākaua and the "Sweet ʻEmalia" in* Hilo One, *composed this while cold and homesick in San Francisco in 1894, where she participated in the World Exhibition on behalf of Hawaiʻi. The original melody was lost so Bill Aliʻiloa Lincoln wrote new music in the 1940s.*

Molokaʻi Nui A Hina

     G   G7   C   G
Ua nani nā hono a Piʻilani
        D7   G
I ke kū kilakila i ka ʻōpua
           G7   C
ʻO kuʻu pua kukui aia i Lanikāula
      G   D7   G
ʻO ka hene wai ʻolu lana mālie

hui

    G   G7
Ua like nō a like lā
   C
Me kuʻu one hānau
 G   D7
Ke poʻokela i ka piko o nā kuahiwi
 G   G7
Me Molokaʻi nui a Hina
 C
ʻĀina i ka wehiwehi
 G   D7   G
E hoʻi nō wau e pili

hui

      G   G7   C
E ka makani ē, e pā mai me ke aheahe
      D7   G
ʻAuhea kuʻu pua kalaunu

  G   G7   C   G
Kiʻekiʻe Hālawa i ke alo o nā pali
      D7   G
ʻO ka heke nō ia i kaʻu ʻike
         G7   C
Lupalupa lau lipo i ke oho o ka palai
   G   D7   G
Ma kuʻu poli mai ʻoe e hoʻoheno nei

Beautiful are the bays of chief Piʻilani
Flanked by the majestic cloud banks
My kukui blossom, there at Lanikāula
With the teasing comfort of the calm waters

chorus:
So alike, so very like
The land of my birth
The finest at the heart of mountains
Like Great Molokaʻi, child of Hina
Land of beauty and verdure
I shall return to stay

chorus
Oh breezes, blow gently
Where indeed is my crown flower

Hālawa rises lofty amid the cliffs
It is the finest I've witnessed
Dark and luxurious with lush fern
You'll be held precious in my heart

Credited to Matthew Kāne, the composer-singer who was born on Molokaʻi. The tune was taken from *Tenting Tonight*, an American Civil War song, reflecting the not-uncommon practice of borrowing melodies.

He Mele Aloha

Moloka'i Waltz

[G] He 'āina kaulana 'o Hālawa
Ka heke nō ia i ka'u [D7] 'ike
'Āina ho'ohihi a ka malihini
Hanohano wale i ka waha o ka le[G]hule[D7]hu
[G] Hū wale mai nō ke aloha
[G7] Wai pōhihi i nā [C] pali
[D7] Wailele a'o Moa'ula
Pulupē i ka hunehune [G] kēwai

🎸 *hui*

[G] He nani kū kilakila
[D7] Alo lua i nā pali
Home aloha nō ia
Ku'u one [G] hā[D7]nau
[G] Wailele hune i nā pali
[G7] Kou kāhiko nō [C] ia
Me Molo[Cm]ka'i, [G] 'āina kau[E7]lana
Me [A7] 'oe [D7] nō [G] wau

Hālawa is a renowned land
The finest that I know
Land entrancing to visitors
Praised far and wide
Fondness wells up within
For water streaming over the cliffs
The waterfall of Moa'ula
Drenching with misty droplets

chorus:
Beauty that is so majestic
With cliffs face-to-face
It's a beloved home
Sands of my birth
Waterfalls cascading on the cliffs
They are your adornment
Moloka'i, famous land
With you I belong

Also known as Moloka'i 'Āina Kaulana, *this song is by Matthew H. Kāne.*

He Mele Aloha

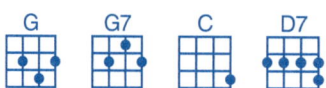

Muliwai

    G   G7   C   G
Aia i ka muliwai ia home nani
        D7   C G
Ka ʻiʻini pau ʻole a ka puʻuwai

         There at the riverside is that beautiful home
         The never ending desire of the heart

    G   G7   C   G
He nani ia home i kaʻu ʻike
      D7   C   G
He pakika he paheʻe i ka papahele

         This home is beautiful in my estimation
         Slipping and sliding on the floors

    G   G7   C   G
Na wai nō ʻoe e pakele aku
      D7   C G
He uila i ka maka aʻo ka ʻōpua

         Who shall help you to escape away?
         There's lightning in the face of the clouds

    G   G7   C   G
He manaʻo nui koʻu lā i laila
     D7   C G
I kahi a nā manu e hiaʻai nei

         I think often of that place
         The place where birds will find their delight

    G   G7   C   G
Haʻina ʻia mai ana ka puana
     D7   C G
Aia i ka muliwai ia home nani

         The story is told in the refrain
         There at the riverside is that beautiful home

A muliwai is the pool at the mouth of a stream which typically sits behind a sand bar, enlarged by ocean water left there by high tide, serving as a safe and nutrient-rich nursery for hinana (young ʻoʻopu) and other fresh-water and marine juvenile fish. This song is credited to Charles Pokipala, Sr. and Daniel Kapahuonaaliʻi Pokipala about their family home in Waikīkī. The song describes the well-polished floors of a large and lovely home and the hosts and their many guests (birds).

He Mele Aloha

My Hawaiian Souvenirs

         C   Am   C
A photograph, a calabash, a paper lei
 Gb-   G7
Are my Hawaiian souvenirs

Each token brings back memories all thru the day
                              C
And may they last for many years

    A7   Dm
When I am old and gray
 D7   G7
I'll have the pleasure to say to you
     C   Am   A7
A photograph, a calabash, a paper lei
 F   G7   C
Are my Hawaiian souvenirs

This plaintive song from the 1930s by Johnny Noble is typical of the hapa-haole genre in that it is musically more complex and poetically less so than most Hawaiian songs.

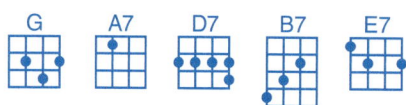

My Little Grass Shack in Kealakekua, Hawai'i

I want to go
G **A7**
Back to my little grass shack in Kealakekua, Hawai'i
D7 **G**
I want to be with all the kāne and wāhine that I knew long ago
B7 **E7**
I can hear old guitars a'playing on the beach at Hōnaunau
A7
I can hear the old Hawaiians saying —
D7
   "E komo mai nō kāua i ka hale wela ka hao"
G **A7**
It won't be long 'til my ship will be sailing back to Kona
D7 **B7**
A grand old place that's always fair to see
E7
I'm just a little Hawaiian and a homesick island boy
A7
I want to go back to my fish and poi
G **A7**
I want to go back to my little grass shack in Kealakekua, Hawai'i
D7 **G**
Where the humuhumunukunukuapua'a go swimming by
D7 **G**
Where the humuhumunukunukuapua'a go swimming by

Another favorite at the Kodak Hula Show, this was composed by Bill Cogswell, Tommy Harrison and Johnny Noble in 1933. The Hawaiian line means "let's you and I go in the house while the time is right."

My Sweet Gardenia Lei

    C   G7   C
My sweet gardenia lei
  G7   C
You gave to me
     G7   C
Upon a moonlit night
G7   C
At Waikīkī

🎸 *chorus:*

   C   C7
All those memories
         F
Of you are here

Haunting me now
     D7
Your faint perfume
 G7
I cannot forget

          C
A lover's melody
  G7   C
Just meant for two
    G7   C
A flower scented night
   G7   C
When I met you

       G7   C
'Till you return to me
 G7   C A7
Again some day
      D7
Singing me a song
          G7   C
Of my sweet gardenia lei

Flowers continue, through the years, to be a favorite vehicle for expressing love in song in Hawai'i, as shown here in this song by Bernie Ka'ai and Danny Kua'ana.

My Sweet Sweeting

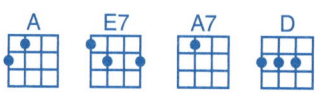

    A   E7
Ku'u 'ohu lei ānuenue
                  A
Ko'iaweawe nei i ke pili
          E7
'O ka pai a ka makani Kiu
              A A7
Ka 'iniki 'ana iho welawela

hui

  D   A
Ho'i mai kāua e pili
E7   A   A7
My sweet sweeting
  D   A
'A'ohe pili hemo 'ole i ke kau
E7   A
My sweet sweeting

My adornment a rainbow lei
Lies spreading over the pili grass
When lifted by the Kiu wind
One feels a sharp pinch

chorus:
Come let us be together
My sweet sweeting
For no tie can last forever
My sweet sweeting

    A   E7
Ko 'awihi 'ana ka'u i 'upu ai
                A
'O ko leo nahe a pa'ē mai
            E7
I ho'ohenoheno iho ai au
              A
I ke ala o pi'i ka manene

Your wink I fondly recall
Your sweet voice has been heard
It makes me love so dearly
This pathway to the shudders of delight

This love song by J.K. Namo'olau and Kalani Peters from 1908 has a timeless quality.

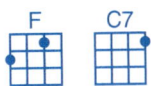

My Yellow Ginger Lei

My **F** yellow ginger **C7** lei
Reveals her scent through the **F** day
Enchanting moments with **C7** you
Make me love **F** you

Ku'u **F** lei 'awapuhi mele**C7**mele
I pu**F**īa me ke 'ala onaona
Ho'ohihi ka mana'o iā **C7** 'oe
E ku'u lei 'awa**F**puhi

My yellow ginger lei
Suffused with sweet scent
My thoughts are entranced by you
My dear ginger lei

You're **F** as lovely as can **C7** be
My yellow **F** ginger lei
My heart is yearning for **C7** you
My 'awa**F**puhi

Ha'**F**ina 'ia **C7** mai
Ana ka **F** puana
My lei 'a**C7**wapuhi
Makes me love **F** you

This composition is variously attributed to John Papa, Sr. as well as to John Ka'ōnohiokalā Keawehawai'i. 1940s.

Nā Ali'i

[F] Aloha nā 'ahahui o nā ali'i
[G7] Nā ali'i mai nā kūpuna mai
[C7] E pa'a i nā 'ōlelo kaulana
[F] E hele a moe i ke [C7] ala
[F] Hū wale a'e nā ho'omana'o 'ana
[G7] No nā ali'i kaulana
[C7] Ua pau, ua hala lākou
A koe nō nā [F] pua
[C7] Ua pau, ua hala lākou
A koe nō nā [F] pua

[F] E lei i ka lei ha'aheo o Hawai'i
[G7] Ka wehi ho'i o nā ali'i i hala
[C7] E pa'a ka mana'o me ka lōkahi
[F] E mau ke ea o ka 'āina i ka [C7] pono
[F] He ali'i 'o Kalani ua kaulana
[G7] Ka Napoliona o ka Pākīpika
[C7] E lei i ka wehi ha'aheo o Hawai'i
Nā hulu mamo like [F] 'ole
[C7] E lei i ka wehi ha'aheo o Hawai'i
Nā hulu mamo like [F] 'ole

Hail societies of the chief
Chiefs from ancestral times
Remember the famous saying
"Go and sleep safely on the byways"
Memories well up
Of the famous chiefs
They are gone, they have passed away
And their descendants live on
They are gone they have passed away
And their descendants live on

Wear the proud lei of Hawai'i
The adornment of departed chiefs
May all unite in recalling
That the life of the land is perpetuated in righteousness
The royal one is a famous chief
Napoleon of the Pacific
Wear the proud adornments of Hawai'i
The mamo-feather leis
Wear the proud adornments of Hawai'i
The mamo-feather leis

[F] 'Imi nui 'o Maleka o lōli'i
[G7] Ka wehi ho'i o nā ali'i i hala
[C7] 'A'ole nō na'e e like aku
[F] Me ka mea no'eau he [C7] kupua
[F] He ali'i 'o Kalani ua kaulana
[G7] Ke 'ahi kananā o ka Pākīpika
[C7] Nāna nō i ulupā nā pae moku
A pau ma lalo [F] ona
[C7] Nāna nō i ulupā nā pae moku
A pau ma lalo [F] ona

America, in readiness, is seeking
The adornment of departed chiefs
There is nothing, though, to compare
With the wisdom that is heroic
The royal one is a chief
Fierce fighter of the Pacific
He struck the island group
And all were subdued under him
He struck the island group
And all were subdued under him

Composed by Samuel Kuahiwi around 1928, this tribute to the departed chiefs contains two famous sayings. The first is "E hele a moe i ke ala," known as Kamehameha's "Law of the splintered paddle," which guaranteed the safe passage for women, children and the infirm. The second is "Ua mau ke ea o ka 'āina i ka pono," Kamehameha III's 1843 statement that became Hawai'i's motto, and translates "The life of the land is perpetuated in righteousness." Syncopation is important in this song, and depends on the singer gliding the two words "nā" and "ali'i" together, as is suggested in the original spelling of the title "Na 'lii."

He Mele Aloha

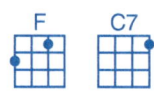

Nā Hala O Naue

F
Nani wale nā hala, 'eā, 'eā
C7   F
O Naue i ke kai, 'eā, 'eā

    Beautiful are the hala trees
    of Naue by the sea

F
Ke 'oni a'ela, 'eā, 'eā
C7   F
Pili mai Hā'ena, 'eā, 'eā

    Swaying there
    Hā'ena draws near

F
'Ena aku nā maka, 'eā, 'eā
C7   F
O nā manu i ka pua, 'eā, 'eā

    The eyes are bright
    As birds search for blossoms

F
A 'ike i ka lehua, 'eā, 'eā
C7   F
Miki'ala i laila, 'eā, 'eā

    On spying the lehua
    They rush to be there

F
I laila nō au, 'eā, 'eā
C7   F
Me ka mana'o pū, 'eā, 'eā

    I too am there
    With the same intention

F
Nani wale ka nahele, 'eā, 'eā
C7   F
I puīa i ke 'ala, 'eā, 'eā

    The forest is beautiful
    Suffused with perfume

F
Ke 'ala laua'e, 'eā, 'eā
C7   F
'O ka pua mokihana, 'eā, 'eā

    The scent of laua'e fern
    And mokihana berry

F
'Oni aku nā Hono, 'eā, 'eā
C7   F
Ka pua o Pi'ilani, 'eā, 'eā

    One of Maui's own moves forth
    The blossom of chief Pi'ilani

F
'O ko'u lei ia, 'eā, 'eā
C7   F
'O ua la'i lani, 'eā, 'eā

    That indeed is my lei
    That heavenly serenity

F
Ha'ina ka inoa, 'eā, 'eā
C7   F
'O Kaleleonālani, 'eā, 'eā

    Tell then of the name
    Kaleleonālani

J. Kahinu wrote this song, which is often performed with the pū'ili, or split bamboo. Kaleleonālani is the name given to Queen Emma, wife of Kamehameha IV, after the deaths of her son and husband. 1888.

He Mele Aloha

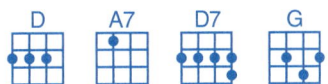

Nā Hoa Heʻe Nalu

   D   A7
ʻEu mai e nā hoa ē
 D   D7
Hō aʻe hoʻi i kahakai ē
    G   D
I laila nō ka leʻaleʻa ē
     A7   D
Ka puni hoʻi a kākou ē

 D   A7
Kū aku e hākilo ē
    D   D7
I nā kūlana papa heʻe nalu ē
   G   D
A ʻau aku i waho ē
    A7   D
I nā nalu o laila ē

  D   A7
Mālama i ka papa ē
     D   D7
O kāpeku hoʻi a lilo ē
      G   D
Paʻa iho a paʻa pono ē
    A7   D
I ko wā e ʻau ai ē

  D A7
I ka nalu pūkī ē
        D   D7
Haʻaheo hoʻi kūlana ē
      G   D
Me he ʻiwa ke kīkaha ē
      A7   D
Hoʻolaʻilaʻi i luna ē

 D   A7
Haʻina mai ka puana ē
    D   D7
No nā hoa leʻaleʻa ē
      G   D
Kīkaha mai me he ʻiwa ē
    A7   D
A hoʻi mai i ka ʻāina ē

Get up friends
Let's go to the beach
To have fun
Doing our favorite thing

We'll stand and watch
The surf line
And travel out
To the surf there

Watch the board
Or it will slip and get lost
Hold on, hold tight
When you go out on the sea

On the high-shooting wave
Proud stance
Like a seabrid gliding
Poised aloft

Tell the story
Of my companions in fun
Gliding like a seabird
And returning to land

Here's one for surfers and lovers by Mary Kawena Pukui and Irmgard Farden Aluli.
Translation by Mary Kawena Pukui.

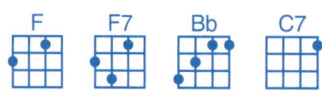

Nā Kuahiwi ʻElima

    [F]   [F7]   [Bb]   [F]
Hoihoi ka piʻina aʻo Waimea
   [C7]   [F]   [C7]
I ka pā mai a ke kēhau anu
  [F]   [F7]   [Bb]   [F]
ʻAkahi hoʻi au a ʻike maka
    [C7]   [F]
I nā wailele pālua i ka pali aʻo Waipiʻo
    [C7]   [F] [C7]
I nā wailele pālua i ka pali aʻo Waipiʻo

Happy the ascent to Waimea
In the cool, breezy mist
First sight I see
The double waterfalls in the cliffs at Waipiʻo

 [F]   [F7]   [Bb]   [F]
Kilakila Maunakea me kona nani
   [C7]   [F]   [C7]
Helu ʻekahi o ke kiʻekiʻe
 [F]   [F7]   [Bb]   [F]
Pili mai Maunaloa, mauna kamahaʻo
    [C7]   [F]
Home noho o ka wahine Pele mai Kahiki
    [C7]   [F] [C7]
Home noho o ka wahine Pele mai Kahiki

Majestic is Maunakea with her beauty
Foremost and highest
Close by is Maunaloa, wondrous and awesome mountain
Home where dwells the woman Pele from Tahiti

     [F]   [F7]   [Bb]   [F]
Hanohano Hualālai e kū maila
   [C7]   [F]   [C7]
E hoʻohiwahiwa ana a i nā Kona
 [F]   [F7]   [Bb]   [F]
Aia lā nā kuahiwi o Kohala
  [C7]   [F]
Ke holo aʻela mai uka a ke kai
  [C7]   [F] [C7]
Ke holo aʻela mai uka a ke kai

Magnificent Hualālai rises
Adorning all Kona
There, the mountains of Kohala
Run from the uplands to the sea

  [F]   [F7]   [Bb]   [F]
Ma ʻō aku o ʻAlenuihāhā
     [C7]   [F]   [C7]
Haleakalā o Maui o Kama
 [F] [F7]   [Bb]   [F]
Haʻina ka puana i lohe ʻia
  [C7]   [F]
Mahalo i ka nani o nā kuahiwi ʻelima
  [C7]   [F]
Mahalo i ka nani o nā kuahiwi ʻelima

Beyond the ʻAlenuihāhā channel
Haleakalā of Maui of Kama
Tell the theme that it may be heard
Worthy admiration for the beauty of the five mountains

A travelogue song that addresses the mountains coming into view on a ride up to Waimea and then down to Kawaihae, where Maui comes into view. Helen Desha Beamer was often inspired to compose while enroute to visit friends, an old custom she perpetuated. 1953. Translation by Mahiʻai Beamer.

He Mele Aloha

Nā Lei O Hawai'i

   C C-   G7   D7   G7 C
Nani Hawai'i ka moku o Keawe
         A7   D7
Lei ha'aheo i ka lehua
       G7   C
A me ka maile a'o Pana'ewa

Beautiful is Hawai'i, island of Keawe
Proudly garlanded with lehua
And the maile of Pana'ewa

  C   C-   G7   D7   G7 C
Kilakila 'o Maui lā iā Haleakalā
      A7 D7
Ua kapu Roselani
        G7   C
A no'u ho'okahi wale nō

Maui is majestic with Haleakalā
The roselani blossom is forbidden
You are for me alone

  C   Cd   G7   D7   G7 C
Kaulana Moloka'i i ka ulu kukui
    A7D7
O Lanikāula
        G7   C
A me ka wailele a'o Moa'ula

Moloka'i is renowned for the kukui groves
Of the priest Lanikāula
And the waterfall of Moa'ula

  C   C-   G7   D7   G7 C
'Ohu'ohu O'ahu i ka 'ilima
         A7   D7
He kohu manu 'ō'ō
         G7   C
Hulu melemele o ke kuahiwi

O'ahu is adorned with 'ilima
Like the beautiful 'ō'ō bird
Golden feathered one of the mountains

  C   C- G7   D7   G7 C
Lei Kaua'i i ka mokihana
     A7   D7
Laua'e o Makana
     G7   C
'O ka'u aloha nō ia

Kaua'i wears a lei of mokihana
Fragrant laua'e fern of Makana
That is what I love

  C C- G7   D7   G7 C
'O Ni'ihau, Kaho'olawe, Lāna'i
        A7 D7
Ho'oheno me ka pūpū
       G7   C
Ka hinahina me ke kauna'oa

Ni'ihau, Kaho'olawe, Lāna'i
Graced with precious shells
With hinahina and kauna'oa

  C   C- G7   D7   G7 C
Ha'ina 'ia mai ana ka puana
     A7 D7
Lei o Hawai'i
      G7   C
Nā lei o Hawai'i, e ō mai

Let the story be told
Hawai'i is adorned with lei
Oh garlands of Hawai'i, do respond

Known also as Song of the Islands, *this Charles E. King song is played during school May Day celebrations in Hawai'i as a processional for the princess and attendants for each island. 1915.*

Nā Makani ʻEhā

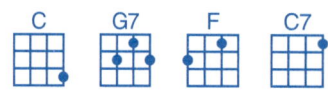

C
He wahine ʻoe no Hālawa mai
G7
He nani maoli nō
Ka heke nō ʻoe i kaʻu ʻike lā
C   C7
He wehi no kuʻu nui kino
F
Hoʻi mai i ʻaneʻi
C
I ka uluwehi o ke Koʻolau
G7   C
Me ka lei i ka makani Hoʻolua

You are a woman from Hālawa
A true beauty indeed
You are unsurpassed in my eyes
An adornment for my whole being
I am returning here
The lushness of the mountains
With the lei of the Hoʻolua wind

C
He wahine ʻoe no Wailau mai
G7
He nani maoli nō
G7
Ka heke nō ʻoe i kaʻu ʻike lā
C   C7
He wehi no kuʻu nui kino
F
Hoʻi mai i ʻaneʻi
C
I ka uluwehi o ke Koʻolau
G7   C
Me ka lei i ka makani ʻEkepue

You are a woman from Wailau
A true beauty indeed
You are unsurpassed in my eyes
An adornment for my whole being
I am returning here
The lushness of the mountains
With the lei of the ʻEkepue wind

C
He wahine ʻoe no Pelekunu mai
G7
He nani maoli nō
G7
Ka heke nō ʻoe i kaʻu ʻike lā
C   C7
He wehi no kuʻu nui kino
F
Hoʻi mai i ʻaneʻi
C
I ka uluwehi o ke Koʻolau
G7   C
Me ka lei i ka makani Puʻupilo

You are a woman from Pelekunu
A true beauty indeed
You are unsurpassed in my eyes
An adornment for my whole being
I am returning here
The lushness of the mountains
With the lei of the Puʻupilo wind

He Mele Aloha

[C]
He wahine 'oe no Waikolu mai
[G7]
He nani maoli nō
[G7]
Ka heke nō 'oe i ka'u 'ike lā
[C]   [C7]
He wehi no ku'u nui kino
[F]
Ho'i mai i 'ane'i
[C]
I ka uluwehi o ke Ko'olau
[G7]   [C]
Me ka lei i ka makani Kili'o'opu

You are a woman from Waikolu
A true beauty indeed
You are unsurpassed in my eyes
An adornment for my whole being
I am returning here
The lushness of the mountains
With the lei of the Kili'o'opu wind

[C]
Ha'ina mai ka puana lā
[G7]
Nā u'i maoli nō
Me he pua 'a'ala onaona lā
[C]   [C7]
Nā wehi no ku'u nui kino
[F]
Ho'i mai i 'ane'i
[C]
I ka uluwehi o ke Ko'olau
[G7]   [C]
Nā makani 'ehā o Moloka'i Nui a Hina

So the story is told
Of the true beauties
Like sweet fragrant blossoms
Adornments for my whole being
I am returning here
The lushness of the mountains
With the four winds of Great
    Moloka'i, child of Hina

The four great valleys of Moloka'i and their winds are celebrated in this joyful song by Dennis Kamakahi. 1980.

He Mele Aloha

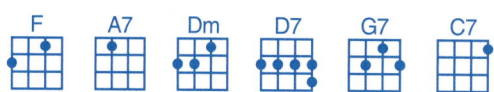

Nā Moku ʻEhā

F   A7   Dm   A7
Hanohano Hawaiʻi lā lei ka lehua lā
D7   G7   C7   F
Kuahiwi nani lā ʻo Maunakea

Grand is Hawaiʻi adorned with lehua
The beauitiful mountain Maunakea

F   A7   Dm   A7
Kilakila ʻo Maui lā lei ka roselani lā
D7   G7   C7   F
Kuahiwi nani lā ʻo Haleakalā

Majestic is Maui adorned with roselani
The beautiful mountain Haleakalā

F   A7   Dm   A7
Haʻaheo Oʻahu lā lei ka ʻilima lā
D7   G7   C7   F
Kuahiwi nani lā aʻo Kaʻala

Proud is Oʻahu adorned with ʻilima
The beautiful mountain Kaʻala

F   A7   Dm   A7
Kaulana Kauaʻi lā lei ka mokihana lā
D7   G7   C7   F
Kuahiwi nani lā aʻo Waiʻaleʻale

Renowned is Kauaʻi adorned with mokihana
The beautiful mountain Waiʻaleʻale

F   A7   Dm   A7
Haʻina ʻia mai ana ka puana lā
D7   G7   C7   F
Nā moku ehā o ka Pākīpika

May the story be told
Of the four isles of the Pacific

Hawaiʻi's great mountains are honored in this song by J. Kealoha. 1920.

He Mele Aloha

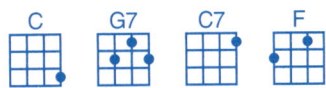

Nā Pua Lei ʻIlima

C　　　　　　G7　　C　　C7
Nani wale nā pua lei ka ʻilima
F　　C　　　G7　　　　C
ʻO ka uʻi hoʻoheno o Kākuhihewa

Lovely indeed are the ʻilima blossoms, strung as a lei
The cherished beauty of Kākuhihewa's land

C　　　　　G7　　　C　　C7
Hoʻohihi ka manaʻo lā i laila
F　　C　　　G7　　　C
Nā pua lei ʻilima e kaulana nei

The mind is entranced by the thought
Of the blossoms of the lei ʻilima, so renowned

C　　　　　G7　　　C　　C7
Kūlana hiehie me ka hanohano
F　　C　　　G7　　　C
Haʻaheo i ka maka ke ʻike aku

Held in esteem and honored
A thing of pride to behold

C　　　　G7　　C　　C7
Kaulana nā pua lei ka ʻilima
F　　C　　　G7　　C
Ke kikowaena o nā ʻailana

Famous are the blossoms of the lei ʻilima
The very heart of the island chain

C　　　　　G7　　　C　　C7
ʻOhuʻohu wale ai nā malihini
F　　C　　　G7　　　C
Ka nani kaulana poina ʻole

They adorn visitors in glory
The famous and unforgettable beauty

C　　　　　G7　　C　　C7
Haʻina ʻia mai ana ka puana
F　　C　　　G7　　　C
Nā pua lei ʻilima e kaulana nei

The story is told in the refrain
Of the blossoms of the lei ʻilima, so renowned.

The beautiful ʻilima blossoms of Oʻahu are likened to the children of Hawaiʻi in this song credited to Kauʻi Zuttermeister.

He Mele Aloha

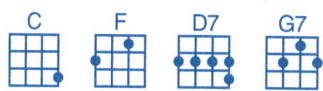

Nāmolokama Lā

C
Kipa aku ana ke aloha
F   D7
I ka hale kamaʻāina
G7
ʻIke ana i ka hau anu
                C
Kolonahe ʻolu i ka laʻi

Ua laʻi malu kāua
F   D7
Ka nohona i ke konakona
G7
ʻIke ana i ka puʻeone
              C
Pua rose aʻo nā moku

Love has made a visit
To the familiar home
We experience the cold chill
The gentle breeze feels nice in the quiet
We are both pleasantly contented
As we remain close together
Seeing the sand bars
Pua Rose and the islets

*hui*

C
Aia i ka luna lā Nāmolokama lā
F   D7
Pumehana hoʻi kāua
G7
Kiani ana i ka lau o ka maile
           C
ʻOni ana nō i ke kuahiwi lā
F   D7
ʻOhuʻohu hoʻi kāua
G7   C
I ka ua nui kaulana o Hanalei

chorus:
There above is Nāmolokama
You and I share our warmth
In the gentle movement through the maile leaves
Moving toward the mountain
You and I are bedecked
By the famous heavy rain of Hanalei

Alfred U. ʻAlohikea and Hanalei are forever linked together in people's minds by his mele pana for this beautiful place. 1928.

He Mele Aloha

Nani Haili Pō I Ka Lehua

C
E ō e Liliʻu i ko inoa
G7   C
Nani Haili pō i ka lehua

Noho ia uka i ke onaona
G7   C
Honi ke kupa i ke ʻala

  Answer, Liliʻu, to your name song
  Haili is beautiful, dense with lehua
  Those uplands dwell in fragrance
  The native inhales the perfume

C   G7
Wai hōʻū nō i ka poli o ka ipo hīnano
            F   G7
Nānā aku he nani wale nō ka nahele
C
ʻIlihia ʻokoʻa i ka maikaʻi o nā pua
G7   C
I kui au a hoʻolawa i ko aloha

  Moisture bedews the bosom of the sweet lover
  Behold the forest so beautiful
  Utterly thrilled by the flowers' beauty
  That I string until enough for your love

C
E ō e Liliʻu i ko inoa
G7   C
Nani Kīlauea paʻa i ka noe

Pō luna ʻo Uēkahuna i ke ʻala
G7   C
Nalo akula nā lehua neʻe i ka papa

  Answer, Liliʻu, to your name song
  Kīlauea is beautiful, covered in mist
  Uēkahuna is thick with fragrance
  Low-spreading lehua is hidden on the plain

C   G7
ʻIke ʻole au i nā hala o Halaaniani
          F   G7
I ke ālai ʻia mai e ka ua nahunahu
C
E ake au e hoʻi mai ka Puʻulena e pili
G7   C
E moe aloha māua me ka moani

  I cannot see the hala of Halaaniani
  It is screened by the driving rain
  I wish the Puʻulena would return to stay
  We would lie as lovers in the gentle breeze

Konia, Bernice Pauahi's mother, composed this name song for her hānai daughter, Liliʻuokalani. 1888. Translation by Dixon Stroup.

He Mele Aloha

Nani Hanalei

[A] 'O Hanalei ku'u [D] aloha [A] [A7]
[D] Ka nani a'o Ha[A]nalei
[E7] Ho'ohihi ana 'oe i ku'u aloha lā, ē
[B7] Hana[E7]lei nō e ka [A] 'oi

Hanalei is what I love
The beauty of Hanalei
You entrance my heart
Hanalei is unsurpassed

[A] Ho'ohihi ho'i ko'u ma[D]na['A]'o [A7]
[D] Ka nani a'o Ha[A]nalei
[E7] E pakika, e pahe'e, ē
[B7] Ka li[E7]mu o Manu['A]akepa

My thoughts are enamoured
By the beauty of Hanalei
To slip and to slide
On the mosses of Manu'akepa

[A] Hanohano a'o Ha[D]na[A]lei [A7]
[D] I ka ua nui 'a[A]na lā
[E7] I ka wailele a'o Molokama lā, ē
[B7] Ka ma[E7]kani 'Āpa['A]'apa'a

Grand is Hanalei
In the pouring rain
With the waterfalls of Molokama
And the 'Āpa'apa'a wind

[A] Ha'ina mai ka pu[D]a[A]na [A7]
[D] Ka nani a'o Ha[A]nalei
[E7] Ho'ohihi ana 'oe i ku'u aloha lā, ē
[B7] Hana[E7]lei nō e ka [A] 'oi

Tell, then, the story
Of the beauty of Hanalei
You entrance my affections
Hanalei is unsurpassed

Kai Davis writes about Hanalei and Manu'akepa, a section of land in Hanalei, noted for the slippery moss that resembles seaweed growing in the sandy grasslands there. 1940s.

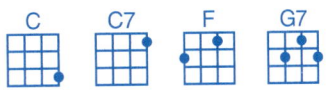

Nani Kaua'i

   C   C7 F   C
Aloha a'e au i ku'u 'āina
        G7   C
I ke kū kilakila o Wai'ale'ale

   C   C7 F   C
'O ke one kaulana a'o Nohili
         G7   C
'Apo iho a pa'a pono lā i ko poli

  C   C7 F   C
Nā hala onaona a'o Māpuana
    G7   C
E naue 'oe i ka 'oni a ke kai

   C   C7 F   C
Inā paha 'oe a'e 'ike ana
        G7   C
I ka nani o ka wai 'ānapanapa

 C   C7 F   C
Hō'oni'oni iki iho ana 'oe
         G7   C
A he honehone i ke kumu o ka hana

  C   C7 F   C
Ha'ina 'ia mai ana ka puana
    G7   C
Ua nani Kaua'i i ka mālie

I express my affection for my beloved land
For the lofty majesty of Wai'ale'ale

The famous sands of Nohili
Grasp and hold them dear to your heart

The fragrant hala trees of Māpuana
You shall move along to the sway of the sea

Perhaps you shall behold
The beauty of the sparkling waters

You have been touched and stirred
A sweet memory in all that you do

May the story be told
Kaua'i is beautiful in the calm

A haunting song of love for the beauty of Kaua'i by Lizzie 'Alohikea. 1918.

Nani Nuʻuanu

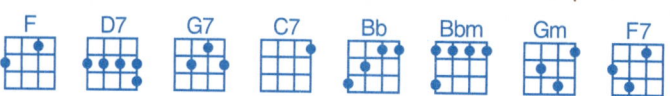

[F] Nani Nuʻuanu i ka ua a [D7] lī[G7]hau
[C7] Kilihune i ke oho o ka pa[F]lai [F7]
[Bb] I laila [Bbm] kuʻu lani ʻelo [F] ē [D7]
[Gm] Ua pulu i ka [C7] huna wai ʻō[F]helo [F7]

hui

[Bb] Eia aku nei paha ʻo Ka[F]la[D7]ni
[G7] I ke kui lei kā[C7]makahala
[F] Wili ʻia me [D7] ka ʻawapuhi [Gm] [Bbm]
[F] Onaona i [D7] ka lau [G7] naʻe[C7]naʻ[F]e

[F] Lamalama ē ke [D7] kino o Ka[G7]lani
[C7] Wehiwehi i ka liko ʻākō[F]lea [F7]
[Bb] Ilihia [Bbm] i ke ʻala a[F]nu[D7]hea
[Gm] He mau he [C7] moani ke [F] pi[F7]li

Nu‘uanu is beautiful, refreshed in the gentle rain
Misting down upon the fern fronds
There my heavenly one is drenched
Wetted with droplets of rosy mist

chorus:
Here perhaps is the heavenly one
Stringing the kāmakahala lei
Entwined with the ginger blossoms
Sweet with heady fragrance

The body of the heavenly one is aglow
Adorned in ʻākōlea buds
Awesome with the cool fresh scent
Ever fragrant in embrace

Kauʻi Wilcox makes full use of her garden to describe her beloved. Translation by Carol Silva.

He Mele Aloha

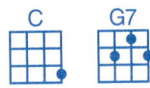

Nani Wale Līhuʻe

    C
ʻAnoʻai wale ka hikina mai
    G7   **C**
Ka ʻikena i ke anu o Wailua
G7 C
ʻElua māua me ka haliʻa
  G7   **C**
I ka piko waiʻolu o Kēmamo

The arrival was by chance
Experiencing the cold of Wailua
The two of us with memories
Of the cool summit waters of Kēmamo

🎸 *hui*

    C
Nani wale Līhuʻe i ka laʻi
   G7   **C**
I ka noe a ka ua Paʻūpili
     C
ʻO ke ahe mai a ka makani
       G7   **C**
ʻO ka Mālualuakiʻiwai o Lehua

chorus:
Lovely Līhuʻe is peaceful
In the mists of the Paʻūpili rain
And the gentle touch of the wind
The Mālualuakiʻiwai of Lehua island

 C
Hoʻonā aʻe ana i ke aloha
    G7   **C**
Pehea lā ia e pau ai
G7 C
ʻAʻole hoʻi naʻe hiki
  G7   **C**
Ua ʻolu, nahe ʻolu i ka noe

Trying to soothe the affections
How indeed can it be done
But it just isn't possible
After finding pleasure and comfort

 C
Hiʻipoi ʻia iho ke aloha
   G7   **C**
I mehana ia pō anuanu
G7 **C**
Mili ʻia i ka lā o ka makemake
  G7   **C**
I ka lā a ka ʻanoʻi e hiki mai ai

Hold love's dream fast
To warm you on a cold night
Cherish it on a good day
On the day your wishes come true

In this mele by Leleiōhoku and Mrs. Kamakau, winds and weather suggest a range of experiences enjoyed by these lovers, from the soft Paʻūpili rain that moistens the pili grass to the Mālualua, a gusty north wind. Published in Holstein, 1897, as Wailua Alo Lahilahi.

Niu Haohao

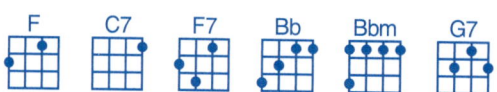

   F   C7
Na wai, na wai nō 'oe a'e
      F
Pakele aku, pakele aku
   C7
I ka wai, ka wai o ka niu
       F   F7
O ka niu haohao, niu haohao
    Bb   Bbm
He ma'ū, ma'ū, ma'ū
     F
I ka pu'u ke moni
  C7   F
Kāohi, kāohi mālie ai ke kīleo

Who, who indeed
Can save you, save you
From the juice, the juice
Of the young coconut, young coconut
So moist, moist, moist
In the throat when swallowed
Pressing gently, gently over the palate

hui

   F
He pakika (he pakika)
   G7
He pahe'e (he pahe'e)
   C7
He pakika i kahi wai
     F
O ka 'āina nui

chorus:
Slick
Slippery
Slick with water
From the continent

Bina Mossman writes about the smooth consistency of the young coconut, so delectable. 1924.

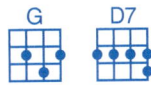

No Ka Pueo

G	D7 G
No ka Pueokahi ke aloha	

D7 G
Nēnē 'au kai o Maui

Love for the *Pueokahi*
The Maui nēnē bird that sails the sea

G   D7   G
Kōwelo ko hae Hawai'i
D7   G
Ma ka 'ilikai a'o Māmala

Your Hawaiian flag waves
Over the sea at Māmala

G   D7 G
Mālama iho 'oe ke aloha
D7   G
I kuleana no'u e hiki aku ai

Keep your love
As a reason for me to get there

G   D7 G
Ha'ina 'ia mai ka puana
D7   G
No ka Pueokahi ke aloha

Tell the refrain
Love for the *Pueokahi*

Composed by Samuel Kalani Kā'eo. The Pueokahi *was a ship named for a place near Hāna, Maui, which was named, in turn, for a pueo (owl or demigod). Māmala is the bay between Diamond Head and Barbers Point, encompassing Waikīkī and Honolulu Harbor. While early versions started with "No ka Pueokahi...," many contemporary versions are "Na ka Pueokahi...." The difference being, in the first instance, love for the* Pueokahi, *and in the second, love delivered by the* Pueokahi.

He Mele Aloha

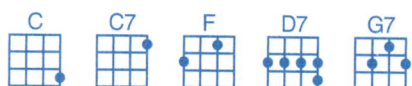

Noho Paipai

   C   C7   F   C
Pupue iho au e mehana
        D7   G7   C
Hone ana 'o Uese i ku'u poli

I crouch down to keep warm
Thoughts of my Sweetie tease my heart

  C   C7   F   C
Me he ala nō e 'ī mai ana
      D7   G7   C
'Auhea ku'u lei roselani

As though saying to me
Give me your attention, oh my roselani lei

  C   C7   F   C
Malihini 'oe, malihini au
       D7   G7   C
Ma ka ihu kāua kama'āina

You are a stranger, I am a stranger too
By means of a kiss, we are acquainted

  C   C7   F   C
Inā 'o you me a'u
       D7   G7   C
Kau pono i ka noho paipai

If you were here with me
We would rock together on a rocking chair

  C   C7   F   C
Ha'ina 'ia mai ka puana
      D7   G7   C
Hone ana 'o Uese i ku'u poli

This is the end of my song
Dreams of my Sweetie tease my heart

This "rocking chair hula" was a traditional piece in Hawaiian song popularized by Johnny Almeida in the mid '40s. Translation by Mary Kawena Pukui.

205
He Mele Aloha

Now is the Hour

F
Now is the hour
     C7   F
When we must say goodbye
Bb   Bbm   F
Soon you'll be sailing
G7   C7
Far across the sea
F   Bb   F
While you're away
   C7   F   F7
Oh please remember me
Bb   Bbm   F   D7
When you return you'll find me
G7   C7   F
Waiting here

Maewa Kaihan, Clement Scott and Dorothy Stewart found their inspiration for this melody in a traditional Māori farewell song. 1913.

Old Plantation

    F   C7
Pua wale mai nō ke aloha
 A7   Dm   G7   C7
Ka paia puīa i ke ʻala
   F   F7   Bb
I ka wai huʻihuʻi aniani
Bbm   F   D7   G7 C7 F
Koʻiawe ka huila wai
    A   Dm
Aia i laila ka ʻiʻini
      C   G7   C   C7
Ka ʻanoʻi a koʻu puʻuwai

Love and affection always well up in me
For the bowers, fragrant with scent
Bubbling waters refreshing and sparkling
Dance on the water wheel
The charms and pleasures are there
The real desire of my heart

🎸 hui

    F   C-   C7
Old Plantation nani ʻoe
                      F
Home pumehana i ke aloha
   A7   Dm   Bb
I ka ʻolu o ka niu
Bbm F   D7   G7 C7 F
I ka poli o ke onaona

chorus:
Old Plantation, you are beautiful
Lovely home that holds my affection
In the shades of waving palms
A sweet and gentle embrace

     F   C7
Nahenahe ke ʻala o nā pua
 A7   Dm   G7   C
I ka pē ʻia e ke kēhau
  F   F7   Bb
Hoʻolaʻi nā manu i laila
Bbm F D7 G7 C7 F
Hoʻoipo i ke oho o ka niu
    A   Dm
Luhe ehu ka palai i ka nuʻa
   C   G7   C C7
I ka ʻolu o ka Old Plantation

The perfume of the flowers is gentle
Wetted by the touch of the misty dew
The birds delight in being there
Romancing the fronds of the palms
The ferns are in luxuriant abundance
In the comfort of Old Plantaiton

Mary Jane Montano and David Nape wrote this about the home of the Ward sisters at Kulaokahuʻa, where the Neal Blaisdell Center now stands. Also known as **Kuʻu Home**, *this song is a well known example of "mele pana," a song of a special place. The third line, first verse, is often sung "I ka wai aniani huʻihuʻi," but the phrasing here is as originally composed by Montano. 1904.*

On the Beach at Waikīkī

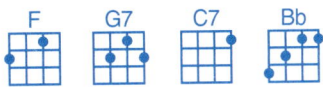

He Mele Aloha

F
"Honi kāua wikiwiki"
G7
Sweet brown maiden said to me
C7
As she gave me language lessons
F   **Bb**   **F**
On the beach at Waikīkī

F
"Honi kāua wikiwiki"
G7
She then said and smiled in glee
C7
But she would not translate for me
F   **Bb**   **F**
On the beach at Waikīkī

F
"Honi kāua wikiwiki"
G7
She repeated playfully
C7
Oh those lips were so inviting
F   **Bb**   **F**
On the beach at Waikīkī

F
"Honi kāua wikiwiki"
G7
She was surely teasing me
C7
So I caught that maid and kissed her
F   **Bb**   **F**
On the beach at Waikīkī

F
"Honi kāua wikiwiki"
G7
You have learned it perfectly
C7
Don't forget what I have taught you
F   **Bb**   **F**
Said the maid at Waikīkī

G.H. Stover and Henry Kailimai collaborated on this song about stealing a quick kiss. 1915.

'Ōpae Ē

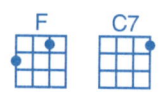

[F] 'Ōpae ē, 'Ōpae ho'i
[C7] Ua hele mai au, ua hele mai au
[F] Na kuahine

Ai iā wai? Ai iā puhi
[C7] Nui 'o puhi a li'ili'i au
[F] 'A'ole loa

[F] Pipipi ē, Pipipi ho'i
[C7] Ua hele mai au, ua hele mai au
[F] Na kuahine

Ai iā wai? Ai iā puhi
[C7] Nui 'o puhi a li'ili'i au
[F] 'A'ole loa

[F] Pūpū ē, Pūpū ho'i
[C7] Ua hele mai au, ua hele mai au
[F] Na kuahine

Ai iā wai? Ai iā puhi
[C7] Nui 'o Puhi a li'ili'i au
[F] 'A'ole loa

Oh shrimp, shrimp, come
I have come
For my sister
Who has her? The eel has her
The eel is big and small am I
No indeed

Oh little rock snail, rock snail, come
I have come
For my sister
Who has her? The eel has her
The eel is big and small am I
No indeed

Oh shell, shell, come
I have come
For my sister
Who has her? The eel has her
The eel is big and small am I
No indeed

He Mele Aloha

[F] Kūpeʻe ē, Kūpeʻe hoʻi
[C7] Ua hele mai au, ua hele mai au
[F] Na [F] kuahine
Ai iā wai? Ai iā puhi
[C7] Nui ʻo puhi a liʻiliʻi au
[F] ʻAʻole loa

Oh reef snail, oh reef snail, come
I have come
For my sister
Who has her? The eel has her
The eel is big and small am I
No indeed

[F] ʻOpihi ē, ʻOpihi hoʻi
[C7] Ua hele mai au, ua hele mai au
[F] Na [F] kuahine
Mai makaʻu, naʻu e pani
[C7] I ka maka a ʻike ʻole
[F] Kēlā puhi

Oh limpet, oh limpet come
I have come
For my sister
No fear, I shall close
The eyes, until they see nothing
Of that eel

This children's favorite by Pilahi Pākī and Irmgard Farden Aluli, which they may have based on a traditional song, tells the story of a maiden from the village of Kahakuloa, Maui who was kidnapped by an eel. Her brother appeals to various sea creatures to help rescue her. Each one refuses for fear of the great puhi. Only the ʻopihi agrees to help. They clamp themselves onto the eyes of that puhi, blinding it, allowing the brother to rescue his sister.

Pa'ahana

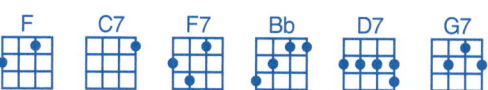

    F   C7   F
He inoa kēia no Pa'ahana
   C7   F   F7
Kaikamahine noho kuahiwi

tag

 Bb   D7 G7 C7   F
He mele he inoa no Pa'ahana

This is a name song for Pa'ahana
The girl who lived in the mountains

tag:
A song, a name song for Pa'ahana

  F   C7   F
Na'u noho aku ia wao kele
    C7   F   F7
Ia uka 'iu'iu Wahiawā

I lived in the rain forests
The distant uplands of Wahiawā

 F   C7   F
'Ōpae 'oeha'a o ke kahawai
        C7   F F7
'O ka hua o ke kuawa ka'u 'ai ia

Clawed shrimps of the streams
And guava fruit are my meals

  F   C7   F
Mai kuhi mai 'oe ka makuahine
    C7   F F7
A he pono kēia e noho nei

Don't mistakenly think, mother
That I am glad to live here

  F   C7   F
'O kahi mu'umu'u pili i ka 'ili
     C7   F F7
'O ka lau lā'ī ko'u kapa ia

A single mu'umu'u clings to my skin
My blankets are ti leaves

 F   C7   F
Pīlali kukui kau lā'au
    C7   F F7
Lau o ke pili ko'u hale ia

Kukui gum on the trees
And pili grass becomes my house

 F   C7   F
I hume iho au ma ka pūhaka
   C7   F F7
I nalo iho ho'i kahi hilahila

I bind my loins
And hide my private parts

He Mele Aloha

    F   C7   F
I hoʻi iho hoʻi au e peʻe   I went back to hide
       C7   F   F7
ʻIke ʻē ʻia mai e ka ʻenemi   But was seen by the enemy

    F   C7   F
Lawe ʻia aku au a i Mānana   I was taken to Mānana
        C7   F   F7
Mākaʻikaʻi ʻia e ka malihini   And exhibited for strangers

     F   C7   F
Haʻina ʻia mai ana ka puana   Tell the refrain
        C7   F   F7
He mele he inoa no Paʻahana   A song, a name song for Paʻahana
Bb   D7 G7   C7   F
He mele he inoa no Paʻahana   A song, a name song for Paʻahana

The story is not told as to just why Paʻahana hid in the mountains in this old song of cruelty. She was captured by a hunter, taken to Mānana, on Oʻahu, and put on exhibit. 1899.

He Mele Aloha

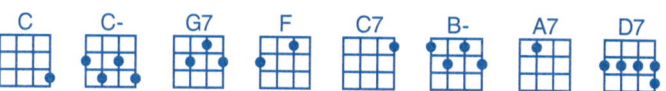

Pāʻuʻau Waltz

C C- C   G7
Haʻaheo Pāʻuʻau i ka nani

C   G7
Kilakila i ka pai a ka Moaʻe

C C- C   C7 F
E walea ana paha i ka ʻolu

B-   C   A7   D7 G7   C
I ka hoʻoheno a ka iʻa hāmau leo

Proud is Pāʻuʻau in its beauty
Majestic is the stirring of the trade winds
Delighting in the pleasant comfort
Cherished for the pearl oyster sought in silence

C   D7 G7   C
Pau ʻole koʻu hoʻohihi

C   G7
I ka nani o Pāʻuʻau

Na wai e ʻole ka ʻiʻini

C
Ua noho a kupa i laila

My delight is boundless
For the beauty of Pāʻuʻau
Who would not be desirous
Having lived as a familiar of that place

C   D7 G7   C
Uluwehi wale ia home

C7   F
Makaʻala i ke kai o Pōlea

F   B-   C   A7
Hoʻolale aʻe ana e ʻike i ka nani

D7 G7 C
O Pāʻuʻau

That home is verdant and lush
Surrounded by the sea of Pōlea
Urging one to witness the beauty
Of Pāʻuʻau

Pāʻuʻau was a home on a peninsula extending into Pearl Harbor. This song by John U. Iosepa tells how, when harvesting for pearls, one had to approach the oysters very quietly so as not to warn them, or else they might clam up! Hawaiians described the pearl oyster as "iʻa hāmau leo," or fish of silenced voice. Early 1900s.

He Mele Aloha

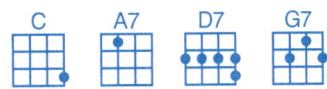

Pālolo

  C   A7   D7
Hoʻi ke aloha a i Pālolo
         G7   C
I ka ua Līlīlehua e kilihune nei

Love returns to Pālolo
To the Līlīlehua rain misting down

  C   A7   D7
Ka ua nō ia ʻolu ka manaʻo
      G7   C
Hōʻoni aʻe nei i kuʻu puʻuwai

It is the rain that soothes the mind
Stirring up feelings in my heart

  C   A7   D7
Kani a ka leo o ke kolohala
      G7   C
I ka ulu kukui honehone nei

The call of the pheasant sounds
Melodious in the kukui groves

  C   A7   D7
Pumehana kāua i ke aloha
      G7   C
I ka pili i ke anu o ke kuahiwi

You and I are warmed by love
Together in the cold of the mountain

  C   A7   D7
Ua lawa kāua e ke aloha
      G7   C
Honi iho nei hoʻi i ka puʻuwai

We two are satisfied my love
Having been touched in the heart

  C   A7   D7
Haʻina ʻia mai ana ka puana
      G7   C
I ka ua Līlīlehua e kilihune nei

Tell the story through the refrain
Of the Līlīlehua rain misting down

Līlīlehua is the name of a chilly rain and wind, famous in Pālolo, Oʻahu, referred to in this song by Charles E. King. 1917.

He Mele Aloha

Pane Mai

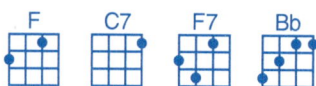

F / C7 / F F7
Ua ala ʻoe e kuʻu ipo
Bb / F C7
Kāhea ana au iā ʻoe
F / C7 / F
I ka lipolipo o ka pō
Bb F C7 F
Pane mai, pane mai

You've awakened my love
I call unto you
In the darkness of the night
Answer me, answer me

🎸 *hui*

Bb / F
Huli, huli kou kino
Bb / F C7
Pumehana i ka laʻi
F / C7 / F
Kīpuni ʻia kāua me ke aloha
Bb F C7 F
Pane mai, pane mai

chorus:
Turn, turn your body (to me)
Pleasantly warm in the calm
You and I are encircled with love
Answer me, answer me

F / C7 / F F7
Hoʻomaha ʻoe i kuʻu poli
Bb / F C7
Honi aku a honi mai
F / C7 / F
He aloha wau iā ʻoe
Bb F C7 F
Pane mai, pane mai

Rest here in my arms
I kiss you, you kiss me
For I love you
Answer me, answer me

F / C7 / F F7
ʻOluʻolu ʻoe e kuʻu ipo
Bb / F C7
I kēia hoʻoipoipo nei
F / C7 / F
I ka wai welawela nui
Bb F C7 F
Pane mai, pane mai

You are so pleasant my sweet
At making love
Feelings surge
Answer me, answer me

This composition by Robert Cazimero reminds us that the urge to hold a dear one can come at any time, even waking you from a deep sleep. 1980s.

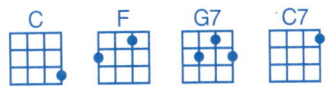

Pāpālina Lahilahi

[C] [F] He aloha wau iā [C] 'oe lā
[G7] Kou pāpālina lahi[C]lahi [C7]
[F] I ka ho'opulu mau 'ia [C] lā
[G7] I ka hunehune o ke [C] kai

I love you
Your dainty cheeks
Always moistened
From sea spray

[C] [F] He aha nō ho'i [C] kāu lā
[G7] 'O ke alawiki 'ana [C] mai? [C7]
[F] Ua 'ike iho nō 'oe [C] lā
[G7] A he pua 'oe ua 'ako [C] 'ia

What indeed is the reason
For hurrying this way?
You've seen for yourself
You're a blossom already plucked

[C] [F] Hā'awi hemolele [C] 'ia lā
[G7] Mai ke po'o a ka [C] hi'u [C7]
[F] He aha nō ho'i [C] kāu la
[G7] 'O ka pūlalelale 'ana [C] mai?

Freely given
From head to toe
What, then, is the reason
For this hurry to possess?

[C] [F] Ha'ina mai ka puana [C] lā
[G7] Kou pāpālina lahi[C]lahi [C7]
[F] Ha'ina hou ka puana [C] lā
[G7] He aloha wau iā [C] 'oe

The story is told
Of your dainty cheeks
And it's told again
That I love you

Attributed to Alice Johnson who asks, "What's the rush? Once love is in the works the relationship can unfold at our leisure."

Pauoa Liko Ka Lehua

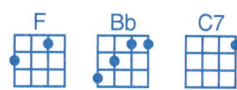

F Bb F C7	F
Aia i Pauoa liko ka lehua	At Pauoa the lehua buds emerge
Ka ʻiʻini pau ʻole a ka makemake	The boundless desire of the heart

Makemake nō wau lā ʻike lihi
I ka lawe haʻaheo o ke kīkala

I so wish to catch a glimpse
Of the proud sway of those hips

Pālua, pākolu i ke kekona
I ka hoʻi ʻākau hoʻi i ka hema

Two or three per second
Back and forth, right and left

Hemahema ka pilina ua lolelole
Ua ʻewa ka palena me ka nihoniho

The match is uneven
The hem and the fringe are crooked

Nihoniho mai nei ko pelekoki
I ka iho makawalu o ka lihilihi

Your petticoat is scalloped
Descending, there's an abundance of lace

A he lihi kuleana koʻu i laila
I ka loʻu ʻūmiʻi a ka huapala

And I have some small privilege there
Through the squeezing embrace of the sweetheart

He aloha kahi wai o ʻAuwaiolimu
Ia wai lomi lima me kuʻu aloha

Beloved are the waters of ʻAuwaiolimu
Waters caressed by me and my love

Haʻina ʻia mai ana ka puana
Aia i Pauoa liko ka lehua

Tell the tale in the refrain
There at Pauoa the lehua buds emerge

This song from the 1920s about a loved one from Pauoa is variously attributed to Emma Bush, Samuel Kanahele and Charles W. Booth, and it may well be that several composers contributed to it. High in Pauoa valley it is said that the leaves of the lehua bud forth but the flowers do not bloom for lack of sun. ʻAuwaiolimu Street is so named for the mossy waterway that once ran there. It exemplifies kuʻi, a favorite feature of Hawaiian poetry and music. While rhyme is not a part of Hawaiian composition, linking the end of a line with the start of the next line is. This song contains "ke kuʻi ʻana o ke kani like" (linking with the same sound) between each verse.

Pidgin English Hula

C
Honolulu pretty girl stop
D7
Too muchee guru looking
G7
Number one sweet, naughty eyes make
  C   G7
Oh! oh! oh! oh!
C
You bet I know you no got chance
D7
'Nother fella she sweetheart
F   C   A7
But today pilikia got
D7   G7   C
She too much huhū for him

hui

    F
    Ahsamala you last night?
    C
    You no come see māmā. I tink so
    G7
    You no likee me no more
    C
    You too muchee like 'nother girl
    F
    'Nother fella likee me too
    C
    He number one guru looking
              D7
    He too much aloha
    G7   C
    Ha ha ha ha ha ha ha auē
    G7   C
    Ha ha ha ha ha ha ha auē

Subtitled "Ah-sa-ma-la-you," this song by Charles E. King of the '30s speaks of pretty girls and a lot of aloha.

218
He Mele Aloha

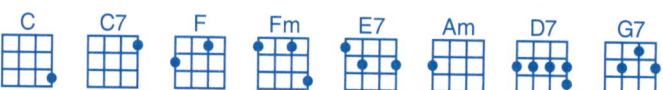

Pō Laʻilaʻi

C Kāua i ka holo **C7** holo
F I ka pō ma **Fm** hina laʻi **C** laʻi
E7 E kilo hoʻo **Am** na **D7** nea
G7 I nā hōkū o nā **C** lani

Let's go for a walk
On a clear moonlit night
To gaze with interest
At the stars in the heavens

C Kō mai ana ke **C7** ʻala
F O ka pua o **Fm** ka pī **C** kake
E7 I halihali **Am** ʻia **D7** mai
G7 I ka makani ko **C** lonahe

A fragrance is brought to us
Of the pīkake blossom
Carried here
By a gentle breeze

C Hoʻolono ana i **C7** ke kani
F Honehone **Fm** a ka ʻuku **C** lele
E7 Me ka mele hoʻo **Am** hauʻ **D7** oli
G7 Hoʻolana a ka **C** puʻuwai

Listen to the sound of the
Sweet refrains of the ʻukulele
With its cheerful melody
Uplifting the heart

C Huli aku kāua **C7** i uka
F I ka ʻāʻā **Fm** a nā **C** kukui
E7 Ua like me **Am** nā **D7** hōkū
G7 E kau ana i nā **C** pali

Let's turn to the uplands
Towards the bright lights
Like the many stars
Nestling on the hillside

C Haʻina mai ka **C7** puana
F No ka pō ma **Fm** hina laʻi **C** laʻi
E7 Hoʻolono ana **Am** i ke **D7** kani
G7 Honehone a ka **C** ʻukulele

This is my song
For the moonlit night
Listening to the sound of the
Sweet refrains of the ʻukulele

Mary Kawena Pukui was inspired by the touch of the moonlight through the bedroom window as she drifted off to sleep one night. Written in collaboration with Maddy Lam, the two formed a prolific songwriting partnership.

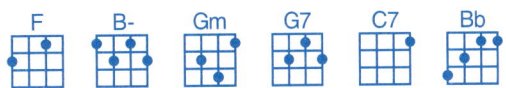

Pōhai Ke Aloha

| F | B- | Gm | G7 C7 | F | C7 |
Pōhai ke aloha lā i ke kino
| F | B- | Gm | G7 | C7 | F | C7 |
Ko mino'aka mai, me ka waimaka
| F | C7 | F | Bb |
Kehakeha i ka wai puhilani ho'opulu
| F | C7 | F | C7 |
Ana i o'u pāpālina

Love encircles one
You smile at me, with tears
Glorious, with heavenly flowing tears wetting
My checks

| F | B- | Gm G7 C7 | F | C7 |
Ka ne'e mai a ke ao hekili
| F | B- Gm G7 | C7 | F | C7 |
I ke alo o nā kumu hau 'ekolu
| F | C7 | F | Bb |
Kama lani, kama nui, kama iki ka home
| F | C7 | F | C7 |
O nā ali'i holokai

The approach of the thundercloud
Before the three hau trees
Royal child, great child, tiny child, at the home
Of the seafaring chiefs

| F | B- | Gm | G7 C7 | F | C7 |
E ō mai ku'u lani, lei loke o Maui
| F | B- | Gm G7 C7 | F | C7 |
I mānai 'ia me ke aloha
| F | C7 | F7 | Bb |
Mali 'ia iho i ka hā'upu
| F | C7 | F |
A kāua i ho'okō ai

Respond, my royal one, rose garland of Maui
Strung as a lei, with love
Brought together by the memories
That we have shared

Mekia Kealaka'i wrote the music, the lyrics are often attributed to Lena Machado. Mary Kawena Pukui says of the hau trees referred to in the second verse, kama lani, kama nui, kama iki, "Hau trees that spread out thickly on the beach were often used as shelters by fisherfolks, just as we use tents today... A little trimming here and there and the shelter was very comfortable indeed. Being resting places for chiefs, the three hau trees would naturally be named to distinguish them from others." Another understanding of the second verse is that it refers to three coconut trees depicting the father, Kamanui, the mother, Kamalani, and the son, Kamaiki, which served as beacons for the ships that sailed in and out of the bay area in Ewa, where Mekia Kealaka'i had his home.

Pretty Red Hibiscus

F6
Pretty red hibiscus
Gm
I've admired you right from the start
C7
Pretty red hibiscus
      F   **G7**   **C7**
You're the flower of my heart
F
Everyday you're fairer
        Gm
Than the fairest flower that grows
C7   **C7**
Pretty red hibiscus
      F   **Bbm**   **F**
You're beautiful everyone knows

chorus:
F7   **Gm**   **D7**   **Gm**
Tho you may not be scented
            D7   **Gm**
Like the other flowers are
E7   **F7**   **E7** **Eb7** **D7**
But when the day has ended
        G9   **C7**
You're as fair as the evening star

Of all the hapa-haole songs that Johnny Noble wrote, it was this one, written in collaboration with Rube Wolf, he most wished to be remembered for. 1936.

Pua ʻĀhihi

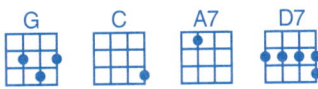

G   C   G   A7
Me ʻoe ka ʻanoʻi e ka ʻāhihi
    C   G   D7   G
Ka lei milikaʻa a kaʻu aloha

O ʻāhihi you are the source of my desire,
The lei caressed lovingly by my affection

G   C   G   A7
He aloha makamae ka i hiki mai
   C   G   D7   G
He ʻala honehone i ka puʻuwai

It is a pure love that has come to me
A fragrance that teases the heart

G   C   G   A7
He waiwai ʻoe i kaʻu ʻike
    C   G   D7   G
Ua kehakeha i luna aʻo Lanihuli

You are precious in my sight
Strikingly beautiful atop Lanihuli

G   C   G   A7
Huli mai nō ʻoe. ʻolu kāua
    C   G   D7   G
I mehana hoʻi au a i kou poli

Turn then to me, let us share comfort
Let me be warmed in your embrace

G   C   G   A7
Haʻina ka puana no kuʻu lei
   C   G   D7   G
Ka pua ʻāhihi aʻo Lanihuli

The story is told for my lei
The ʻāhihi blossom of Lanihuli

This song by Mary Kawena Pukui and Maddy Lam speaks of the ʻāhihi, a low spreading and dainty-leaved lehua tree found in Nuʻuanu. Hihi means entangled or entwined, and, as is often the case, this song has everything to do with being entwined. Lanihuli is the dramatic peak on the west side of the Pali lookout. 1950.

He Mele Aloha

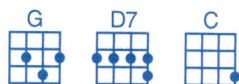

Pua Carnation

   G   D7
'Auhea wale ana 'oe
              C G
Pua carnation ka'u aloha
          D7
A ke lawe 'ia ala 'oe
             C G
E ka makani pā kolonahe

  G   D7
Ko aloha ka i hiki mai
         C G
Hō'eha i ka pu'uwai
            D7
Noho 'oe a mana'o mai
         C G
Ho'i mai kāua e pili

Where indeed are you
Pua carnation, my beloved
For you are being carried away
By the gentle touch of the breeze

Your love came to me
Bringing pain to the heart
Do, then, think of me
Let us reunite as one

Charles E. King wrote this while sitting on the lānai at Grove Farm Homestead, Kaua'i. Love, as variable as the breezes, can bring pangs to the heart. Think of me and let's come back together. 1916.

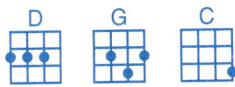

Pua Hone

D	G D
'O 'oe ka wahine a ke aloha
                                   C D
I laila i ka uluwehi ku'u pua hone i ka la'i

 D   G D
Honi ana i ke hau no Makiki
                           C D
'O wau kou aloha i ka noe kuahiwi

 D   G D
He u'i nō 'oe i ke kula
                       C D
I wili 'ia me ka 'ie'ie o Leilono

 D   G D
Ha'ina mai ana ka puana
                                 C D
Ku'u pua hone i ka la'i, he nani maoli nō

Translation:

You are the woman of my affection
There in the beauty of the land is my honey flower in the calm

Kissing the dew of Makiki
I am your love in the mountain mist

You are a beauty on the plain
Entwined with the 'ie'ie vine of Leilono

Tell of the refrain
Of my honey flower in the calm, a true beauty

Dennis Kamakahi composed this song, rich in kaona, as an engagement present for his wife. 1977.
Translation by Dennis Kamakahi.

Pua 'Iliahi

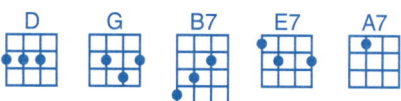

D	G
He aloha nō, he aloha
	D
Ka liko pua 'iliahi
B7	E7
E please mai ho'i 'oe ke aloha
A7	D
'Oiai ua ano, ua meha

Beloved indeed, beloved is the tender bud of sandalwood
Come, share the pleasure of you, my dear
While all is tranquil and secluded

| D | G |
'Ano'ai wale ke 'ike aku
| | D |
I ka malu 'ulu o Kawehiwehi
| B7 | E7 |
Ke kai honehone nei i ku'u poli
| A7 | D |
Ke hone nei i ku'u poli

Such a delight to see
The shady breadfruit grove of Kawehiwehi
The sea speaks softly to my heart
Teasing away at my heart

| D | G |
Pehea kāua e ka hoa
| | D |
Ka 'ano'i a ke aloha
| B7 | E7 |
Maile lau lipolipo i ka wao
| A7 | D |
Ka hanu 'a'ala o ku'u ipo

What then are we to do
Oh choice of my heart
Like perfume of maile deep in the forest
Is the fragrance of my darling

| D | G |
Ha'ina mai ka puana
| | D |
Nā dewdrops a ke aloha
| B7 | E7 |
Ha'ina hou ka puana
| A7 | D |
He aloha nō he aloha

This is the end of my song
About the dewdrops of love
Again I offer my song
A song of love to my beloved

This song by Bill Ali'iloa Lincoln tells of the tender leaf buds of the sandalwood tree, dainty and delicate. Combined with the scent of maile in a shady secluded spot, the poet creates a romantic setting with a sweetheart. 1897.

He Mele Aloha

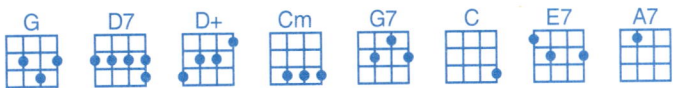

Pua Līlia

G
'Auhea wale 'oe e ka ua
D7
Ke nihi a'e nei i nā pali
Ka helena o ia pua i 'ako 'ia
D+   G D7
Ke popohe mai nei ia uka
G
Ia uka ho'i a'u e walea ai
G7   C
Ke 'ala onaona o ku'u pua
Cm   G   E7
He pua 'oe na'u e lei mau ai
A7   D7   G
Ke 'ala ku'u pua līlia

Where could you be, oh rain
Moving softly over the cliffs
The appearance of this flower which was chosen
Blossoming forth in the highlands
Those lofty heights where I enjoyed
The sweet perfume of my sweet bloom
You are a flower to always wear as my lei
The sweet scent of my lily blossom

Alfred U. 'Alohikea wrote this in 1916. George Kanahele's Hawaiian Music and Musicians *is a excellent source for those seeking a deeper technical understanding of Hawaiian music, as evidenced by his comments on* Pua Līlia. *" 'Alohikea's compositions are characteristically Hawaiian in expression....[Pua Līlia] has a very wide range marked by large leaps which enable the Hawaiian singer to use the much-admired quality of "breaking" the voice, produced by changing voice registers... He also leads into a phrase by a half-step movement upward which is contrasted to larger intervallic leaps that follow. This contrasting pattern clearly reveals 'Alohikea's skill as a composer who knew what was pleasing to the Hawaiian ear... He uses the familiar device of grouping three notes together, occasionally five, ending on a prolonged pitch. If musically 'Alohikea's songs sound more Hawaiian than others, it is attributable partly to his philosophy of composition and partly to his understanding of his Hawaiianness." (Kanahele 15)*

He Mele Aloha

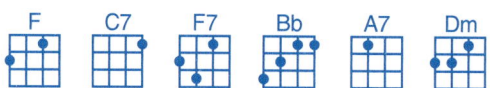

Pua Līlīlehua

| F | C7 | F | F7 |
'Auhea wale ana 'oe
| Bb | F | C7 |
E ka pua līlīlehua
| F | A7 | Dm |
A he ipo ho'ohenoheno
| Bb | F | C7 | F |
E ho'ohihi ai nō ka mana'o

This is to you
O sage blossom
A cherished sweetheart
That attracts the mind

| F | C7 | F | F7 |
Iā 'oe e 'imi ana
| Bb | F | C7 |
I nā nani o ka 'āina
| F | A7 | Dm |
Eia nō lā au ma 'ane'i
| Bb | F | C7 | F |
E kali ana i kou ho'i mai

While you go seeking
Among the beauties of the land
Right here I remain
Waiting for your return

| F | C7 | F | F7 |
E 'alawa mai ho'i 'oe
| Bb | F | C7 |
I nei mau maka onaona
| F | A7 | Dm |
He mau maka poina 'ole
| Bb | F | C7 | F |
E kapalili ai ko pu'uwai

Glance quickly this way
At these inviting eyes
These unforgettable eyes
That make your heart flutter

| F | C7 | F | F7 |
Hilo pa'a 'ia ke aloha
| Bb | F | C7 |
I ka lino hilo pāwalu
| F | A7 | Dm |
'A'ohe mea e hemo ai
| Bb | F | C7 | F |
Me a'u 'oe a mau loa

Love is bound fast
With an eight-strand tie
There's nothing to separate
You're with me forever

| F | C7 | F | F7 |
Ha'ina mai ka puana
| Bb | F | C7 |
No ka pua līlīlehua
| F | A7 | Dm |
A he ipo ho'ohenoheno
| Bb | F | C7 | F |
E ho'ohihi ai nō ka mana'o

The story is told
For you o sage blossom
A cherished sweetheart
That attracts the mind

Mary Kawena Pukui and Kahauanu Lake composed this for Ma'iki Aiu Lake, and it is danced today with much aloha by her many students and disciples. Ma'iki was raised in Pālolo, and was thus given the lyrical name Līlīlehua after the famous rain goddess of that name, a legendary lady of Pālolo who was courted by a mo'o. The lady had a human sweetheart; of course the mo'o was jealous. Līlīlehua is also a little wild sage, one which makes a small paintbrush-like flower with red bristles about an inch high. Translation by Mary Kawena Pukui.

He Mele Aloha

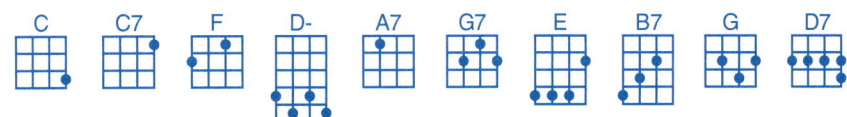

Pua Mae ʻOle

C   C7 F   D-   C A7

  C   C7 F   D-   C A7
Kuʻu pua, kuʻu pua mae ʻole
 F   G7   C   G7
Nou mau koʻu liʻa ʻana
 C C7 F   D-   C   A7
He nohea ʻoe i kuʻu maka lā
 F   G7   C
A no nā kau a kau

My blossom, my unfading flower
My hopes are always for you
You are beautiful in my sight
Now and forever

hui

 E   B7   E
Nani, he uʻi ka wahine lā
   G   D7   G7
A he lei wehi no nā kūpuna
 C C7 F   D-   C A7
Kuʻu pua, kuʻu pua mae ʻole
 F   G7   C
Nou kuʻu mele nei

chorus:
Beautiful, the woman is lovely
And an adorning lei for the elders
My blossom, my unfading flower
For you is this song of mine

John "Squeeze" Kamana left us not only this song, but the story of its creation. Squeeze had the music in his mind as early as 1933, in the days when he would sit under the tree on the beach by the Moana Hotel playing music and watching his young daughter, Leone Kananipuamaeʻole, play in the water. But it wasn't until 1954, that the poetry came to him, a song complete, when he visualized her running up from the water, blossoming from a small child into a beautiful grown woman. It was the Prize Song for Kamehameha School song contest in 1955, and a favorite of Alfred Apaka.

Pua O Ka Mākāhala

'Auhea wale ana 'oe, ē
Ka pua o ka mākāhala
Mai ho'ohala mai 'oe, ē
I ka pilina ua pa'a

Where indeed are you
O blossom of the mākāhala
You should not find fault
In a relationship that is secure

Keu nō paha ua pa'a, ē
Kou mana'o i 'ane'i
Pili 'ia aku 'oe, ē
Ko lā he kanaka u'i

One would think it was settled
Your thoughts would be right here
And yet you are lingering elsewhere
In these days of your beautiful youth

Nele i ka mea poepoe, ē
Pau ka pilina ua pa'a
Ha'ina mai ka puana, ē
Ka pua o ka mākāhala

But lacking the round thing, coin
That stable tie is ended
Tell the story in the refrain
The blossom of the mākāhala

Katie Stevens 'Ī'ī writes of the mākāhala, a twining shrub. While the plant may be on one's property, the flowers may wander afar. This metaphor describes a lover who strays, enjoying the prowess of youth and beauty, but when the money is gone, the affair is done. 1916.

He Mele Aloha

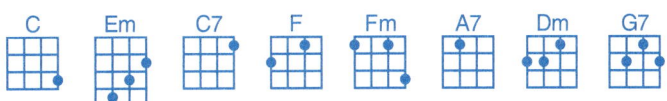

Pua ʻŌlena

C   **Em**
 Pua ʻōlena, pua moe wale
 C7   **F**
 I ka nahele e moe nei
 Fm
 Ka ua noe makaliʻi
       C   **A7**   **Dm**
 E ala mai, hōʻike mai i kou nani
      G7   **C**
 Pua ʻōlena, pua ʻōlena
	ʻŌlena flower, blossom that sleeps
	 In the forest, slumbering
	 The fine, misty rains appear
	 Awaken, display your beauty
	 ʻŌlena flower, ʻōlena flower

C   **Em**
 Pua ʻōlena, dream filled beauty
       C7   **F**
 Of my garden deep in slumber
            Fm
 Kissed by misty summer rain
                  C   **A7**   **Dm**
 Come with me, come let's see of your beauty
      G7   **C**
 Pua ʻōlena, pua ʻōlena	

C   **Em**
 Lau ʻōlena, lau pālulu
 C7   **F**
 E peʻe nei kau mōhala
        Fm
 ʻO ka makani hāwanawana
            C   **A7**   **Dm**
 Hōʻike nei, pua ʻōlena, i kou nani
      G7   **C**
 Pua ʻōlena, pua ʻōlena
	ʻŌlena leaf, sheltering
	 Your blossoming forth is concealed
	 The wind whispers to you
	 ʻŌlena flower, show your beauty
	 ʻŌlena flower, ʻōlena flower

C   **Em**
 Haʻina mai ka puana
       C7   **F**
 Pua moe wale, pua moe ʻole
      Fm
 I ka nahele o Hanalei
                  C   **A7**   **Dm**
 Come with me, come let's see of your beauty
      G7   **C**
 Pua ʻōlena, pua ʻōlena
	The story is in the refrain
	 Of the slumbering flower
	    not really asleep
	 In the forest of Hanalei
	 Come with me, come let's see of
	    your beauty
	 ʻŌlena flower, ʻōlena flower

The ʻōlena blossom hides under the thickness of its own leaves, emerging to be seen only briefly during its flowering span, then returning to dormancy in this song by James Kalei Kaholokula, Sr. The choice of a particular flower is an effective metaphor in Hawaiian poetry, allowing particular attributes to invoke images or imply kaona.

He Mele Aloha

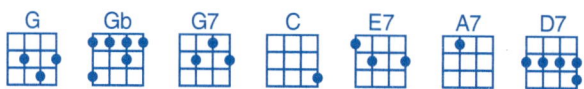

Pua Tuberose

| G Gb G G7 C E7 A7
E kau mai ana nō ka hali'a
D7 G
No sweet tuberose poina 'ole

The sudden remembrance comes to me
For the sweet tuberose, so unforgettable

G Gb G G7 C E7 A7
Me he ala nō e 'ī mai ana ia'u
D7 G
He welina pau 'ole me ia pua

As though it were saying to me
An endless affection is there with this flower

G Gb G G7 C E7 A7
Aloha ku'u pua 'ala onaona
D7 G
I wili 'ia me maile lauli'i

Beloved is my sweetly fragrant flower
Entwined with the dainty leafed maile

G Gb G G7 C E7 A7
Ke hea nei ku'u lei 'ala onaona
D7 G
E ho'i mai kāua lā e pili

My sweetly fragrant lei beckons to me
To return so that we may be together

G Gb G G7 C E7 A7
Ha'ina 'ia mai ana ka puana
D7 G
Ku'u pua tuberose poina 'ole

The story is told in the refrain
Of my dear tuberose, so unforgettable

Kimo Kamana compares memories of a sweetheart to the heady scent of tuberose twined with fragrant maile beckoning for a return to love. 1928.

He Mele Aloha

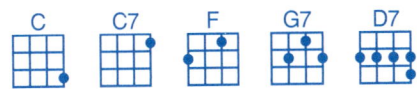

Puamana

C   C7   F   C
Puamana, ku'u home i Lahaina

G7
Me nā pua 'ala onaona
D7   G7   C
Ku'u home i aloha 'ia

Puamana, my home in Lahaina
With abundant sweet smelling flowers
My home, much beloved

C   C7   F   C
Ku'u home i ka ulu o ka niu
G7
'O ka niu kū kilakila
D7   G7   C
He napenape mālie

There is my home, in the grove of coco palms
The coconut trees standing majestic
Gently swaying and rustling

C   C7   F   C
Home nani, home i ka 'ae kai
G7
Ke kōnane a ka mahina
D7   G7   C
I ke kai hāwanawana

Beautiful home, home at the edge of the sea
Bright beams of moonlight
Dance on the whispering sea

C   C7   F   C
Ha'ina 'ia mai ka puana
G7
Ku'u home i Lahaina
D7   G7   C
I piha me ka hau'oli

The refrain is told
Of my home in Lahaina
So filled with happiness

This was Irmgard Farden Aluli's first hit, composed in 1937, and telling of the Farden family home in Lahaina. An English version was later written and recorded as the popular Sea Breeze by Genoa Keawe. Irmgard Aluli was 65 years old when, in 1978, she started playing music with her two daughters, Mihana and Neaulani, and later her niece, Luanna and her third daughter 'Ā'ima. The elegant and popular group sang every weekend for the next 20-plus years. Translation by Carol Silva.

He Mele Aloha

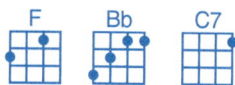

Pulupē Nei ʻIli I Ke Anu

[F] Uluwehi nā luna i Lani[Bb]hu[F]li
Pulupē i ka nihi a ka [C7]ua
A [F]ʻo ʻoe a ʻo wau i [Bb]lai[F]la
I ke [C7]onaona o ka na[F]hele

The heights of Lanihuli are verdant
Soaked by the sweep of the rain
And you and I are there
Amid the sweet scents of the forest

🎸 hui

[F] Pulupē nei ʻili i ke [Bb]a[F]nu
A he anu mea ʻole i ka mana[C7]ʻo
[F]ʻO ka ʻike iā ʻoe, e ke a[Bb]lo[F]ha
Hoʻi [C7]pono ka ʻiʻini iā lo[F]ko

chorus:
My skin is wet and chilled
But the cold is as naught to me
The sight of you, my love
Brings desire right back to the heart

[F] I laila liʻa ka ma[Bb]na[F]ʻo
Pūkuʻi i ke anu a ka [C7]ua
Ko[F]lonahe aʻela i ka [Bb]u[F]ka
Me ke [C7]kēhau o ka na[F]hele

There desires are stirred
Crouching in the chill of the rain
As it gently slips through the uplands
With the cool dew of the forest

[F] E maliu mai ʻoe, e ke [Bb]a[F]loha
Kuʻu dear love o ka pō la[C7]ʻi
[F]Buenos once more, e ke [Bb]ho[F]a
Koʻu [C7]time huli hoʻi kē[F]ia

Give me your attention, my beloved
My dear love of the still night
Good bye once more, my companion
It's time to take my leave

This traditional song describes beautiful Lanihuli, the peak above the western side of the Pali lookout. Chill and cold often appear in Hawaiian poetry to describe the physical sensations of love and desire. The images of crouching with a loved one in the cool rain of a fragrant forest portrays quite an intimate setting. 1916.

233
He Mele Aloha

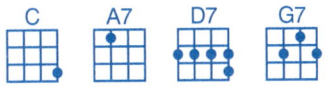

Punalu'u

    C   A7
Onaona 'o Punalu'u
        D7
Sweet i ka līlia
         C
Ke 'ala o ka hīnano
G7   C
Ho'ohenoheno i ka poli

   C   A7
He nani nō ka 'ikena
         D7
Ke kai e nehe nei
       C
Ke kai hāwanawana
G7   C
Nanea ho'olohe aku

 C   A7
He beauty nō ka naupaka
        D7
Pua pili kahakai
          C
He ho'okahi nō 'ao'ao
G7   C
Ka lihilihi o ia pua

  C   A7
He ho'okahi nō 'oe
         D7
Ke 'ike iā Punalu'u
         C
Ke ahe a ka makani
G7   C
He 'olu'olu ka 'āina

  C   A7
Ha'ina mai ka puana
        D7
No Punalu'u aloha
        C
Ke 'ala o ka hīnano
G7   C
Ho'ohenoheno i ka poli

Fragrant is Punalu'u
Sweet with the scent of lilies
The perfume of the hīnano blossom
Stirs affection in the heart

Beautiful is the scene
Of the ocean nuzzling the shore
The sea that softly whispers
A delight to listen to

The naupaka is a beauty
A blossom that clings to the shore
There's but one side
To the petals of that flower

There's but one of you
When one sees Punalu'u
The gentle touch of the breeze
Brings comfort to the land

Tell, then, the story
Of beloved Punalu'u
Where the perfume of hīnano blossoms
Stirs affection in the heart

Composed by Mary Kawena Pukui and Irmgard Aluli honoring the beauty of Punalu'u's coast line, on O'ahu.

He Mele Aloha

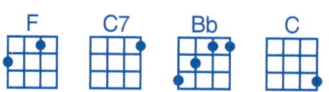

Pūpū Hinuhinu

    C7   F   C7
Kāhuli aku, kāhuli mai
        Bb   C   F
Kāhuli lei 'ula, lei 'ākōlea
 C7   F   Bb   F
Kōlea, kōlea, ki'i i ka wai
 C7   F   C7   F
Wai 'ākōlea, wai 'ākōlea

     Forest shells here and there
     Red lei of forest shells, like a lei of 'ākōlea
     Plover, plover, fetch the nectar
     Nectar of 'ākōlea, Nector of 'ākōlea

🎸 *hui*
   F   C7   F   C7
Pūpū hinuhinu
   F   Bb   F   C7
Pūpū hinuhinu ē

opening chorus:
Shiny shells
Shiny shells

  F   Bb   F Bb
O ke kahakai, kahakai ē
  F   C7   F
Pūpū hinuhinu ē

Of the shore, the shore
Shiny shells

 F   Bb   F Bb
E lohe kākou ē
 F   C7   F
Pūpū hinuhinu ē

Let us listen
Shiny shells

 F   Bb F Bb
E moe, e moe ē
 F   C7   F
Pūpū hinuhinu ē

Rest, rest well
Shiny shells

Pūpū hinuhinu ē
 F   Bb   F Bb
E moe, e moe ē,
 F   C7 F
E moe ē

Rest, rest well
Do rest well

When Nona Beamer was a child, her Sweetheart Grandma, Helen Desha Beamer, wrote this song in English about shiny seashells, for her mo'opuna. Years later, when Nona was herself a mother, she composed a version in Hawaiian, incorporating a stanza from an old chant about the native Hawaiian land shells and golden plover in recollection of many happy days at the black sand beach on the island of Hawai'i. This song and hula is a favorite of Hawaii's children. 1950.

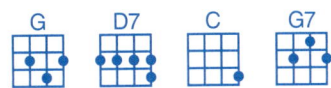

Pūpū A'o 'Ewa

    G   D7   G
Nani Ka'ala hemolele i ka mālie
    D7   G
Kuahiwi kaulana a'o 'Ewa
   G   G7   C
E ki'i ana i ka makani o ka 'āina
        D7   G
Hea ka Moa'e, "Eia au e ke aloha"

Beautiful is Ka'ala, flawless in the calm
Renowned mountain of the 'Ewa district
Fetching the wind of the land
The Moa'e wind beckons, "Here I am my love"

🎸 *hui*

     G
    Pūpū a'o 'Ewa
                 G7
    I ka nu'a nā kānaka
       C
    E naue mai a e 'ike
        D7
    I ka mea hou o ka 'āina
      G   G7
    A he 'āina ua kaulana
      C
    Mai nā kūpuna mai
       G   D7   G
    Alahula Pu'uloa ke ala hele no Ka'ahupāhau
      D7   G
    Alahula Pu'uloa ke ala hele no Ka'ahupāhau

chorus:
Shells of 'Ewa
Amid throngs of people
Hasten here and learn
The news of the land
A land renowned
From the ancient ones
Pu'uloa is a famous pathway
The pathway for Ka'ahupāhau

 G   D7   G
Kilakila 'o Polea noho i ka 'olu
    D7   G
Ia home ho'ohihi a ka malihini
           G7   C
E walea ana i ka 'olu o ke kiawe
    D7   G
I ka pā kolonahe a ke Kiu

Majestic is Polea settled in comfort
A home delightful to visitors
Relaxing in the cool shade of the kiawe trees
And the soft blowing of the Kiu wind

Kawaihau Glee Club was said to have sung this song regularly. This song is also known as Ka'ahupāhau, *who was the benevolent shark goddess of the loch Pu'uloa. The people of this area revered her, and she in turn took care of them while in these waters. 1870s.*

236
He Mele Aloha

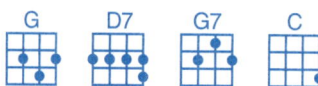

Pu'uohulu

    G   D7   G   G7
'O ka loku hala 'ole
   C   D7   G   D7
A ka ua i Mā'ili
   G   D7   G
Ili hewa ka mana'o i 'ane'i
        D7   G
Ka waiho lahalaha i ka la'i

The ceaseless deluge
Of the rain at Mā'ili
Brings on a disturbing thought
Affecting my peace of mind

🎸 *hui*

    G   D7   G   G7
'O 'oe ka i huia ihola
    C   D7   G D7
Ka mana'o e puapua'i ala
  G   D7   G
Eia a'e 'o Pu'uohulu
    D7   G
Hulu nō au ua hiki nō

chorus:
You're the one that has brought about
The feelings that well up in me
Pu'uohulu hill appears
And I feel the same, but it's okay

G   D7   G   G7
Na'u i lāhui i ka leo
  C   D7   G D7
'Ike i ka makani Kaiāulu
      G   D7 G
Ka makani o ka 'āina
  D7   G
I laila ho'ola'i nā manu

It is I who forbade the discussion
Take note of the Kaiāulu breeze
The famous breeze of the land
That is where the birds poise aloft

Eliza Ha'aheo Holt uses the pouring rains as a symbol of grief over a lost love. Mā'ili, Wai'anae, is known for its gentle Kaiāulu wind. 1897.

He Mele Aloha

Pu'uwa'awa'a

C F G7 C
Kipa i ka 'olu o Pu'uwa'awa'a
Ab C
E hi'i 'ia maila e Hualālai
G7 E7 Am D7
Ia home i puīa me ke aloha
G D7 G G7
Pihanakalani wehi i ka pua

hui

C F G7 C
'O ka 'olu'olu nō me ka nahenahe
F G7 C
Ke kuini maoli pua o ka home
G7 E7 Am D7
Ke ali'i hele loa 'oe 'o Kina'u
G D7 G G7
Ke ali'i wahine o Pu'uwa'awa'a
C F G7 C
Pumehana ke aloha o Lope Haina
B7 Em G7
Keiki o ka 'āina ha'aheo
C F G7 C Ab
Hanohano Hawai'i ua ki'eki'e
C Am F G7 C
Kilohana nā kuahiwi 'ekolu

Visit the comfort of Pu'uwa'awa'a
In the embrace of Hualālai
That home imbued with love
Mystic garden filled with flowers

chorus:
Pleasantness and gentleness
Reign in this home
Kīna'u, your rule is extensive
As the chiefess of Pu'uwa'awa'a
Robert Hind gives warm welcome
Son of the proud land
Glorious is Hawaii, majestic
With the adornment of the three mountains

The Hawai'i ranches each vied with the next in beauty and hospitality, and none out did Pu'uwa'awa'a, owned by the Hinds. Mary E. Low wrote the words and Ernest Kaleihoku Ka'ai the music to this mele pana. 1920s.

Queen's Jubilee

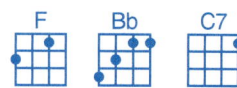

F	Bb F	Bb F

Mahalo piha mōʻī o ʻEnelani
Kuʻi kou kaulana nā ʻāina pau
Nā kai ʻākau, nā one hema
ʻIkea kou ʻihi mana nui
Eia mākou i kou kapa kai
I kou lā nui jubilī
I hiʻi mai i ko mākou aloha
Ma luna ou ka malu o ka lani

All hail to thee Great Queen of England
Fair Queen who rul'st o'er land and sea
From Northern seas to southern shores
Thy sway is known both far and near
We come to thy shores most gracious Lady
On this great day of thy Jubilee
To bring kind greetings from afar
May Heaven bless thee, long mayst thou reign

Hauʻoliʻoli ʻemepela o ʻĪnia
I kēia makahiki jubilī
ʻĀkoakoa nā aliʻi ʻaimoku
A puni ke ao holoʻokoʻa
E hiʻilani, e mililani
Ua hui pū ʻia me Hawaiʻi
E uhi mai ka lani i kona nani
E ola ka mōʻī i ke akua

All hail, all hail, Empress of India
In this thy year of Jubilee
Now kings and queens and princes great
Have all assembled here today
To pay due homage and reverent love
Hawaiʻi joins with loyal fervor
May heaven shed her smiles on thee
God bless the Queen, long may she live

Written by Queen Liliʻuokalani for Queen Victoria on the occasion of her 50th year jubilee in 1887. Translation by Liliʻuokalani.

He Mele Aloha

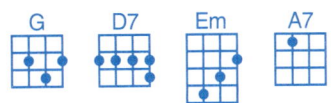

Queen's Prayer

    G   D7   Em
'O kou aloha nō
 A7   D7
Aia i ka lani
       G   C
A 'o kou 'oia'i'o
    G   D7   G
He hemolele ho'i

Oh Lord thy loving mercy
Is high as the heavens
It tells us of thy truth
And 'tis filled with holiness

   G   D7   Em
Ko'u noho mihi 'ana
  A7   D7
A pa'ahao 'ia
     G   C
'O 'oe ku'u lama
    G   D7   G
Kou nani, ko'u ko'o

Whilst humbly meditating
Within these walls imprisoned
Thou art my light, my haven
Thy glory my support

   G   D7   Em
Mai nānā 'ino'ino
 A7   D7
Nā hewa o kānaka
   G   C
Akā e huikala
    G   D7   G
A ma'ema'e nō

Oh look not on their failings
Nor on the sins of men
Forgive with loving kindness
That we might be made pure

  G   D7   Em
No laila e ka Haku
  A7   D7
Ma lalo o kou 'ēheu
   G   C
Ko mākou maluhia
    G   D7   G
A mau loa aku nō
  C G
  'Āmene

For Thy grace I beseech thee
Bring us 'neath thy protection
And peace will be our portion
Now and forevermore
    Amen

Originally entitled Ke Aloha o Ka Haku, *this saddest and most forgiving of songs was written by Queen Lili'uokalani in 1895 after seven weeks of imprisonment. She entitled the translation* The Lord's Mercy. *Translation by Lili'uokalani.*

He Mele Aloha

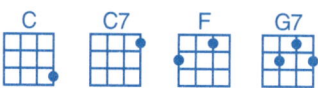

Radio Hula

```
  C        C7    F       C
He aha nei hana a ka radio
       G7              C
A ka nui manu aʻe liʻa mau nei
```
What is the radio doing
That so entices the flocks of birds

```
  C       C7     F      C
Ua hana ʻia oe me ka noʻeau
       G7              C
Na ka ʻili puakea piha akamai
```
You were crafted with skill
By the fair-skinned ones, so smart

```
  C       C7      F        C
Me he ala nō e ʻī mai ana iaʻu
      G7              C
E kiss mālie ʻoe, e ke aloha
```
It's as though you were saying to me
Kiss gently, oh my love

```
  C       C7      F      C
Nāna i hoʻohui nā ʻailana
          G7             C
ʻIke ʻia ʻo Hawaiʻi nō e ka ʻoi
```
That one has united all the islands
It's known that Hawaiʻi is the best

```
   C       C7     F      C
Haʻina ʻia mai ana ka puana
         G7              C
Be still, mālie ʻoe, e ke aloha
```
Let the story be told in the song
Be still, be calm, my love

By Lizzie ʻAlohikea, in the 1920s.

He Mele Aloha

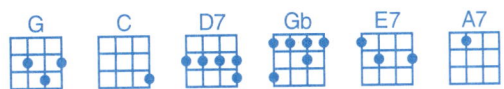

Roselani Blossom

G	C D7
'Auhea wale ana 'oe	Where could you be
Gb G	O bud of the lokelani blossom
E ka liko pua lokelani	You are a heavenly being for me
E7 A7	Now and forever
He lani nui 'oe na'u	
D7 G	
No nā kau a kau	

G · C D7
Kau nui aku ka mana'o
         Gb G
I ka wai a'o 'Īao
  E7   A7
Ua inu au a kena
D7   G
I ka 'ono a'o ia wai

One's thoughts are always drawn
To the waters of 'Īao
I have slaked my thirst
On that sweet water

G   C D7
Eia i ka pu'uwai
           Gb G
Ka 'i'ini no ka ipo li'a
    E7   A7
'O ka li'a 'oe a loko
D7   G
Honehone i ku'u manawa

Here in the heart
Is the yearning for the beloved
You are the innermost desire
Teasing at my emotions

G   C D7
Ua like nō a like
       Gb G
Ka 'ano'i a ke aloha
    E7   A7
He aloha i hi'ipoi 'ia
D7   G
I 'apo pūlama 'ia

Just exactly the same
Is the desire and the affection
An affection that is cherished
Embraced as precious

G   C D7
Ha'ina mai ka puana
        Gb G
'O Maui nō ē ka 'oi
   E7   A7
Ka liko pua lokelani
D7   G
Ku'u lei 'ala onaona

Tell the story in refrain
Maui indeed is the finest
The bud of the lokelani blossom
Is my garland of fragrance

John Kameaaloha Almeida speaks with a passion that transcends even this flower special to Maui, and the satisfaction of having slaked his thirst on the waters of 'Īao.

Royal Hawaiian Hotel

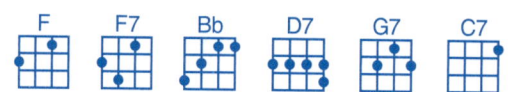

    F   F7
Uluwehiwehi ʻoe i kaʻu ʻike lā
  Bb   D7   G7
E ka Royal Hawaiian Hotel

          You are glorious in my sight
          Oh, Royal Hawaiian Hotel

hui

  G7   C7
A he nani lā, ke hulali nei
               F
A he nani maoli nō

chorus:
Lovely, sparkling there
Truly a thing of beauty

 F   F7
Ka moena weleweka moe kāua lā
 Bb   D7   G7
He pakika he paheʻe maikaʻi nei

The beds are velvet, let us lie down
So smooth and slippery

 F   F7
Ka paia māpala ʻōmaʻomaʻo lā
 Bb   D7   G7
He pipiʻo mau ē ke ānuenue

The walls are green marble
The rainbow arches above

 F   F7
ʻO ka hone a ke kai i ka puʻu one lā
 Bb   D7   G7
Me ke ʻala līpoa e moani nei

The sea murmurs on the sand dunes
And the scent of līpoa is carried in

 F   F7
ʻO ka holu nape a ka lau o ka niu lā
 Bb   D7 G7
I ke kulukulu aumoe

The coconut fronds rustle
In the late night hours

 F   F7
E ō e ka Royal Hawaiian Hotel
 Bb   D7   G7
Kou inoa hanohano ia lā

We laud you, Royal Hawaiian Hotel
Your name is a grand one

Mary Pūlaʻa Robins wrote this song for the grand opening of the Royal Hawaiian Hotel in 1927.

243
He Mele Aloha

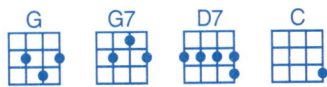

Sanoe

'Auhea 'oe e Sanoe (G G7 C)
Ho'opulu liko ka lehua (D7 G D7)
Eia ho'i au (G G7 C)
Ke kali nei i ka leo (G D7 G)

hui

'O ka pane wale mai nō (G G7 C)
'Olu au me he wai ala (D7 G)
Honehone me he ipo ala (G7 C)
Paila i ka nui kino (D7 G)

E kala nēia kino (G G7 C)
I piliwi ai i laila (D7 G D7)
Pehea e hiki ai? (G G7 C)
E kō ai 'o ka mana'o? (G D7 G)

Ke hea mai nei Water Lily (G G7 C)
E ao mai 'oe iā kāua (D7 G D7)
Eia a'e nō 'o Pelo (G G7 C)
Manu 'āha'i 'ōlelo (G D7 G)

Lohe aku nei nā kuhina nui (G G7 C)
A he 'ahahui ko Loma (D7 G D7)
Ke 'oni a'ela i luna (G G7 C)
E like me Likelike (G D7 G)

Where are you, Sanoe
You who dampens the young lehua leaf buds
Here I am
Waiting for your voice

chorus:
With just your response
I am content like a water's flow
Attuned to the sweet sound as if from a sweetheart
That tingles throughout my person

My entire being has so long
Believed in what is there
How can it come to be?
How can my wishes come to pass?

Water Lily is calling
For you to be watchful over us
Here comes Pelo
A bird who spreads the news

The great leaders have heard
And Rome has its own association
It moves skyward
Similar to Likelike

This song, written to honor Likelike by Princess Lili'uokalani and her friend, Elizabeth Achuck, is full of court intrigue, which is discussed in The Queen's Songbook. *Sanoe (kanoe), the mist, referred to the Queen's people, the Queen awaits their will. 1870s. Translation by Hui Hānai.*

Sassy

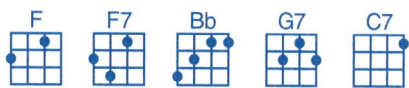

[F]Kaikamahine no Iwilei [F7]lā
[Bb]Sassy hoʻi kāu lewa [F]ʻana
Ua maʻa wale i ka ʻai ʻalamihi [G7]lā
[C7]Sassy hoʻi kāu lewa [F]ʻana

[F]Kaikamahine no Kalihi [F7]lā
[Bb]Sassy hoʻi kāu lewa [F]ʻana
Ua maʻa wale i ka inu pia [G7]lā
[C7]Sassy hoʻi kāu lewa [F]ʻana

[F]Kaikamahine no Kapālama [F7]lā
[Bb]Sassy hoʻi kāu lewa [F]ʻana
Ua maʻa wale i ka ʻai laiki [G7]lā
[C7]Sassy hoʻi kāu lewa [F]ʻana

[F]Kaikamahine no Kakaʻako [F7]lā
[Bb]Sassy hoʻi kāu lewa [F]ʻana
Aia i ka papa ABC [G7]lā
[C7]Sassy hoʻi kāu lewa [F]ʻana

[F]Wahine haole no ka Moana Hōkele [F7]lā
[Bb]Sassy hoʻi kāu lewa [F]ʻana
ʻElua kālā me ka hapalua [G7]lā
[C7]Sassy hoʻi kāu lewa [F]ʻana

Girl of Iwilei
Sassy straying
Always eating black crabs
Sassy straying

Girl of Kalihi
Sassy straying
Always drinking beer
Sassy straying

Girl of Kapālama
Sassy straying
Always eating rice
Sassy straying

Girl of Kakaʻako
Sassy straying
There in the ABC class
Sassy straying

White woman of the Moana Hotel
Sassy straying
Two dollars and a half
Sassy straying

[F]Kaikamahine no Wai[F7]kīkī lā
[Bb]Sassy hoʻi kāu [F]lewa ʻana
Ua maʻa wale i ke [G7]ʻai līpoa lā
[C7]Sassy hoʻi kāu [F]lewa ʻana

Girl of Waikīkī
Sassy straying
Always eating seaweed
Sassy straying

[F]Kaikamahine no Wai[F7]ʻalae lā
[Bb]Sassy hoʻi kāu [F]lewa ʻana
Ua maʻa wale i ke [G7]kau ʻēkake lā
[C7]Sassy hoʻi kāu [F]lewa ʻana

Girl of Waiʻalae
Sassy straying
Always riding a donkey
Sassy straying

[F]Haʻina ʻia mai ana [F7]ka puana lā
[Bb]Sassy hoʻi kāu [F]lewa ʻana
Ua maʻa wale i ke [G7]kau ʻēkake lā
[C7]Sassy hoʻi kāu [F]lewa ʻana

Tell the refrain
Sassy straying
Always riding a donkey
Sassy straying

This song, composed in the 1890s and credited to J. Kokolia as well as to Solomon Hiram, "honors sassy girls in various places, beginning with the then notorious Iwilei district in Honolulu and eastward as far as Waiʻalae, mentioning alleged characteristics of each place. This use of place names and descriptive epithets is popular in songs..." (Elbert 90).

He Mele Aloha

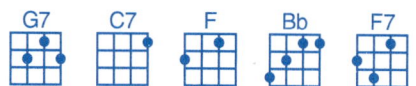

Song of Old Hawai'i

G7   C7   F
There is a melody
G7   C7   F
Forever haunting me
Bb   F
A thousand times retold
      G7   C7
A theme that's never old

          F   C7
There's the perfume of a million flowers
                 F   C7
Clinging to the heart of old Hawai'i
        F   C7
There's a rainbow following the showers
                     F
Bringing me a part of old Hawai'i

F7   Bb   F
There's a silver moon, a symphony of stars
       G7   C7
There's a hula tune, and the hum of soft guitars
     F   C7
There's a trade wind sighing in the heavens
                  F
Singing me a song of old Hawai'i

There are several hapa-haole songs like this one by Gordon Beecher with an introductory passage that few can recall, although "There is a perfume of a million flowers" is familiar to many. 1938.

He Mele Aloha

Stevedore Hula

[Chords: Am E7 G7 C A7 D7]

Am   E7   Am

Eia mai nā kipikoa

E7   Am   G7

Ke holuholu nei kīkala

C   A7   D7

'Ehehē iho ai ko 'aka

G7   C   E7

He suipa lilo mai ho'i kau

Here are the stevedores

Swinging their hips

How catching is your laughter

That sweeps all!

Am   E7   Am

Ne'e i mua me ka hau'oli

E7   Am G7

I 'ō i 'ane'i kau mai i luna

C   A7   D7

Go all around a lūlū lima

G7   C   E7

'O Uese 'oe let-a-go your blouse

Glide on forward with gusto

Near and far and way up high

Go all about shaking hands

You, Sweetie, let-a-go your blouse

Am   E7   Am

Nā kipikoa ua kaulana

E7   Am G7

Nā keiki Hawai'i hana no'eau

C   A7   D7

Hā'awi ke aloha me ka 'eha koni

G7   C E7

Me ka Hawaiian hospitality

The stevedores are renowned

The Hawaiian boys so clever in their work

Give love with a throbbing passion

With Hawaiian hospitality

Am   E7   Am

Ha'ina hou mai ana ka puana

E7   Am G7

Nā keiki Hawai'i hana no'eau

C   A7   D7

Hā'awi ke aloha me ka 'eha koni

G7   C

He suipa lilo mai ho'i kau

The story is told again

About those Hawaiian boys so clever in their work

Give love with a throbbing passion

That sweeps all

Also known as Kipikoa, *Bina Mossman composed this song for her husband in the 1930s. The use of scattered English or Anglicized phrases is common in this era of Hawaiian music. For instance, "uwese" for sweetie, or "suipa" for sweep, and of course that kolohe "let-a-go your blouse."*

Sweet Lei Mamo

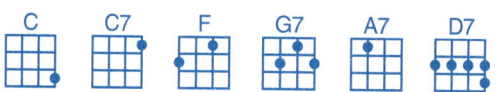

     C   C7
Wehiwehi ka uka i ka nahele
   F   C
Ka popohe lau o ka palai
C7   F   C
Hau lipolipo i ke onaona
     G7   C
Hoa pili o ke 'a'ali'i

The forest adorns the highlands
The lush fronds of fern
Hau, dense with fragrance
Is a companion of the 'a'ali'i

hui

 C   G7
Sweet lei mamo
         C
Lei o ke aloha
  C   C7   F A7 D7
Kāhiko nani o'u
G7   C
Sweet lei mamo

chorus:
Sweet garland of yellow lehua
Garland of affection
My beautiful adornment
Sweet garland of yellow lehua

    C   C7
Ka uhi pa'a a ka noe
 F   C   C7
Ka luna 'olu o Kilohana
 F   C
I laila ho'i au i 'ike ai
    G7   C
Kahi wai hu'i o Leialoha

The soft mist enfolds
The gentle peaks of Kilohana
It is there that I witnessed
The bracing cool waters of Leialoha

     C   C7
Honehone leo o ke kāhuli
    F   C
Leo le'a o ka wao kele
C7   C
Ka 'i'iwi ka hoa e like ai
    G7   C
My sweet Lei Mamo

The sweet trill of the land shell
Cheery voice of the rain forest
The 'i'iwi is one that compares
To my sweet garland of yellow lehua

It is assumed that the mamo referred to here is the yellow lehua, much prized for lei and mentioned here with other forest plants. The yellow feathers of the mamo bird were also fashioned into precious garlands worn by royalty in ancient times.

Sweet Lei Mokihana

   C   F   C   G7   C A7
Sweet lei mokihana 'auhea 'oe
   D7   G7   C
Ku'u lei nani 'oe poina 'ole

   C   F   C   G7   C A7
Ho'ohihi ka mana'o iā Hanalei
   D7   G7   C
Hanohano nō 'oe he nani maoli nō

   C   F   C   G7   C A7
Ka' ehu o ke kai a'o Hā'ena
   D7   G7   C
Laua'e o Makana, 'o Nāmolokama

   C   F C   G7   C A7
Ha'ina 'ia mai ana ka puana
   D7   G7   C
Sweet lei mokihana poina 'ole

Sweet lei of mokihana, this is for you
You are my lei of beauty so unforgettable

One's thoughts are captivated by Hanalei
You are truly grand, so beautiful indeed

The spray of the sea at Hā'ena
The laua'e of Makana, and Nāmolokama's cascading falls

Tell the story in the refrain
The sweet lei of mokihana is unforgettable

George Mānoa Huddy III wrote of the mokihana, an anise-scented, hard green berry, found in abundance only on Kaua'i. It was designated as Kauai's official lei by the Hawai'i Territorial Legislature in 1923. 1950s.

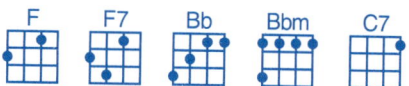

Sweet Leilani

    F   F7   Bb Bbm
Sweet Leilani, heavenly flower
F   C7   F
Nature fashioned roses kissed with dew
C7   F
And then she placed them in a bower
C7   F   C7
It was the start of you

    F   F7   Bb Bbm
Sweet Leilani, heavenly flower
F   C7   F
Tropic skies are jealous as they shine
C7   F
I think they're jealous of your blue eyes
C7   F   C7
Jealous because you're mine

    F   F7   Bb Bbm
Sweet Leilani, heavenly flower
F   C7   F
I dreamed of paradise for two
C7   F
You are my paradise completed
C7   G7   C7 F
You are my dream come true

"Few individual musicians have given Hawaiian music more national, if not international, exposure than Harry Owens. His biggest hit, Sweet Leilani, as recorded by Bing Crosby, was played on every radio station and every jukebox in the US. It was on the Hit Parade radio program for 28 consecutive weeks, a record that never was equaled. It was actually credited for helping to revive the American record industry during the Depression." (Kanahele 281) Sweet Leilani won the Oscar for best song in 1938.

Sweet Someone

Gm   **C**
Sweet someone
Gm   **C**
Whoever you may be
F   **Dm**
Sweet someone
F   **Dm**
You suit me to a "T"

Gm   **C**
Although you pay no attention
F   **D7**
To me at all
G7
One kiss and needless to mention
Bb   **C**
I had to fall

Bb   **C**
How I wonder
Bb   **C**
Who's keeping us apart
F   **Dm**
Don't blunder
F   **Dm**
And give away your heart

Gm   **C**
And when I whisper "I love you"
F   **D7**
And then you'll know
Gm   **C**
Sweet someone
Bb   **G7**   **C**   **F**
That you belong to me

This song by Gordon Waggner and Baron Keyes, while not a big hit on the mainland, captured the affection of the Hawaiian audience, and was on the best selling list in Hawai'i for many months. 1927.

Tewetewe

    G   C   G
'O'opu nui tewetewe
          C   G
Ta'a mai ana tewetewe
         D7
Pā i ka lani tewetewe
        G
Tōheoheo tewetewe

Big goby fish, arching
Moving along, arching
Touching the sky, arching
Froglike and strutting, arching

🎸 *hui*

  D7   G
Teketeke tewe tewe tewe

 G   C   G
'O'opu nui tewetewe
        C   G
Pa'a i ka lima tewetewe
        D7
Ke 'oni nei tewetewe
       G
Kūpaka nei tewetewe

Big goby fish, arching
Held fast in the hand, arching
Writhing there, arching
Bucking, arching

 G   C   G
'O'opu nui tewetewe
       C   G
Te tomo nei tewetewe
       D7
I ka 'upena tewetewe
      G
A kāua tewetewe

Big goby fish, arching
Entering now, arching
The fish net, arching
You and I crafted, arching

 G   C   G
'O'opu nui tewetewe
        C   G
E akahele 'oe tewetewe
         D7
O hemo a'e nei tewetewe
         G
Pa'a 'ole iā tāua tewetewe

Big goby fish, arching
Do be careful, arching
Lest you slip loose, arching
We haven't a good grasp, arching

Although this is not about fish, 'o'opu is a native freshwater goby; there are five species that are endemic to Hawaiian streams.

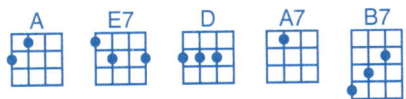

That's the Hawaiian in Me

A
I don't like shoes upon my feet
To be at ease is such a treat
E7
And smile at everyone I meet
A
That's the Hawaiian in me

A
I love to sing and dance for you
And give a lei to cheer you thru
E7
And with that goes a kiss or two
A
That's the Hawaiian in me

A7
It's great to be in Hawai'i
D
And be a native too
B7
But it's greater still to play around
E7
And carry on as I do

A
So right out here in Hawai'i
Where everything is heavenly
E7
I'm just as happy as can be
A
That's the Hawaiian in me

The original composition by Margarita Lane was augmented and arranged by Johnny Noble. 1936.

Toad Song

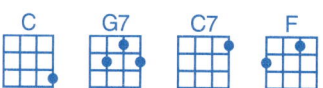

[C] He kani kapalili i ka pōuliuli 'o ke mele alo[G7]ha a polo[C]ka
E konikoni ana i ke ki'owai lepo me ka leo hea[G7]hea i ka i[C]po [C7]
[F] 'O ka hōkū 'imo'imo o ka lani lipolipo ke [C] kukui e hō'ike mai nei
He mana'olana kona i ka ho'oniponipo me ka [G7] ipo ho'ohenoheno ā[C]na

[C] Ua 'oli'oli 'o ia i ka pā 'olu'olu o ke kiliki[G7]lihune o ka [C] ua
I ho'olalilali i ka 'ili pu'upu'u ma ke [G7] kua 'ōma'oma'o o[C]na [C7]
[F] He kakali wale kona i ka lohe 'ia aku o [C] kāna mele o ke aumoe
A 'ume'ume 'ia kahi hoa kīkīkō'ele e ka [G7] leo mīkololo[C]hua

[C] Mai kinohi loa mai a i kēia pō ua lohe [G7] mau 'ia kāna [C] mele
Ma nā ki'owai lepo o nā 'āina like 'ole a [G7] hiki auane'i i 'ane'[C]i [C7]
[F] Ma waho iki aku o ka lumi moe o'u i ke [C] kulukulu o ke aumoe
Ha'ina ka puana no ka maka pu'upu'u i pili [C7] hala 'ole ke alo[C]ha

[C] A sound of wobble bobble in the glooming that's a looming
   it is the [G7] lovely crooning of the [C] Bufo
A throbbing and a bobbing in the muddle of the puddle
   with a [G7] voice of invitation to the [C] ipo [C7]
[F] The winking and the blinking of a star up afar
   is the [C] light by which one might be seeing
He's a foggin' in his noggin to be squeezin' and a teasin'
   with the [G7] one true love of his [C] dreamin'

[C]He's happy, snappy fellow in the touch, oh so mellow
      of the [G7]wisty misty falling of the [C]showers
That bring a slimy shine to the lumpy, bumpy kind of the
      [G7]dark green skin on his [C]shoul[C7]ders
He'll just [F]wait for a date til his song of the late night
      [C]hour finds the ear of his beloved
And brought for his selection is a mate of sweet perfection
      [G7]who is drawn by the eloquence [C]bestowed

[C]From the very start of time to the evening of this rhyme his
      [G7]crooning always found a willing [C]ear
In the muddy bogs and strands of so many different lands
      [G7]eventually arriving even [C]here [C7]
Just [F]there, close outside of this room where I reside
      wide [C]awake in the deepening of midnight
So let the tale be told of the lumpy, bumpy toad
      that has [G7]never failed to win his lovely [C]birthright

Puakea Nogelmeier writes of a trilling toad that becomes a metaphor for human relations — sing your own song, and there is someone just your flavor. This makes much use of devices of word play and sound repetition, which created a challenge when doing a lyric translation. The umpah goes something like "Oom mama oom bebe oom mama oom bebe oom ma oom." 1994.

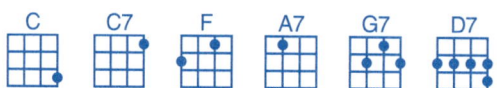

To You Sweetheart, Aloha

    C   C7   F A7 D7
To you, sweetheart, aloha
G7   C   G7
Aloha from the bottom of my heart
        C   C7
Keep the smile on your lips
      F   A7   D7
Brush the tear from your eyes
G7   C   G7
One more aloha, then it's time for goodbye

    C   C7   F A7 D7
To you, sweetheart, aloha
G7   E7
In dreams I'll be with you dear, tonight
        A7
And I'll pray for that day when
   D7
We two will meet again
      G7   C
Until then, sweetheart, aloha

Harry Owens published this song in 1935. Owens "gave up all other music for Hawaiian as soon as he landed in Honolulu. He tried to develop a blending of Hawaiian and the 'sweet corn' (his phrase) sound of mainland ballads to produce a new sound." (Kanahele 282).

Tūtū

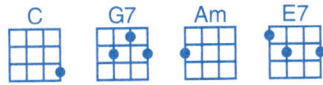

C G7 C
Aia i Kaʻalaʻalaʻa
G7 C
Kuʻu wahi kupuna wahine
G7 C
Ua nui kona mau lā
G7 C
ʻO ka noho ʻana i ke ao nei
Am E7 Am
Kāna hana i ke kakahiaka
E7 Am
ʻO ka wehe i ka Paipala nui
Am E7 Am
Kiʻi akula i nā makaaniani
E7 Am G7
A penei e kau ai

There lived at Kaʻalaʻalaʻa
My aged dear old Grandma
Her days were full of numbers
That she lived in this world of care
Her first duty in the morning
Was to turn to the great Bible
Then searching for her glasses
Sheʻd place them on her nose

hui

C G7 C
E aloha kākou iā ia
G7 C
E mālama kākou iā Tūtū
G7 C
E hoʻāno kākou iā ia
G7 C
Kō kākou kupuna wahine

chorus:
Now we must all show her reverence
We must all love our dear Tūtū
We must all do honor to her
Our dear Grandma Tūtū

C G7 C
A kau mai e ke ahiahi
G7 C
Hoʻomākaukau e pule
G7 C
Kiʻi akula i nā makaaniani
G7 C
Auē! Ua nalowale!
Am E7 Am
Aia kā i ka lae!
E7 Am
I ka lae kahi kau ai
E7 Am
Ua poina loa ʻia
E7 Am G7
I luna i ka lae!

As the hour of eve drew near
Sheʻd prepare for eveʻs devotions
And how she seeks her glasses
But lo, they are not there
She has placed them on her forehead
High up above her brow
And there she soon forgot them
High up above her forehead

"This hula was composed by Queen Liliʻuokalani for a benefit for Kaumakapili Church in Pālama, Honolulu. Maria Heleluhe took the role of tūtū and seven little girls, all uniformly dressed, acted as grandchildren. The Queen trained the girls to sing this song and accompanied them on her guitar, singing with them. The song was a great success, and lots of nickels, dimes and quarters were showered on the singers. One little girl was so tired of singing that she cried after five encores and they had to stop singing." (Elbert 92-3). 1890s. Translation by Liliʻuokalani.

258
He Mele Aloha

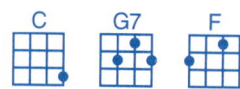

Ua Like Nō A Like

| C G7 F C |
| Ua like nō a like |
| G7 C |
| Me ka ua Kanilehua |
| G7 F C |
| Me he ala e ʻī mai ana |
| G7 C |
| Aia i laila ke aloha |

So like, so very like
The Kanilehua rain
That seems to say
There is the one to love

hui

| C G7 F C |
| ʻO ʻoe nō kaʻu i ʻupu ai |
| G7 C |
| Kuʻu lei i hiki ahiahi |
| C7 F G7 C |
| ʻO ke kani a nā manu |
| G7 C |
| I nā hola o ke aumoe |

chorus:
You are the one that I think of
My darling who comes at evening time
Like the song of the birds
Filling the late night hours

| C G7 F C |
| Ma ʻaneʻi mai kāua |
| G7 C |
| He welina paʻa i ka piko |
| G7 F C |
| A nāu nō wau e ʻimi ana |
| G7 C |
| A loaʻa i ke aheahe a ka makani |

Let us two draw together
An intensity sealed deep within
You've been searching for me
And found me in the whispering breeze

Alice Everett compares love to the cherished attributes of Hilo, its rain, birds and flowers. 1882.

Ua Noho Au A Kupa

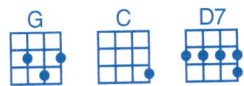

Aia i ka wēkiu ka pua lehua
Ke ona 'ia lā e nā manu
Pili 'ia e ka makani Waiolohia
La'ahia au i ka Maluakele

The lehua blossom is in the lofty reaches
So attractive to all the birds
Attended to by the refreshing Waiolohia breeze
I am devoted, like the Maluakele, the tradewinds

hui

Ua noho au a kupa i ko alo
A kama'āina lā i ka leo
Ka hi'ona a ka mana'o i laila
I 'ane'i ka waihona a ke aloha

chorus:
I've grown familiar with your presence
And accustomed to your voice
Your image is there in my mind
Love's refuge is right here

Pa'ē mai ana ka leo o ka hikihiki
Hiki mai ana ke 'ala o ka fesia
Sila 'ia ke aloha welawela
E ho'i nō kāua lā e pili

The voice of the land shell trills
The perfume of the freesia comes to me
The passion of love is set
Let us come back together again

This old hīmeni by Edward Nainoa dates back to at least the 1890s.

Ua Mau *on following page: Moses W. Ka'aneikawaha'ale Keale, was a well-known Christian leader on Ni'ihau also known as Keale Te Kaula ("Keale, the prophet"). Keale started his first church in Waimea, Kaua'i, and was led to Ni'ihau where he was greatly loved and respected as a kahu and for his gift of prophecy. Many songs were written in his honor and he in turn wrote many prayers and hymns for his church that are still used today. (huapala.com). 1880s.*

260
He Mele Aloha

Ua Mau

hui

C   F   C
Hōsana 'ia ke Akua
G7   F   C
Ma nā lani ki'eki'e
       F   C
Ka waiho 'ana mai
  G7   C
I ko kākou ola

chorus:
Praised be God
In the high heavens
For granting to us
Our salvation

C   F   C
Ua mau mai ē ka pono
G7   F   C
Mai ka Makua lani mai
     F   C
Ke hui nei mākou
  G7   C
I kona loko maika'i

Righteousness is eternal
From the Heavenly Father
We all join together
In his goodness and grace

C   F   C
Ke hui mai mākou
G7   F   C
Makua me keiki
      F   C
Lōkahi pū ka mana'o
  G7   C
I ho'okahi pu'uwai

Let us come together
Parents and children alike
Our thoughts be united
And our hearts be as one

C   F   C
Eia nō mākou
G7   C
Ke mele 'oli aku nei
     F   C
Ma ka inoa o ka Haku
  G7   C
Iēhowa Sāpāōta

Here we all are
Singing in joy
In the name of the Lord
Jehovah Almighty

C   F   C
E ala like nā hoa
G7   F   C
E paio no ka pono
       F
E mau ē ke kūpa'a
  G7   C
Me ka pono o ka 'Uhane

May all the brethren arise
And battle for righteousness
Forever faithful
In the goodness of the Holy Spirit

He Mele Aloha

[C] Kaulana [F] kēia [C] hui
[G7] Ma nā hana [F] o ka [C] pono
'O ka [F] hui Kula [C] Sābati
[G7] O ka welona a ka [C] lā

Renowned is this assembly
In the works of righteousness
The Sunday School assembly
Of the glorious setting sun at Niʻihau

[C] Eia [F] kākou a [C] pau
[G7] I ʻākoakoa [F] mai [C] nei
E ʻike [F] i nā [C] hana
[G7] Kaulana ʻo Iubi[C]lē

Here we all are
Assembled together
To witness the endeavors
Renowned is the Jubilee

[C] E nā [F] hoa luhi [C] nei
[G7] E hoʻōla [F] ana ka [C] manaʻo
Ma ka [F] pono o ka [C] ʻUhane
[G7] E ola [C] ai kākou

Oh, fellow laborers
Reviving the intentions
Through the righteousness of the Spirit
By which we thrive

[C] Hoʻokahi [F] nō [C] mākia
[G7] Nāna i kuhi[F]kuhi [C] mai
Nā [F] hana e [C] ulu ai
[G7] Ka pono no [C] kākou

There is but one motto
That has advised us
In the works that inspire
For the good of us all

[C] Nāna i [F] alakaʻi [C] aʻe
[G7] Iā kākou [F] a [C] pau
Me ke [F] ao māla[C]malama
[G7] O ka lanakila [C] mau

That is what guided
Every one of us
With the shining light
Of eternal victory

[C] Hauʻoli [F] pū [C] kākou
[G7] I kēia [F] lā mai[C]kaʻi
Hoʻi [F] Kula [C] Sābati
[G7] O ka welona a ka [C] lā

We all share our joy
On this fine day
The return of the Sunday School
Of the glorious setting sun

He Mele Aloha

'Uhe'uhene

F / G7
Ho'ohihi 'oe ke 'ike
C7 / F
'Olu nō ho'i oe ke lilo iā 'oe
                C7
A he mea nui na ka makua i milimili
                   F
Pūlama 'ia ua hi'ipoi 'ia ua makamae
       G7
'A'ole nō he hewa
C7   A7
I laila 'oe e lawai'a ai
  D7
'O ka maunu nō ka mea nui pololei
     G7
A i hei nō ho'i i kāu makau

hui

C7   F
'Uhe'uhene 'uhe'uhene lā
        C7
(Kani e kō aka)
                    F
'Uhe'uhene 'uhe'uhene lā

F   G7
Ke lilo ho'i iā 'oe
C7   F
Kāu hana nui 'o ke kama a pa'a
                C7
A i hemahema 'oe ko iala lilo nō ia
                  F
Pohō wale ho'i nā hu'i koni a ka pu'uwai
        G7
Eia aku nō ia lawai'a
C7   A7
Huikau ana nā makau a 'olua
  D7
Hō'ike 'ia ke akamai pololei
G7
A i pili pa'a me 'oe

You are entranced by the sight
You'll be delighted to obtain
A treasure cherished by the parents
Embraced and held dear, precious
No flaws indeed
It is there you shall fish
The bait is truly of great importance
To get it snagged upon your hook

chorus:
Teasing, teasing
(Your laughter resounds)
Teasing, teasing

When you make your catch
Your main task is to bind and secure it
And if you are clumsy, it will get away
The throbbing pangs of the heart will go to waste
Here comes that other fisherman
Your hooks may become entangled
But real skill will be displayed
And it will be secure with you

Composer Charles King tells of catching and keeping, but not of fishing, in this song subtitled the Hawaiian Shouting Song. 1930.

He Mele Aloha

'Ūlili Ē

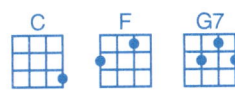
C F G7

    C   F   C
Hone ana ko leo e 'ūlili ē
            G7   C
E kahi manu noho 'ae kai
          F   C
Kia'i ma ka lae a'o Kekaha
       G7   C
'O ia kai ua lana mālie

🎸 *hui*

    C
'Ūlili ē
               G7   C   G7   C
'ahahana, 'ūlili 'ehehene, 'ūlili 'ahahana
'Ūlili ho'i
           G7   C   G7   C
'ehehene, 'ūlili 'ahahana, 'ūlili 'ehehene
                  F   C
'Ūlili holoholo kahakai ē
       G7   C
'O ia kai ua lana mālie

C   F   C
Hone ana ko leo e kōlea ē
              G7   C
Pehea 'o Kahiki? Maika'i nō!
       F   C
'O ia 'āina uluwehiwehi
      G7   C
I hui pū 'ia me ke onaona

Your voice sings out, wandering tattler
Bird who lives by the seashore
Watchful at Kekaha Point
Where the sea is calm

chorus:
Oh 'ūlili, tra la la
Oh 'ūlili, tra la la
'Ūlili who runs along the shore
Where the sea is calm

Your voice sings out, golden plover
How is Tahiti? Just fine!
It is a verdant land
Imbued with sweet fragrance

Harry Naope and George Keahi tell about the wandering tattler and the golden plover in this song from Kekaha, Kaua'i. While the 'ūlili runs along the shorebreak, seeking its food, the kōlea is migratory, preferring to spend the time it spends in Hawai'i in the grass flatlands. 1935.

He Mele Aloha

Uluhua Wale Au

Onaona e ka uka o Ka'ala
Kuahiwi 'au i ke kai
Ho'omahie mai ana i ka nahele
I ka nani o Kūmaipō

hui

Uluhua, uluhua wale au
Uluhua i ka wai a ka Nāulu
Ia wai nihi a'e i nā pali
Kālewa ma uka o Mikilua

'Elua nō pu'u i 'oi a'e
A Halona e hi'ipoi nei
'O ka uhi wai nō me ka lalana
'Ekolu i ke onaona Iāpana

The highlands of Ka'ala are sweetly fragrant
That mountain that juts from the sea
Delightfully perfuming the woodlands
Amid the beauty of Kūmaipō

chorus:
I am discouraged and annoyed
Vexed at the Nāulu rains
That water that sweeps across the cliffs
Drifting inland of Mikilua

But two things are of greater importance
Which Halona does embrace
The watery mist and the rising waters
Being three with the night blooming jasmine

Theresa Cartwright refers to Kūmaipō, Mikilua and Halona, areas in the district of Wai'anae. 1898.

He Mele Aloha

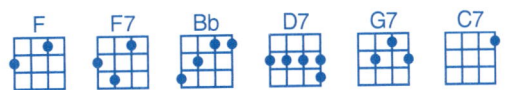

'Ulupalakua

F	F7
Kaulana mai nei
Bb	F
A'o 'Ulupalakua
D7	G7
He 'īnikiniki ahiahi
C7	F
Ka home a'o paniolo

Renowned indeed
Is 'Ulupalakua
Where evenings bring a tingle
The home of the cowboys

F	F7
He wehi e ku'u lei
Bb	F
A'o 'Ulupalakua
D7	G7
Onaona me ka 'awapuhi
C7	F
He beauty maoli nō

You are an adornment, my dear one
Land of 'Ulupalakua
Redolent with ginger
A true thing of beauty

F	F7
Ha'ina mai ka puana
Bb	F
A'o 'Ulupalakua
D7	G7
He 'īnikiniki ahiahi
C7	F
Ka home a'o paniolo

Tell then the refrain
Of 'Ulupalakua
Where evenings bring a tingle
The home of cowboys

John Pi'ilani Watkins wrote this song about the beautiful 'Ulupalakua Ranch and its cowboys in the 1940s. There are not as many paniolo songs as might be expected, when one considers what an attractive and romantic subject the Hawaiian cowboy is.

266
He Mele Aloha

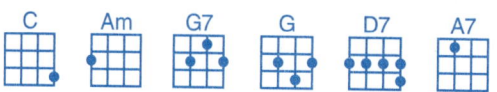

Uluwehi ʻO Kaʻala

    C   Am   G7
Uluwehi ka luna o Kaʻala
                   C
Kāhiko ʻia maila e ka ʻohu
             Am   G
ʻAlawa kuʻu maka i luna
   D7   G7
Ka piʻo a ke ānuenue
   C   Am   G7
ʻAlawa kuʻu maka i lalo
                 E
Ka hulali a ka wai liʻulā
 F   C   A7
ʻAuana i ke kula o Leilehua
   D7   G7   C
Me ka ipo honehone o ke aumoe

🎸 *hui*

   C   A7   D7
Pā mai ka makani he Moaʻe
 G7   C   G7
Hōʻinoʻino nei i ka manaʻo
  C   A7   D7
I laila māua i pili ai
   G7   C
Me ka ipo honehone o ke aumoe

The heights of Kaʻala are verdant
Adorned by the sweeping mists
My eyes glance upward
To behold the arching rainbow
My eyes glance downward
To the sparkling waters in twilight
Wandering the plains of Leilehua
With the gentle sweetheart of midnight

chorus:
The tradewind blows, the Moaʻe
Disturbing one's thoughts
It's there that we two were together
I and the gentle sweetheart of midnight

Kanihomauʻole celebrates the beauty of Mt. Kaʻala, which at 4,000 feet elevation, is the highest peak on Oʻahu. 1916.

He Mele Aloha

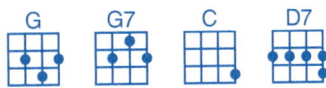

Uluwehi O Ke Kai

G He hoʻoheno ke ʻike aku **G7**
C Ke kai moana nui lā **G**
C Nui ke aloha e hiʻipoi nei **G**
D7 Me ke ʻala o ka līpoa **G**

So precious to witness
The great expansive ocean
A great affection is nourished within
With the fragrance of the līpoa seaweed

G He līpoa i pae i ke one **G7**
C Ke one hinuhinu lā **G**
C Wela i ka lā ke hehi aʻe **G**
D7 Mai manaʻo he pono kēia **G**

The līpoa washes up on the sand
The glittering sand
Scorching hot from the sun to step on
Don't think that this is what must be

G Hoʻokohukohu e ka limu kohu **G7**
C Ke kau i luna o nā moku lā **G**
C ʻO ia moku ʻula lā e hō! **G**
D7 ʻOni ana i ʻō i ʻaneʻi **G**

The limu kohu so alluring
Set atop the reef rocks
Those clumps,ʻula lā e hō!
Waving back and forth

G Haʻina mai ka puana **G7**
C Ka līpoa me ka limu kohu **G**
C Hoa pili ʻoe me ka paheʻe **G**
D7 ʻAnoni me ka līpalu **G**

The refrain is told
Of the līpoa and the limu kohu seaweeds
You are companion to the paheʻe
Mixed together with the līpalu

Most of Edith Kanakaʻole's musical compositions dealt with the relationship between the kanaka and his or her relationship to the environment — a relationship that is not only intuitive, but must also be taught if the environment is to be maintained. In this favorite hula mele, Kanakaʻole describes one's relationship with the ocean through various limu (seaweeds) such as the lipoa, limu kohu, paheʻe and lipalu. These each have diverse characteristics, as do sweethearts. 1970s.

Wahīkaʻahuʻula

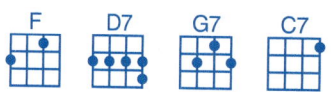

    F   D7   G7
He inoa kēia nou e ka lani
  C7   F
E ka uʻi nohea o Hawaiʻi nei

This is a name song for you, oh Royal One
Handsome beauty of this land, Hawaiʻi

F   D7   G7
ʻO ʻoe nō ka heke i kaʻu ʻike
  C7   F
ʻO ka helu ʻekahi o ke onaona

You are the finest in my vision
Foremost in sweetness and grace

F   D7   G7
Ua kaʻapuni au a puni Kaleponi
  C7   F
Ua ʻike i ka nani o American Beauty

I've travelled all around California
I've seen the splendor of American Beauty

F   D7   G7
ʻO ʻoe nō ka heke i kaʻu ʻike lā
  C7   F
Ka hau nani o Hawaiʻi nei

You though, are the fairest I've witnessed
The beautiful cool dew of Hawaiʻi

F   D7   G7
Nāna e haulani o Hale Aliʻi
  C7   F
Ka paepae kapu o Līloa

The one who is a familiar at the Palace
The sacred stone platform of Līloa

F   D7   G7
Haʻina ka puana i lohe ʻia
  C7   F
ʻO Wahīkaʻahuʻula he inoa ē

Tell the refrain, that it be heard
A name song for Wahīkaʻahuʻula

This mele by Ruth Lilikalani honors Princess Abigail Kawānanakoa, whose name Wahīkaʻahuʻula, means "wrap in a feather cape." Within the family, it was played only for the princess and was quite solemn. 1923.

269
He Mele Aloha

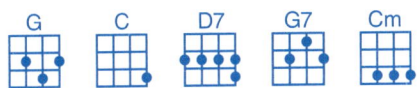

Wahine ʻIlikea

🎸 *hui*

    G C   G C   G   C   G D7
Pua kalaunu ma ke kai o Honouliwai
       G   C   G   C
Wahine ʻilikea i ka poli o Molokaʻi
      C G
Nō ka heke

chorus:
Crown flower by the sea of Honouliwai
Fair-skin woman in the bosom of Molokaʻi
The foremost one

C
Nani wale nō

Nā wailele uka
         G   G7
ʻO Hina, ʻo Haha, ʻo Moʻoloa
C   Cm
Nā wai ʻekolu i ka uluwehiwehi
    G   D7
O Kamalō i ka mālie

So beautiful indeed
Are the upland waterfalls
Hina, Haha and Moʻoloa
The three waterfalls in the lush greenery
Of Kamalō, in the calm

C
Nani wale nō

Ka ʻāina Hālawa
  G   G7
Home hoʻokipa a ka malihini
 C   Cm
ʻĀina uluwehi i ka noe ahiahi
     G   D7
Ua lawe mai e ka makani Hoʻolua

So beautiful indeed
Is the land of Hālawa
Hospitable home of the newcomer
Verdant land in the evening mist
Brought by the Hoʻolua wind of the North

Dennis Kamakahi wrote this for the beauty of the mountains above Kamalō, Molokaʻi, an area he referred to as the fair skinned woman. He composed this song in 1975, with a cadence that calls for motion.

Wai O Ke Aniani

[F]
E aloha aʻe ana wau lā
[C7] [F] [F7]
Aloha kuʻu pua ka lehua lā
[Bb] [F]
E moani ke ʻala i ka poli lā
[C7] [F]
ʻUheʻuhene i ka wai o ia pua

I offer up my affection
How I love my lehua blossom
Whose fragrance stirs the heart
Delighting in the nectar of this flower

🎸 *hui*

[F]
Huʻi au konikoni

I ka wai konikoni
[C7] [F] [F7]
Wai huʻihuʻi o ke aniani

chorus:
I'm chilled, throbbing
For the water, throbbing
Cool water of the glass

🎸 *tag*

[Bb] [F]
Huʻi au, i ka wai
[C7] [F]
Wai huʻihuʻi o ke aniani

tag:
I'm chilled by the waters
The cool waters of the glass

[F]
Ua laʻi nō ke ʻala
[C7] [F] [F7]
I ka liko o ka pua pīkake
[Bb] [F]
ʻO ka noe a ka ua liʻiliʻi
[C7] [F]
Ka ʻuhene a ka wai i ka ʻili

Soft is the fragrance
Of the pīkake bud
The misting of the fine rain
The teasing of the water upon the skin

[F]
ʻO ka noe a ka ua liʻiliʻi
[C7] [F] [F7]
I ka uka o Kāʻilikahi
[Bb] [F]
Hoʻokahi pua nani o ka liko
[C7] [F]
Ka ʻōnohi wai ānuenue

The misting of the light rain
Inland at Kāʻilikahi
There is just one beautiful flower bud
Like a glimmering center of attention

He Mele Aloha

[F]
E aloha a'e ana wau lā
[C7]   [F]   [F7]
Aloha ku'u pua ka 'ilima lā
[Bb]   [F]
E moani ke 'ala i ka poli lā
[C7]   [F]
'Uhe'uhene i ka wai o ia pua

I offer up my affection
I love my 'ilima blossom
Whose fragrance stirs the heart
Delighting in the nectar of this flower

[F]
E aloha a'e ana wau lā
[C7]   [F]   [F7]
Aloha ku'u puakenikeni lā
[Bb]   [F]
E moani ke 'ala i ka poli lā
[C7]   [F]
'Uhe'uhene i ka wai o ia pua

I offer up my affection
How I love my puakenikeni blossom
Whose fragrance stirs the heart
Delighting in the nectar of this flower

[F]
Ha'ina mai ka puana lā
[C7]   [F]   [F7]
Aloha ku'u pua lei aloha lā
[Bb]   [F]
E moani ke 'ala i ka poli lā
[C7]   [F]
'Uhe'uhene i ka wai o ia pua

Tell the refrain
How I love my precious lei of flowers
Whose fragrance stirs the heart
Delighting in the nectar of this flower

This song revels in the fragrant nectar of various flowers, recalled as a lei that stirs the heart. The chorus and second and third verses of this version appeared in Holstein, 1897, under the title Wai Hui O Ke Aniani. *It may have been expanded with the other blossom verses over time.*

He Mele Aloha

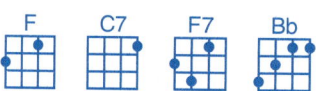

Wai'alae

Ua 'ike nō ho'i 'oe (F ... C7)
I ka 'i'ini a ka mana'o (F)
Ho'okahi māpuna leo (F7 ... Bb)
Ua lawa ia i ka makemake (C7 ... F)
Aia hiki ko aloha (F ... C7)
Ku'u home i Wai'alae (F)
Ko aloha hiki aumoe (F7 ... Bb)
Pulupē i ke kēhau (C7 ... F)

You indeed are acquainted
With the longing in my heart
Just a word from you
Is sufficient to satisfy the desire
When your love comes to me
To my home in Wai'alae
Your love in the still of the night
Is refreshing like the moistening dew

This Spanish-style waltz by Mekia Kealaka'i was featured in the 1912 Broadway play Bird of Paradise, *the first time Hawaiian music was featured in a successful Broadway show, which helped to popularize Hawaiian music internationally.*

He Mele Aloha

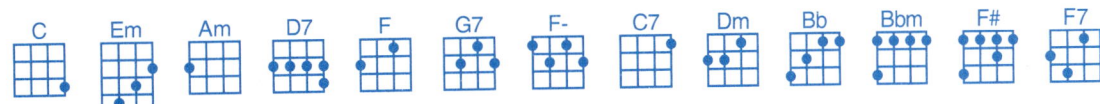

Waikā

   C   Em   Am
Kū akula ʻoe i ka Malanai
  D7
A ke Kīpuʻupuʻu
 F   G7   C   G7
Nolu ka maka o ka ʻōhāwai a Uli
      C   C7   F   F-
Niniau ʻeha ka pua o koaiʻe
        C
ʻEha i ke anu
   G7   C
Ka nahele aʻo Waikā

C7 F   Am   Dm   G7
Aloha Waikā iaʻu me he ipo lā
         C7   F   C7
Me he ipo lā ka maka lena o ke koʻolau
  F   Am   Dm   G7
Ka pua i ka nahele o Mahuleia
 Bb   Bbm   F
E lei hele i ke alo o Moʻolau
         C7   F   F7
He lau ka huakaʻi hele i ka pali loa
   Bb C7   F# F7
A he aloha ē, a he aloha ē
   Bb C7   F
A he aloha ē, a he aloha ē

You are touched by the gentle Malanai breeze
And the gusty Kīpuʻupuʻu wind-driven rain
The grotto of Uli is lush and wet
Wearied and bruised is the koaiʻe flower
Pained by the cold
Is the forest of Waikā

Waikā, love me as a sweetheart
Dear to my heart is the yellow koʻokoʻolau blossom
The flower in the tangled woods of Mahuleia
Go adorned to face the wilds of Moʻolau
Many are the difficult journeys to undertake
And this, it is love
And this, it is love

John Kinohou Spencer, Sr., took the words to Waikā *from an ancient chant and wrote the music based on the way Lokalia Montgomery chanted it. The original chant is said to have been a name song for Kamehameha that was inherited by his son, Liholiho. The Kīpuʻupuʻu was a band of warriors who named themselves after Waimea's icy rain. But even a Hawaiian war song has veiled reference to love making. 1950s.*

Waikaloa

| C |
| Aia i Waikaloa |
| F   C |
| Home hoʻokipa malihini |
| A7   D7 |
| Pumehana me ke aloha |
| G7   C |
| I ka leo o ka makamaka |

There at Waikaloa
Is a home so welcoming to guests
Warmed by much love
Through the voices of dear friends

| C |
| Huli aku au mahalo |
| F   C |
| I ka nani aʻo Kaʻuiki |
| A7   D7 |
| ʻO ia nani nō ia |
| G7   C |
| ʻO ka hale ipu kukui |

Turn did I to admire
The beauty of Kaʻuiki
There is another beauty there
The lighthouse

| C |
| ʻO ka noe a ka Uakea |
| F   C |
| Kaulana nei aʻo Hāna |
| A7   D7 |
| Me ka ua Mālualua |
| G7   C |
| E uhai ana i ka noe |

The misting of the white Uakea rain
For which Hāna is famous
Then the Mālualua rain
Seems to follow the mist

| C |
| Haʻina mai ka puana |
| F   C |
| Waikaloa i ka hanohano |
| A7   D7 |
| Home hoʻokipa malihini |
| G7   C |
| He beauty maoli nō |

Thus ends my story
Of Waikaloa in its glory
A home that welcomes guests
A true beauty indeed

John Piʻilani Watkins wrote this Maui song. Waikaloa is the area beside Hāna bay looking directly at the fortress hill of Kaʻuiki, jutting out to sea, with the lighthouse on the point Uakea is the famous misty white rain of the Hāna district.

Opposite: Many songs were written by homesick and cold Hawaiians, including this favorite by Andy Cummings. He recalled "It was a cold and foggy night in November 1938, and we were walking back to our hotel from the theatre (in Lansing, Michigan). I thought of Waikīkī with its rolling surf, warm sunshine, palm trees and...."

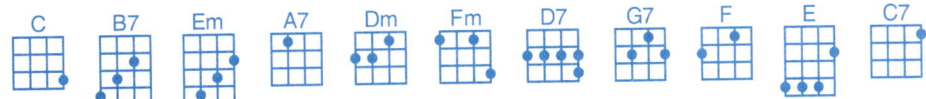

Waikīkī

C / B7
There's a feeling deep in my heart
Em / A7
Stabbing at me just like a dart
Dm / G7 / C / G7
It's a feeling heavenly

C / B7
I see mem'ries out of the past
Em / A7
Memories that always will last
D7 / G7
Of that place across the sea

G7 / C / C7
Ah —— Waikīkī
F / Fm
At night when the shadows are falling
C / D7
I hear your rolling surf calling
G7 / C
Calling and calling to me

G7 / C / C7
Ah —— Waikīkī
F / Fm
'Tis for you that my heart is yearning
C / D7
My thoughts are always returning
G7 / C / B7
Out there to you across the sea

E / B7
Your tropic nights and your wonderful charms
E / B7
Are ever in my memory
E / B7
And I recall when I held in my arms
Em / G7
An angel sweet and heavenly

C / C7
Waikīkī
F / Fm
My whole life is empty without you
C / D7
I miss that magic about you
G7 / C
Magic beside the sea

He Mele Aloha

Waiomina

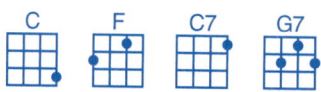

   C   F   C   C7
Kaulana 'Ikuā me Ka'au'a lā
  F   C
Nā 'eu kīpuka 'ili
       G7
Nā āiwaiwa o 'Europa lā
               C
No Waimea ē ka 'eu
  G7   F   C
I ka ua Kīpu'upu'u
  G7   F   C
I kahua Waiomina

Famous are 'Ikuā and Ka'au'a
The lively ropers
The wondrous ones of Europe
From Waimea comes such spirit
From the Kīpu'upu'u rain
To the arenas of Wyoming

 C   F   C   C7
'Olua nā moho puni o ke ao lā
  F   C
Nā 'eu kīpuka 'ili
            G7
'A'ohe kupu'eu nāna e 'a'e lā
               C
No Waimea ē ka 'eu
  G7   F   C
I ka ua Kīpu'upu'u
  G7   F   C
Me ke anu a'o Kaleponi

You two are the world champions
The lively ropers
No rascal could beat you
From Waimea comes such spirit
From the Kīpu'upu'u rain
And the cold of California

  C   F   C   C7
Na ke kelekalapa i ha'i maila
  F   C
Nā 'eu kīpuka 'ili
           G7
'Ikuā e ka moho puni ke ao lā
               C
No Waimea ē ka 'eu
  G7   F   C
I ka ua Kīpu'upu'u
  G7   F C
Nā kuahiwi 'ekolu

It was the telegraph that announced
The lively ropers
'Ikuā was the world champion
From Waimea comes such spirit
From the Kīpu'upu'u rain
The three famous mountains

[C] Ha'ina 'ia mai ana ka [F] puana [C] lā [C7]	Let the story be known in the telling
Nā [F] 'eu kīpuka [C] 'ili	The lively ropers
'Ikuā ē ka moho puni ke ao [G7] lā	'Ikuā is the world champion
No Waimea ē ka [C] 'eu	From Waimea comes such spirit
I ka [G7] ua Kīpu[F]'upu[C]'u	From the Kīpu'upu'u rain
Nā [G7] kuahiwi [F] 'e[C]kolu	From the three famous mountains

Helen Lindsey Parker tells the story of three cowboys from Waimea, Hawai'i — 'Ikuā Purdy, Archie Ka'au'a, and Ebon "Jack" Low — who competed in the international rodeo competition in Cheyenne, Wyoming in 1907. Ikuā was declared world champion and, it was reported, received a standing ovation. Ka'au'a took third place and Low placed sixth. "Helen Lindsey Parker was an excellent horsewoman. She spent her life on the ranches of the Big Island, understood perfectly the life of the paniolo — and happened to be a musician and singer with a beautiful voice." (Kanahele 293)

Waimea Corral

```
C        C7     F         C
That old Waimea Corral
C7    F    G7    C
I can never forget
   C7     F            D7
Take me back, take me back
    E7              Am
To the people that I knew
     D7        G7     C F  C
At that old Waimea Corral

    C              Cm7         F            C
Gone all the sounds that filled the air before
     C            C7           F          G7
The echo of hooves on the silent turf below
     C           Cm7      C7
Pleading, begging cattle cries
   F                    Fm
In the whispers of the wind
     C    D7       G7     C F  C
At that old Waimea Corral

       C           Cm7       F                  C
The branding is over and cowboys young and old
     C           C7         F               G7
Faces tired and worn and still can wear a smile
     C              C7            F           Fm
Children on horseback, playing in pastures below
     C    D7       G7     C
At that old Waimea Corral
   C7     F            D7
Take me back, take me back
```

A paniolo song from the island of Hawaiʻi.

He Mele Aloha

Waipi'o

	F C A7 D7
C	'O kāu hana mau nō ia

       C   F C A7   D7
'O kāu hana mau nō ia
    G7   F C
'O ka ho'okipa i ke aloha
   F   C   C7 F
A na'u i ho'oheno mua
 A7 D7 G7   C
Ka makani 'o Laulani

You can always be counted on
To offer a loving welcome
I have long held dear
The Laulani breeze of that land

hui

   C   F C   C7 F
He inoa kēia no Waipi'o
    G7   F C
'O ka Halelauokekoa
 F   C   C7 F
I puīa i ke 'ala
 A7 D7 G7   C
Onaona i ka ihu

chorus:
This is a name song praising Waipi'o
And the house, Halelauokekoa
Filled with the fragrance of the flowers
So sweet and welcoming to behold

   C   F C A7   D7
E ka i'a hāmau leo
   G7   F C
E hi'ipoi mālie nei
 F   C   C7 F
I ka mea kāmeha'i
 A7 D7 G7   C
O ua 'āina nei

The renowned pearl oysters
Do gently hold so dear
A thing of wonderous nature
Belonging to that land

Mekia Kealaka'i and George Allen wrote this for Irene Kahalelaukoa I'i, daughter of John Papa I'i, and talks about her home at Kahuaiki, in Waipi'o, 'Ewa, O'ahu. It overlooked the West Loch of Pearl Harbor and thus the reference to the renowned pearl oysters. Translation from Kamehameha School pamphlet "Nā Haku Mele Kane."

280
He Mele Aloha

Waltz Medley

G   D7
Aloha nō wau i ko maka
                    G
Kou ihu waliwali kaʻu i honi
 G7   C   A7
Koe aku kou piko waiʻolu
 D7   G   D7
Ua kapu na ka mea waiwai

   (from Aloha Nō Wau I Ko Maka)

I do love your face
Your sweet little nose I have kissed
Your center of delight remaining untouched
Held on reserve for the fortunate one

G   D7
Someone is tall and handsome
                G
Someone is fair to see
 G7   C   A7
Someone is kissing somebody
D7   G   D7
Under the light of the moon

   (from Aloha No Wau I Ko Maka)

G G7 C   G
Pulupē nei ʻili i ke anu
                D7
A he anu mea ʻole i ka manaʻo
    G G7 C   G
ʻO ka ʻike iā ʻoe e ke aloha
   D7   G
Hoʻi pono ka ʻiʻini iā loko

   (from Pulupe Nei Ili I Ke Anu)

My skin is drenched and cold
But the chill is nothing in my mind
At the sight of you, my love
Desire rushes back into my heart

G   D7
Sweet lei mamo
        G
Lei o ke aloha
      G7 C A7
Kāhiko nani oʻu
D7   G
Sweet lei mamo

   (from Sweet Lei Mamo)

Sweet mamo-feather garland
Lei of loving affection
Beautiful adornment of mine
Sweet mamo feather lei

```
   G                    D7
Uluhua, uluhua wale au
                          G
Uluhua i ka wai a ka Nāulu
   G7              C
Ia wai nihi aʻe i nā pali
      D7           G
Kā lewa ma uka o Mikilua
```

(from Uluhua Wale Au)

I am vexed, simply vexed
Thwarted by the sudden Nāulu rains
Showers that traipse across the cliffs
Sweeping along inland of Mikilua

```
  G            D7      G   G7
Wehiwehi ʻoe e kuʻu ipo
 C        G E    A7       D7
He ʻiʻini ke koʻiʻi waiho iā loko
  G        D7          G  G7
A loko hana nui i ka puʻuwai
 C   Cm  G   E7   A7   D7  G
Ko leo nahenahe e maliu mai
```

(from Wehiwehi ʻoe)

You're a thing of beauty, my beloved
The urgency within is that of desire
So stirring to the heart and emotions
Your gentle voice one must heed

```
   G              D7
E kuʻu lei mae ʻole
                G
Aʻu i kui ai a lawa
  E7        C    A-
I lei hoʻohiehie
  D7         G
No ke ano ahiahi
```

(from Wehiwehi ʻoe)

My dear never-fading garland
That I have strung to my delight
As a garland of elegance
For the peaceful eventide

Although many of the songs themselves are no longer well known, hui from the waltzes Aloha Nō Wau I Ko Maka, Pulupē Nei ʻIli I ke Anu, Uluhua Wale Au, Wehiwehi ʻOe *and* Sweet Lei Mamo *are beautifully strung together. While not apt to be found in any songbook, this and other medleys are commonly sung at kanikapila.*

282
He Mele Aloha

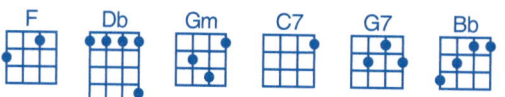

White Ginger Blossoms

[F]White ginger blossoms
[Db]Cool and [F]fragrant
[C7]Sweeter than the [Gm]rose
[C7]Fairer too than [G7]moon[C7]light
[F]White ginger blossoms
[Db]From the mount[F]ains
[C7]Fill the thirsty [Gm]air
[C7]With exotic [G7]fragrance [C7]rare[F]

[F7]Round your lovely throat
You wear my [Bb]ginger lei
[G7]Each white petal nestles
Close and [C7]longs to say
"Let me [Gm]stay [C7]here"
[F]White ginger blossoms
[Db]Cool and [F]fragrant
[C7]By a mountain [Gm]pool
[C7]Guard their sweetness
[G7]All [C7]for [F]you

Although hapa-haole songs often lack the metaphorical content, this one by R. Alex Anderson is true to one of the favorite themes of Hawaiian songs, the flower. 1939.

He Mele Aloha

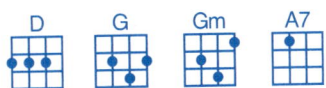

White Sandy Beach

[D]I saw you in my dreams

We were walking hand in hand

On a [G]white sandy [Gm]beach of Hawai'[D]i

We were playing in the sun

We were having so much fun

On a [G]white, sandy [Gm]beach of Hawai'[D]i

[A7]Sound of the ocean, [G]soothes my restless [A7]soul

Sound of the ocean, [G]rocks me all night [A7]long

[D]Those hot long summer days

Lying there in the sun

On a [G]white, sandy [Gm]beach of Hawai'[D]i

[A7]Sound of the ocean [G]soothes my restless [A7]soul

Sound of the ocean, [G]rocks me all night [A7]long

[D]Last night in my dream I saw your face again

We were [G]there in the sun

On a [Gm]white sandy beach of Hawai'[D]i

On a [Gm]white sandy beach of Hawai'[D]i

By Rich Bibbs.

'Ukulele Chords

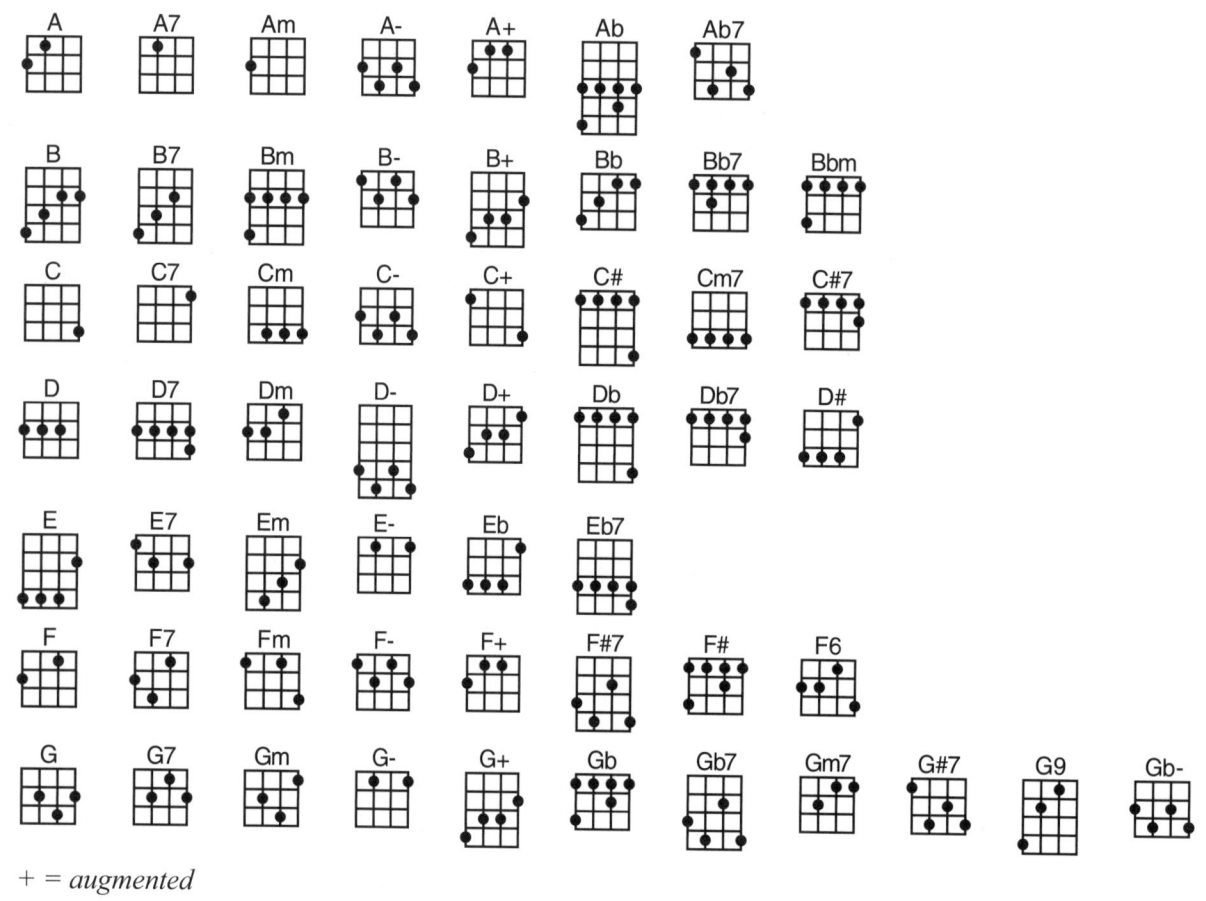

+ = *augmented*
− = *diminished*

Just Starting on the 'Ukulele?

Tuning: Using a piano or note finder, tune the strings to GCEA.

Finger Position: Use your left hand to finger the chords. An easy general rule for fingering is to use your index finger on the first fret, your middle finger on the second fret, and the ring finger on the third fret. This works for chords like F, C and C⁷. You need to adapt, of course, for chords like G⁷. When all four strings are marked within a fret, as in D⁷, bar it with one finger.

Make Music: Strum up and down in area of the sound hole with the index finger of your right hand.

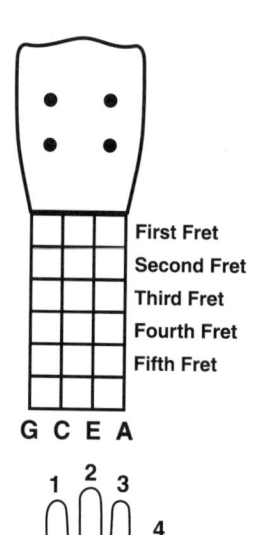

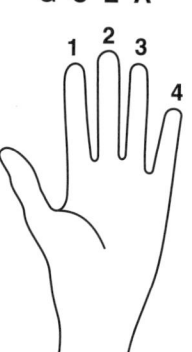

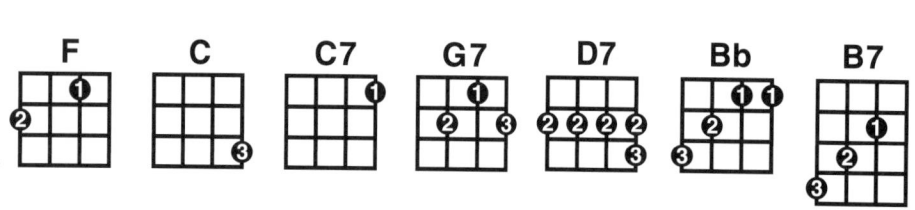

Chord Transpositions

Key

1	2	3	4	5	6	7	8
C	D	E	F	G	A	B	C
G	A	B	C	D	E	F#	G
D	E	F#	G	A	B	C#	D
A	B	C#	D	E	F#	G#	A
F	G	A	Bb	C	D	E	F
Bb	C	D	Eb	F	G	A	Bb

Vamp Chords

1	2^7	5^7
C	D^7	G^7
G	A^7	D^7
D	E^7	A^7
A	B^7	E^7
F	G^7	C^7
Bb	C^7	F^7

Principal Chords

1	4	5^7
C	F	G^7
G	C	D^7
D	G	A^7
A	D	E^7
F	Bb	C^7
Bb	Eb	F^7

Use this chart to transpose a song from one key to another more suitable to you. The row of numbers at the top, in the gray band, correspond to each note in a musical scale. The column of letters on the left, in the gray band, is the key in which the song is chorded. So, in the key of C, C=1, D=2, E=3 and so forth. In the key of G, G=1, A=2, and so forth. Likewise, any chord derivative, for example a seventh or a minor, would be assigned to the corresponding number. In the key of C, $D^m = 2^m$, $E^7 = 3^7$, and so forth.

How to Transpose: To transpose a song to a key of your choice, determine the key your song is played in, which is usually the first chord listed at the top of the song page. Proceed horizontally until reaching the chord that needs to be transposed. Then proceed vertically until reaching the intersection of the new key you wish to use. The chord in the box at the intersection is the solution.

To demonstrate using the song *Nani Kauaʻi*, which is keyed in C, let's change it to the key of A. Draw a table on the page, fill in the chords and numbers that correspond with the chords in this song, then, using the chart above, fill in your new key and fill in the chords that correspond to those numbers found in the table above.

	1	*1^7*	*5^7*	*4*
Existing chords for *Nani Kauaʻi* in key of C	C	C7	G7	F
Proposed new chords in key of A	**A**	**A7**	**E7**	**D**

Now, whenever you see a G^7, for instance, you will know to play a E^7, when you see a F you should play D, and so forth.

Vamp Chords: Vamps are used to begin and end pieces as well as transition between verses in many Hawaiian songs. Chords for vamps in each respective key are included in this chart.

Principal Chords: Principal chords are those most often used in each respective key.

Bibliography

Alama, Kimo. "Kimo Keaulana Alama Mele Collection." Honolulu: Bishop Museum Archives, Ms. Grp. 329.

Almeida, John Kameaaloha. *Na Mele Aloha: A Collection of Hawaiian Lyrics with English Translations by Mrs. Mary Pukui.* Honolulu: John K. Almeida, [n.d.] ca.1946.

Anderson, Alex. *Famous Songs of Hawaii.* Honolulu: Alex Anderson Music, Inc., 1971.

Cunha, A. R., arranger. Coney, W.H., and Solomon Mehuela, translators. *Famous Hawaiian Songs.* Honolulu: Bergstrom Music Co., Ltd., 1914.

Doyle, Emma Lyons. *Makua Laiana.* Honolulu: Star Bulletin Press, 1945.

Elbert, Samuel H., and Noelani Mahoe. *Nā Mele o Hawai'i Nei: 101 Hawaiian Songs.* Honolulu: University Press of Hawaii, 1970. Reprint, 1976.

Emerson, N.B. *Unwritten Literature: The Sacred Songs of the Hula.* Vermont: Charles Tuttle, 1964. 1980 edition.

Hawaiian Evangelical Association. *Leo Hoonani.* Honolulu: Ka Papa Hawaii, 1902.

Hawaiian Music Hall of Fame and Museum. "Ho'oha'i." Kailua: Various issues 1999-2001.

Hodges, Wm. C., and Ernest K. Kaai, eds. *Souvenir Collection of Hawaiian Songs & Views.* Honolulu: Hawaii Promotion Committee, 1917.

Holstein, Edward C., compiler. *Ka Buke Mele o na Himeni Hawaii: I haku a meleia e na kahuli leolea o ka aina o na Home Hawaii Ponoi.* Honolulu: Hawaiian News Company, Ltd., 1897. Reprinted Bishop Museum Press, 2003.

Hopkins, Charles A. K., ed. *Aloha Collection of Hawaiian Songs.* Honolulu: Wall, Nichols Company, Ltd., 1899.

Hui Hānai. *The Queen's Songbook: Her Majesty Queen Lili'uokalani.* Honolulu: Hui Hānai, 1999.

Ka'aihue, Marmionett M., ed. *Songs of Helen Desha Beamer.* Honolulu: Abigail K. Kawananakoa Foundation, 1991.

Kamakau, Samuel. *The Ruling Chiefs of Hawaii.* USA: Kamehameha Schools Press, rev. ed., 1992.

Kamehameha Schools Song contest programs. Honolulu: 1998 – 2002.

Kanahele, George S., ed. *Hawaiian Music and Musicians: An Illustrated History.* Honolulu: The University Press of Hawaii, 1979.

Keakaokalani, and J.M. Bright. *Ka Buke o na Leo Mele Hawaii: Ka buke o na leo mele Hawaii no ka pono a me ka pomaikai o na home Hawaii, na anaina hoolaulea a me na aha mele hoonanea.* Honolulu: Hale Pai Mahu P.C. Advertiser, 1888.

King, Charles Edward. *King's Song Book.* Honolulu: Charles E. King, 1916.

King, Charles Edward. *King's Book of Hawaiian Melodies.* Honolulu: Charles E. King, 1920.

King, Charles Edward. *King's Book of Hawaiian Melodies.* Honolulu: Charles E. King, 1945.

King, Charles Edward. *King's Songs of Hawaii: A Companion to King's Book of Hawaiian Melodies.* Honolulu: Charles E. King, 1950.

Kinney, Ray. *Popular Hawaiian Songs.* New York: Miller Music Corporation, [n.d.] ca.1944.

Liliʻuokalani. *Her Royal Highness Queen Liliuokalani Poet, Composer, Musician.* Honolulu: Lynne Waihee and the Docents of Washington Place, 1994.

Mader, Vivienne. "Vivienne Mader Collection." Honolulu: Bishop Museum Archives. Ms. Grp. 81.

Martin, Kaiulani Kanoa, compiler. Huapala: Hawaiian Hula and Music Archives. Available online at http://www.huapala.org. Accessed 07-28-03.

Noble, Johnny. *Johnny Noble's Royal Collection of Hawaiian Songs.* San Francisco: Sherman, Clay & Co., 1929.

Noble, Johnny. *Aloha Souvenir Collection of Rare Old Hawaiian Songs.* Honolulu: Wall, Nichols Co., [n.d.] ca.1930.

Noble, Johnny. *Johnny Noble's Book of Famous Hawaiian Melodies Including Hulas and Popular Hawaiian Standards.* New York: Miller Music. Inc., 1935.

Noble, Johnny. *Johnny Noble's Collection of Ancient & Modern Hulas.* New York: Miller Music, Inc., 1935.

Ortone, Brett C., compiler. *The Island Music Source Book.* Honolulu: Olinda Road Distribution, 1999.

Pukui, Mary Kawena, and Alfons L. Korn, trans. and eds. *Echo of Our Song: Chants and Poems of the Hawaiians.* Honolulu: University Press of Hawaii, 1973.

Pukui, Mary Kawena, Samuel H. Elbert and Esther T. Mookini. *Place Names of Hawaiʻi.* Honolulu: University Press of Hawaii, rev. ed., 1974.

Pukui, Mary Kawena, and Samuel H. Elbert. *Hawaiian Dictionary.* Honolulu: University Press of Hawaii, rev. ed., 1986.

Pukui, Mary Kawena, trans., and Pat Namaka Bacon and Nathan Napoka eds. *Nā Mele Welo: Songs of Our Heritage.* Honolulu: Bishop Museum Press, 1995.

Royal Collection of Hawaiian Songs. Honolulu: Hawaiian News Co. Ltd., 1907.

Shiraishi, Makoto. *Best 100 Hawaiian.* Japan: Doremi Music Publishing Co., Ltd, 1989.

Songs of Hawaii. New York: Miller Music Corporation, 1950.

State of Hawaiʻi, State Foundation on Culture and the Arts. *Nā Mele Paniolo: Songs of Hawaiian Cowboys.* Honolulu: State Foundation on Culture and the Arts, fifth printing, 1990.

Stone, Scott C. S. *From a Joyful Heart: The Life and Music of R. Alex Anderson.* Waipahu: Island Heritage Publishing, 2001.

Index of Composers

A

Achuck, Elizabeth
    Sanoe 243
Aiu, Maʻiki
    Aloha Kauaʻi 16
Akiu, George
    Lei ʻOhu 153
Allen, George
    Waipiʻo 279
Almeida, John Kameaaloha
    Ā ʻOia! 1
    Green Rose Hula 36
    Holoholo Kaʻa 69
    Kanaka Waiwai 108
    Kuʻu Ipo Pua Rose 139
    Maile Swing 163
    Roselani Blossom 241
ʻAlohikea, Alfred
    Hanohano Hanalei 41
    Ka Ua Loku 94
    Ka Wai O Nāmolokama . . . 96
    Nāmolokama Lā 196
    Pua Līlia 225
ʻAlohikea, Lizzie
    ʻAlekoki 12
    Nani Kauaʻi 199
    Radio Hula 240
Aluli, Irmgard Farden
    E Maliu Mai 30
    Laupāhoehoe Hula 147
    Nā Hoa Heʻe Nalu 189
    ʻŌpae Ē 208
    Puamana 231
    Punaluʻu 233
Anderson, R. Alex
    Blue Lei 25
    *Cockeyed Mayor of
        Kaunakakai* 26
    Haole Hula 44
    I Will Remember You 83
    *Iʻll Weave a Lei of
        Stars for You* 85
    Lovely Hula Hands 155
    Malihini Mele 166
    White Ginger Blossoms . . . 282
Apoliona, Haunani
    Alu Like 21
Auld, Mrs.
    Makalapua 164

B

Beamer, Francis (Pono)
    Kuʻu Hoa 136
Beamer, Helen Desha
    Kaʻahumanu 98
    Kawohikūkapulani 119
    Keawaiki 125
    Kimo Hula 127
    Kinuē 128
    Nā Kuahiwi ʻElima 190
Beamer, Keola
    Honolulu City Lights 70
Beamer, Milton
    Blue Lei 25
Beamer, Nona
    Pūpū Hinuhinu 234
Beckley, Mary
    Ahi Wela 4
Beecher, Gordon
    Song of Old Hawaiʻi 246
Berger, Henry
    ʻAkahi Hoʻi 9
    Hawaiʻi Ponoʻī 47
Bibbs, Rich
    White Sandy Beach 283
Bingham, Hiram
    *Hoʻonani I Ka
        Makua Mau* 75
Bishaw, Keliana
    Kūhiō Bay 134
Booth, Charles W.
    Pauoa Liko Ka Lehua . . . 216
Bosetti, Carlo
    Makalapua 164
Bright, Solomon (Sol)
    Hawaiian Cowboy 48
Brooks, Jack
    Farewell for Just Awhile . . . 34
Burrows, David
    Maile Lauliʻi 161
Bush, Emma
    Pauoa Liko Ka Lehua . . . 216

C

Cartwright, Theresa
    Uluhua Wale Au 264
Cazimero, Robert
    Pane Mai 214

Cogswell, Bill
    *My Little Grass Shack in
        Kealakekua, Hawaiʻi* . . 182
Collins, Lei
    Ke Aloha 121
    Laimana 144
Conjugacion, Tony
    Ka Beauty Aʻo Mānoa 90
Cummings, Andy
    Kaimana Hila 99
    Waikīkī 275

D

Darby, Ken
    Kalua 105
Davis, Kai
    ʻĀina ʻO Molokaʻi 7
    Nani Hanalei 198
de Silva, Kīhei
    Hanohano Wailea 43
Doiron, Lizzie
    Ahi Wela 4
    Mai Poina ʻOe Iaʻu 157
Dudoit, Hannah
    Kalamaʻula 101

E

Edwards, John
    Lei No Kaʻiulani 152
Ellis, William S.
    Hula O Makee 79
Everett, Alice
    Ua Like Nō A Like 258

F

Farden, Rudolph (Randy)
    Beautiful Kauaʻi 24
Flanagan, Barry
    Lei Pīkake 154
Fuller, Solomon
    Me Molokaʻi 170

H

Haʻi, Scott
    ʻAhulili 5
Hakuole, Naha Harbottle
    Makalapua 164

Harrison, Tommy
   My Little Grass Shack in
      Kealakekua, Hawai'i . . *182*
Hawk, Leonard "Red"
   May Day Is Lei Day
      in Hawai'i *170*
Heanu, Mary
   Hilo Ē *64*
Henshaw, Bucky
   Hula Breeze *78*
Hiram, Solomon
   Sassy *244*
Hoffman, Al
   Ke Kali Nei Au *122*
Holt, Eliza Ha'aheo
   Kaula 'Ili *114*
   Pu'uohulu *236*
Hopkins, Louisa
   Aloha Ku'u Home Kāne'ohe. *17*
Huddy, George Mānoa
   Sweet Lei Mokihana *249*

I

'Ī'ī, James
   Makee 'Ailana *165*
'Ī'ī, Katie Stevens
   Pua O Ka Mākāhala *228*
Iosepa, John U.
   Pā'au'au Waltz *212*
Isaacs, Alvin
   Kō'ula *133*

J

Johnson, Alice B.
   Hanohano Olinda *43*
   Ho'okipa Pāka *74*
   Pāpālina Lahilahi *215*

K

Ka'ai, Bernie
   My Sweet Gardenia Lei . . . *183*
Ka'ai, Ernest
   Pu'uwa'awa'a *237*
Ka'apa, Charles
   'Ālika *14*
Ka'apuni, K.
   Kaleponi *104*
Kā'eo, Samuel Kalani
   No Ka Pueo *203*
Kahale, James
   'Iniki Mālie *87*

Kahinu, J.
   Nā Hala O Naue *188*
Kaholokula, James Kalei, Sr.
   Pua 'Ōlena *229*
Kaihan, Maewa
   Now Is the Hour *205*
Kaihumua, 'Emalia
   Moku O Keawe *177*
Kailimai, Henry
   On the Beach at Waikīkī . . *207*
Kalāinaina, Sam Li'a, Jr.
   Heha Waipi'o *58*
Kalākaua
   'Āinahau *8*
   'Akahi Ho'i *9*
   'Alekoki *12*
   Hawai'i Pono'ī *47*
   Koni Au I Ka Wai *132*
Kalama, Sylvester Thomas
   Maui Girl *168*
Kalima, Joe
   Hilo Hula *66*
Kamakahi, Dennis
   E Hīhīwai *27*
   Kōke'e *130*
   Nā Makani 'Ehā *192*
   Pua Hone *223*
   Wahine 'Ilikea *269*
Kamakau, Mrs.
   Nani Wale Līhu'e *201*
Kamana, Kimo
   Pua Tuberose *230*
Kamana, John "Squeeze"
   Pua Mae 'Ole *227*
Kamealoha
   Ka 'Ano'i *89*
Kanahele, Samuel
   Pauoa Liko Ka Lehua *216*
Kanaka'ole, Edith
   Uluwehi O Ke Kai *267*
Kāne, Matthew
   Ka Makani Kā'ili Aloha *92*
   Ku'u Lei Poina 'Ole *142*
   Moloka'i Nui A Hina *178*
   Moloka'i Waltz *179*
Kanihomau'ole
   Uluwehi 'O Ka'ala *266*
Ka'ōpio, Danny
   Ke 'Ala O Ka Rose *120*
Ka'ōpūiki, James
   Hula O Makee *79*
Kapena, Emma
   Aia Hiki Mai *6*
Kapoli
   Ahe Lau Makani *3*

Kauhailikua
   Kananaka *107*
Kauwē, Lot
   Aloha Ka Manini *15*
   He Aloha Nō 'O Honolulu . . *50*
   Ho'okena *73*
   Kupa Landing *135*
Keahi, George
   'Ūlili Ē *263*
Kealaka'i, Mekia
   Lanakila Kawaihau *145*
   Pōhai Ke Aloha *219*
   Wai'alae *272*
   Waipi'o *279*
Keale, Moe
   Hanohano Wailea *43*
Keale, Moses
   Ua Mau *260*
Kealoha, J.
   Nā Moku 'Ehā *194*
Keawehawai'i, John
   My Yellow Ginger Lei *185*
Keku'ewa, Lydia
   Hu'i Ē *76*
Kelepolo, George
   I Kona *81*
Kepilino, Val
   Mele O Lāna'i *171*
Keyes, Baron
   Sweet Someone *251*
King, Charles E.
   'Eleu Mikimiki *33*
   I Mua Kamehameha *82*
   'Imi Au Iā 'Oe *86*
   Kaimana Hila *99*
   Kamehameha Waltz *106*
   Ke Kali Nei Au *122*
   Kilakila 'O Haleakalā *126*
   Ku'u 'Ini *137*
   Ku'u Lei Aloha *140*
   Ku'u Lei Poina 'Ole *142*
   Lei Aloha, Lei Makamae . . *149*
   Lei 'Ilima *151*
   Nā Lei O Hawai'i *191*
   Pālolo *213*
   Pidgin English Hula *217*
   Pua Carnation *222*
   'Uhe'uhene *262*
Kinney, Clarence
   Holoholo Ka'a *69*
Kinney, Ray
   Maile Lauli'i *161*
Kokolia, J.
   Sassy *244*

Kong, Abbie
   Kāneʻohe 110
Konia
   Makalapua............ 164
   Nani Haili Pō I Ka Lehua . 197
Kuaʻana, Danny
   He Uʻi................ 57
   Heha Waipiʻo........... 58
   My Sweet Gardenia Lei... 183
Kuahiwi, Samuel
   Nā Aliʻi 186
Kuakini, Mrs.
   Hiʻilawe 62
Kuni, Joseph
   Lei Nani 151

L

Lake, Kahauanu
   Pua Līlīlehua........... 226
Lake, Maʻiki Aiu
   Aloha Kauaʻi 16
Lam, Maddy
   E Kuʻu Tūtū 29
   He Aloha Kuʻu Ipo....... 52
   Ka Lehua I Milia........ 91
   Ke Aloha 121
   Kīpū Kai.............. 129
   Maile Lei 162
   Pō Laʻilaʻi............. 218
   Pua ʻĀhihi 221
Lane, Margarita
   That's the Hawaiian
     in Me 253
Leleiōhoku
   Adiós Ke Aloha 2
   Aloha Nō Wau I Ko Maka .. 18
   Hole Waimea........... 68
   Kāua I Ka Huahuaʻi...... 111
   Kawaihau Medley 117
   Ke Kaʻupu 123
   Moanikeʻala........... 176
   Nani Wale Līhuʻe....... 201
Libornio, J. S.
   Mai Poina ʻOe Iaʻu...... 157
Likelike, Miriam
   Aia Hiki Mai 6
   ʻĀinahau................ 8
   Kuʻu Ipo I Ka Heʻe
     Puʻe One 138
   Sanoe................ 243
Lilikalani, Ruth
   Wahīikaʻahuʻula........ 268

Liliʻuokalani
   Ahe Lau Makani 3
   Aloha ʻOe............. 19
   He Inoa No Kaʻiulani..... 54
   Ka Wai Māpuna......... 95
   Ka Wiliwiliwai.......... 97
   Kuʻu Pua I Paoakalani ... 143
   Queen's Jubilee........ 238
   Queen's Prayer........ 239
   Sanoe................ 243
   Tūtū 257
Lincoln, William (Bill) Aliʻiloa
   Pua ʻIliahi 224
Lindeman, David
   Honolulu I'm Coming
     Back Again.......... 71
Low, Mary E.
   Puʻuwaʻawaʻa.......... 237
Lucas, Mary Adams
   Makalapua............ 164
Lunalilo
   ʻAlekoki 12
   Hole Waimea........... 68
Lyons, Lorenzo
   Hawaiʻi Aloha 45

M

Machado, Lena
   Pōhai Ke Aloha 219
Mahikoa, Amy Hobbs
   Hula O Makee 79
Makuakāne
   Miloliʻi 174
Manning, Dick
   Ke Kali Nei Au.......... 122
Mattos, Paleka
   Hanohano Ka Lei Pīkake... 42
Maui, Martha K.
   Hiʻilawe 62
Moki
   Lei No Kaʻiulani......... 152
Montano, Mary Jane
   Beautiful Kahana........ 23
   Old Plantation......... 206
Moon, Peter
   He Hawaiʻi Au.......... 53
Mossman, Bina
   He ʻOno 55
   Kaleponi 104
   Niu Haohao........... 202
   Stevedore Hula 247

N

Naeʻole, Sam Kamuela
   Kaulana ʻO Waimānalo... 116
Nāhaleʻā, Albert
   He Punahele Nō ʻOe 56
   Keaukaha............. 124
Nāhinu
   Iā ʻOe E Ka Lā E
     ʻAlohi Nei 84
Nainoa, Edward
   Ua Noho Au A Kupa 259
Nālimu, Keola
   Hilo Hanakahi.......... 65
Nāmāhoe, Charles
   Lei Nani 151
Nāmakelua, Alice
   Haleʻiwa Pāka 38
   He Hawaiʻi Au 53
Namoʻolau, J.K.
   My Sweet Sweeting 184
Naope, Harry
   ʻŪlili Ē 263
Nape, David
   Makalapua............ 164
   Moanalua............. 175
   Old Plantation......... 206
Nāwāhine, Robert K.
   ʻEkolu Mea Nui 32
Nelson, Bob
   Hanalei Moon 40
Noble, Johnny
   For You a Lei........... 35
   Kāneʻohe 110
   Kāua I Ka Huahuaʻi...... 111
   My Hawaiian Souvenirs .. 181
   My Little Grass Shack in
     Kealakekua, Hawaiʻi .. 182
   Pretty Red Hibiscus...... 220
   That's the Hawaiian in Me 253
Nogelmeier, Puakea
   Hanohano Ka Lei Pīkake... 42
   Lei Haliʻa.............. 150
   Toad Song 254
Nott, Carter
   I Will Remember You..... 83
Nuʻuanu
   Kaleleonālani 102
   Pua ʻĀhihi 221

O

Owens, Harry
   Hawai'i Calls 46
   Hula Breeze 78
   Sweet Leilani 250
   To You Sweetheart, Aloha . 256

Owens, Jack
   Hukilau Song 77
   I'll Weave a Lei of Stars
      for You 85

P

Pākī, Pilahi
   'Ōpae Ē 208

Papa, John, Sr.
   My Yellow Ginger Lei 185

Parker, Helen Lindsey
   'Akaka Falls 10
   Maunaloa 169
   Waimina 276

Peters, Kalani
   My Sweet Sweeting 184

Peterson, Mel
   E Naughty Naughty
      Mai Nei 31

Pitman, Jack
   Aloha Week Hula 20

Pokipala, Charles, Sr.
   Muliwai 180

Pokipala, Daniel
   Muliwai 180

Prendergast, Ellen Wright
   Kaulana Nā Pua 115

Pukui, Mary Kawena
   E Ku'u Tūtū 29
   He Aloha Ku'u Ipo 52
   Ka Lehua I Milia 91
   Kīpū Kai 129
   Laupāhoehoe Hula 147
   Nā Hoa He'e Nalu 189
   Pō La'ila'i 218
   Pua 'Āhihi 221
   Pua Līlīlehua 226
   Punalu'u 233

R

Reichel, Keali'i
   E Ho'i I Ka Pili 28
   Kauanoeanuhea 113
   Kawaipunahele 118

Rickard, Alice
   Kaimukī Hula 100

Robins, Mary Pūla'a
   Lē'ahi 148
   Royal Hawaiian Hotel 242

Rosha, Ron
   He Hawai'i Au 53

S

Scott, Clement
   Now Is the Hour 205

Sheldon, William
   Maika'i Ka Makani
      O Kohala 158

Silverwood, F. B.
   Honolulu I'm Coming
      Back Again 71

Smith, M.
   Heha Waipi'o 58

Spencer, John
   Waikā 273

Sproat Family
   Maika'i Ka Makani
      O Kohala 158

Stewart, Dorothy
   Now Is the Hour 205

Stover, G. H.
   On the Beach at Waikīkī . . 207

Swinton, Harry
   Latitū 146

T

Taylor, Emily
   Ku'u Lei 'Awapuhi 141

W

Waggner, Gordon
   Sweet Someone 251

Waia'u, Henry
   Kaua'i Beauty 112
   Kona Kai 'Ōpua 131
   Maika'i Kaua'i 160

Wall, Lilinoe
   Kinuē 128

Watkins, John Pi'ilani
   Honomuni 72
   'Ulupalakua 265
   Waikaloa 274

Wilcox, Kau'i
   Nani Nu'uanu 200

Wolf, Rube
   Pretty Red Hibiscus 220

Woodd, Jennie
   Hale'iwa 37

Z

Zuttermeister, Kau'i
   Nā Pua Lei 'Ilima 195

He Mele Aloha

Mahalo

The seed for this songbook was sown in 1997, when Dixon Stroup, Vicky Hollinger and I compiled a list of Hawaiian song titles, which quickly numbered over 600 mele. We honed it down to about 300 titles, based on a loose standard of *kanikapila* — songs we most love to sing. Dixon, an avid singer and collector of Hawaiian music, passed away two years later, and we had to eliminate several songs because he was the only one among us who remembered them. This drove home how easily songs are lost.

Four of us collaborated on this book.

Vicky Hollinger greatly influenced the final selection of songs with her comprehensive knowledge of Hawaiian music. She also chorded the songs in collaboration with Kimo Hussey. Vicky envisioned a songbook that would enable people to sing these Hawaiian songs correctly.

Kimo Hussey brought formal musical discipline to this project and kept us firmly rooted in the application of musical theory and practice, and proper chording. Kimo saw this book as another step toward a music academy that provides formal training for Hawaiian musicians.

Puakea Nogelmeier, Hawaiian language orthographer, teacher and songwriter, edited the Hawaiian lyrics and English translations and, where needed, generated new translations. Puakea worked on this project to help keep the Hawaiian language growing as a living language, in this case using song as a vehicle to that end.

My motivation for compiling this book was to help those who want to *kanikapila*. I designed this as a workbook, one you can mark up, transpose keys, add verses, or whatever suits your needs and style.

We all agreed to participate in this project *hana manawaleʻa*. Likewise, all of those who have allowed us to include their lyrics have done so without compensation, in the same spirit of *hana manawaleʻa*. In addition, part of the proceeds and any profits will go to the Lunalilo Home.

This book, like Hawaiian music itself, was a collaborative effort, and was made possible only with the support, *manaʻo*, and permission to use creative work from: Coline Aiu, Frankie and Bob Anderson, Haunani Apoliona, Pat Bacon, Amelia Bailey, Keola Beamer and Tom Moffatt and Niniko Music, Mahiʻai Beamer, Nona Beamer, Leah Bernstein and Mountain Apple Company, Mehana Blaich, Miki and Mandy Bowers and all our friends at Hawaiian Sing, Manu Brand, Gladys ʻĀinoa Brandt, Victor K. Bright, Robert Cazimero, Kaili Chun, Tony Conjugacion, Mary Ann Owens Crandall, Barry Flanagan, Sahoa Fukushima, Bucky Henshaw, Irving Jenkins, Robin and Dennis Kamakahi, John "Squeeze" Kamana, Jr., Kekuhi Kanahele and the Edith Kanakaʻole Foundation, Matthew Kaʻōpio, Poomai Kawananakoa, Momiaarona Kepilino, Kahauanu Lake, Clifford Lam, Kekoaokekoolau Lyu, Noelani Kanoho Mahoe, Peter Moon, Corbin Morse, Puakea Nogelmeier, Charles Nakoa and Hui Hānai, John Overton, Kealiʻi Reichel, Barbara Robeson, Carol Silva, Kīhei de Silva, Harry B. Soria, Jr., Mihana Aluli Souza, Tita Spielman, David and Linda Akana Sproat, Nākila Steele, James Stone, Dixon Stroup, Cindy Turner and Hugo de Vries of Turner & de Vries, Ltd., Kilipaki Vaughan, Jennifer Wessner, Linda Wahinekapu Wessner, August Yee and, above all, my husband Gaylord.

Carol Wilcox